IMAGES
of America

NORVELT
A NEW DEAL SUBSISTENCE HOMESTEAD

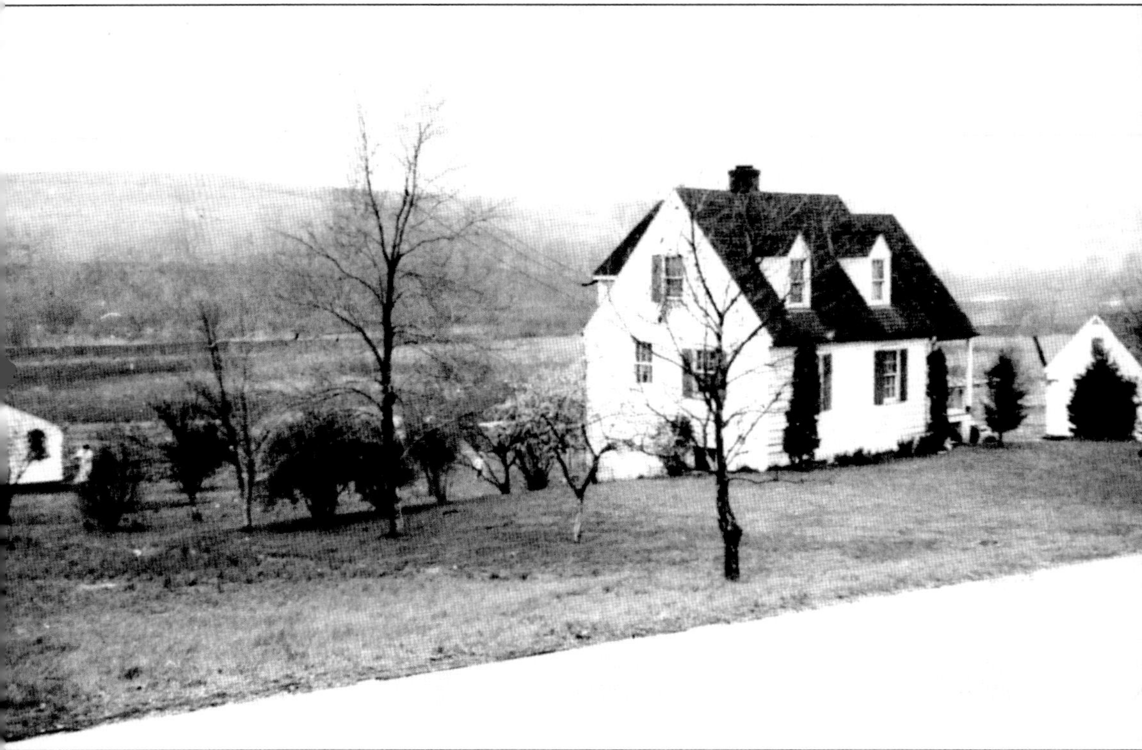

This photograph shows the completed homestead of the Louis Pastore family. Each homestead provided a home, a garage, a poultry house, a garden, a grape arbor, and a chance to start over, as well as share a sense of community with others. (Courtesy of Ann Riggen.)

ON THE COVER: Please see page 22. (Courtesy of Andrea Dominick.)

IMAGES
of America

NORVELT
A NEW DEAL SUBSISTENCE HOMESTEAD

Sandra Wolk Schimizzi with Valeria Sofranko Wolk
Introduction by Michael Carey

ARCADIA
PUBLISHING

ISBN 978-0-7385-7216-1

Published by Arcadia Publishing
Charleston SC, Chicago IL, Portsmouth NH, San Francisco CA

Printed in the United States of America

Library of Congress Control Number:2009929850

For all general information contact Arcadia Publishing at:
Telephone 843-853-2070
Fax 843-853-0044
E-mail sales@arcadiapublishing.com
For customer service and orders:
Toll-Free 1-888-313-2665

Visit us on the Internet at www.arcadiapublishing.com

Dedicated to the original homesteaders who had the foresight, adventuresome spirit, and desire to make a better life for their families and chose to partake in a New Deal subsistence homestead, Westmoreland Homesteads, later named Norvelt. In their honor, the authors' proceeds from this book go to the development of the Westmoreland Homesteads Historical Society.

CONTENTS

ACKNOWLEDGMENTS

There are so many people to thank who helped us in getting this book together. First, I thank Alex Schimizzi, who spent endless hours on photography and layout. A special thanks to Michael Cary, Ph.D., who spent countless hours interviewing and writing to capture the spirit of Norvelt for his upcoming book on Westmoreland Homesteads and for directing the historical committee of the 75th anniversary of the founding of Norvelt and for his assistance with this book.

I am grateful to my parents and grandparents: Joseph J. Wolk and Valeria Sofranko Wolk, who instilled in me an appreciation of the principles and values that brought about the creation of Westmoreland Homesteads, and Anthony and Mary Wolk and Stephen and Theresa Sofranko, original homesteaders who chose to participate in the subsistence homestead. I am also grateful to Anita Wolk Foriska and Chet Czarniak for their editing and Terri Wolk Czarniak for her encouragement.

Along with my mother, who spent countless hours gathering photographs and information to pave the way for this book, I am grateful to Joseph Wolk, Earl Saville, Lois Schlingman, Virginia Boytim Vahaly, Betty Sue Boytim Mondock, Tracey Surma, Kimberly Sulzer, Ann Riggen, Geraldine Dzambo Mizikar, Gail Hoffer, Barbara Kepich, Kathleen Kelley, Dorothy Vidakovich, Pastor David Greer, John Sofranko Sr., John Sofranko Jr., Patty Pavick Kelly, Steve Whisdosh, Edward and Catherine Cibulas, Sally Puskar, Connie Yasher Urban, Shirley Jones Rusinko, Frank and Sophie Pipak, Barbara Pipak Patula, John Kennedy, Helen Bann Stefanek, Dick Soloman, Andrea Urban Dominick, Ellamae Huhn Tepper, Glynnis Cunningham Waters, E. Sharon Jones Smith, Catherine Sherbuck Bosich, Marsha Bosdosh, Patty Ewing Hawse, Doris Weaver, Josey Walton, Keith Pavick, Marie Horrell, and Steve Viazanko, who graciously provided their photographs and memories.

I thank the Westmoreland Homestead Fireman's Department including Lee Speer, Richard Balchik, Ed Ungvarsky, and all of the other volunteers too numerous to mention.

I also wish to thank our editor at Arcadia Publishing, Erin Vosgien, for her expert encouragement, guidance, and gentle prodding that kept us on track.

A special thanks to James Steely of the Westmoreland Historical Society, who has been a longtime leader in keeping the spirit of Westmoreland Homesteads alive in his articles and lectures through the Westmoreland Historical Society.

Most importantly, I want to thank my husband, David Schimizzi, and son, Alex, for their support and Joseph J. Wolk, my father and Valeria's husband, for his memories and support.

—Sandra Wolk Schimizzi

INTRODUCTION

Norvelt recently celebrated its 75th anniversary, a joyous occasion lasting four days with many facets: a homesteaders' reunion picnic, music from multiple bands and orchestras, a banquet, a golf outing, a fireman's fair with ethnic foods and vendor booths, an academic miniconference on Norvelt history, a parade, and a fireworks display. Heavy crowds depleted the food booths on Saturday afternoon, sending vendors scrambling for additional supplies. Lee Speer and the members of his 75th anniversary committee were gratified by the success of the event (and a little relieved, as much money was spent in preparation). When it was over, people remarked how wonderful it all had been.

This event differed a bit from comparable celebrations elsewhere because of the circumstances of Norvelt's founding. Norvelt is a New Deal community, created by the United States government in 1934. In 1933, the area now comprising the village of Norvelt had simply been farmland. By 1935, it was populated with two- or three-acre garden homesteads, minifarms numbering more than 250, all with Cape Cod–style cottages complete with garage, chicken coop ("poultry house," the designers called it), and a graceful grape arbor bridging the space between house and garage.

The enthusiasm for the recent celebration speaks loudly of the historical importance of Norvelt. This community *is* a community, not just a place where people live. One finds, in Norvelt, a palpable sense of shared and common purpose and of fellowship, concepts that get to the original meaning of the word *community*. Problems of modern life aside, people have found happiness here. And that is what the designers and creators of Norvelt intended, which surprises skeptics: Norvelt was a government project whose success is confirmed with each passing year.

Norvelt was created at a time when the American Industrial Revolution had entered its later stages. In the energy industry, coal was being replaced as a fuel by oil and gas. High demand had taken annual coal production to nearly 600 million tons during World War I, but by the late 1920s, demand had slackened to about half of the 1918 rate. Demand fell further with the onset of the Great Depression.

The result was hard times in the coalfields. Miners' and cokers' families lacked food, clothing, and warm places to stay. Clean air and water were in short supply due to mine runoff and smoke from the coke ovens. As jobs disappeared, the miners became stranded—a population of industrial workers dependent on the coal industry, stuck far from traditional towns and urban centers, and with no means of escape. The welfare state had yet to be created, so there were no national programs to turn to—no food stamps, no Medicaid, no TANF (Temporary Assistance for Needy Families). Concerned individuals, churches, and charitable organizations tried to help, but their assistance was too meager and unsystematic in its organization and delivery.

One individual and one organization stand out among those who were concerned and who also made a difference—the American Friends Service Committee (AFSC), run by the Quakers, and Clarence Pickett, the secretary of the AFSC. Pickett spent a lot of time in the coalfields and saw firsthand how traditional relief efforts were inadequate. Relief donations failed to help the recipients become independent, to reduce their need for additional handouts. To change this situation, Pickett took the initiative to introduce new forms of employment: a company making hand-crafted chairs, a weaving shop, a shoe factory. Raised on an Iowa farm, Pickett also urged miners to plant gardens. The fruits and vegetables would help them stave off starvation, although most homes in "patch towns" lacked sufficient fertile soil for gardening.

When Pickett's work was profiled in the *New York Times*, Pres. Franklin D. Roosevelt took notice and sought his advice. Pickett convinced him of the need for federal action to accomplish what the states and private efforts had not been able to do—give the needy a "hand up" out of poverty and dependency and set them on the road to employment and full citizenship. Despite cries of "socialism," Roosevelt did so, signing a bill to create "subsistence homesteads," where people could provide for many of their own food needs with small-scale farming. Section 208 of the National Industrial Recovery Act of 1933 authorized the expenditure of $25 million to purchase land and build subsistence homesteads, including four for stranded populations: Arthurdale, located a little south of Morgantown, West Virginia; Westmoreland Homesteads, as Norvelt was originally called; Tygart Valley, West Virginia; and Cumberland Valley homesteads, Tennessee. Pickett was appointed an administrator in the Division of Subsistence Homesteads and given responsibility for creating these communities.

And thus was Norvelt created. The Westmoreland County site was chosen by Pickett because it was at the center of the great Connellsville coal seam, the purest and one of the largest coal beds in the world, and filled with mining patch towns and stranded miners. The farmland chosen for Norvelt is known for a richness and fertility that would support the new farming operations.

Around 1,500 acres of farmland were acquired by the federal government, which then constructed 250 new houses on tracts ranging in size from two to seven acres. Homesteaders were selected, more than 250 families from over 1,850 applicants, on the basis of "good character" and an apparent suitability for life and work in the community. Having children and being unemployed or underemployed were also primary requirements.

The original name of the community was plainly descriptive: Westmoreland Homesteads. It might have been renamed "Pickettsburg" or something similar, had not Eleanor Roosevelt shown a special interest in the subsistence homesteads project. Working closely with Pickett, she convinced project administrators to install modern conveniences not common in older area homes—indoor plumbing, central heating (a coal furnace in the basement), and electric lighting and outlets. President Roosevelt and some of his advisors thought these were extravagant luxuries for such "simple folk," but Eleanor convinced them that possessing modern conveniences could be an uplifting force in the lives of the much-deprived miners. In gratitude for this and for other efforts by Eleanor on their behalf, residents of Westmoreland Homesteads changed the name of their community to Norvelt in 1937, which they created from the endings of Eleanor's first and last names.

This help was all that the homesteaders needed. From that moment on, the story of Norvelt has been the happy record of a successful community. Of the first generation of homesteaders, very few voluntarily moved away from Norvelt, and today many of the residents are second-, third-, and fourth-generation homesteaders. The original homesteaders were poor, but their descendants find themselves solidly in the middle class, a high proportion of them being successful professionals and business people.

The story of Norvelt is important because the people who know it best, the people who have lived it and continue to develop the story, tell us it is. And they have taken and saved many photographs to illustrate that story, pictures that evoke the past, illustrate the present, and suggest a great future for this wonderful little place.

—Michael Cary
Seton Hill University

One

The Coke and Coal Region

Western Pennsylvania's Connellsville coal or coke seam was famous for having the best bituminous coal and coke in the world. Part of the Pittsburgh coal bed, it was 50 to 60 miles long and 2.5–3 miles wide, spanning Westmoreland and Fayette Counties. Connellsville Coke was a key supplier to iron and steel industries and was used to power locomotives, steamships, and industrial plants. The period from 1870 to 1919 were booming years when hundreds of thousands of coal miners, both men and boys, worked underground in narrow coal seams or tended coke ovens in the Connellsville coke and coal seam. Using crude hand tools, picks, wedges, and explosives, miners cut through 2 to 20 foot-thick coal seams, while laborers shoveled the coal into wooden cars pulled by horses or mules to surface and tipple to be weighed and sorted. Miners often worked 12 hours a day and 7 days a week. Mining was the most dangerous work in the nation. Between 1877 and 1940, 18,000 men and boys died in underground explosions and roof cave-ins in bituminous mines. Countless others were injured and disabled for life.

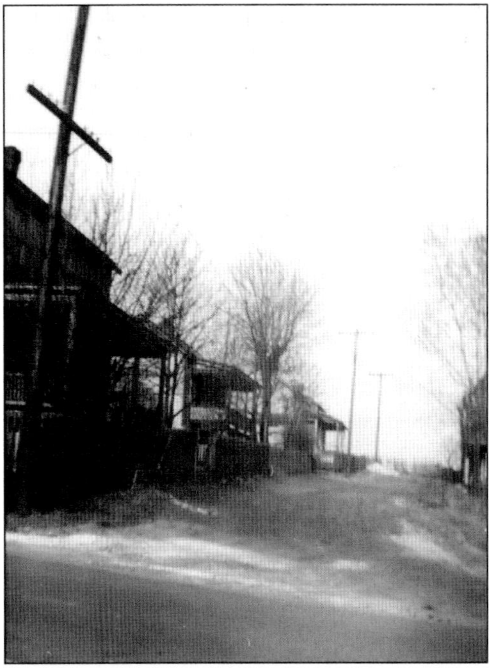

By the 1920s, bituminous coal and coke production in Pennsylvania began to decline drastically due to overproduction and shrinking markets as West Virginia, Illinois, Kentucky, and Ohio passed Pennsylvania's production. To add to the difficulties, the worldwide economic depression developed in most places by 1929. Mining was one of the hardest industries hit. This photograph of Standard, a coal town in nearby Mount Pleasant, shows a typical coal-town street. (Courtesy of Keith Pavick).

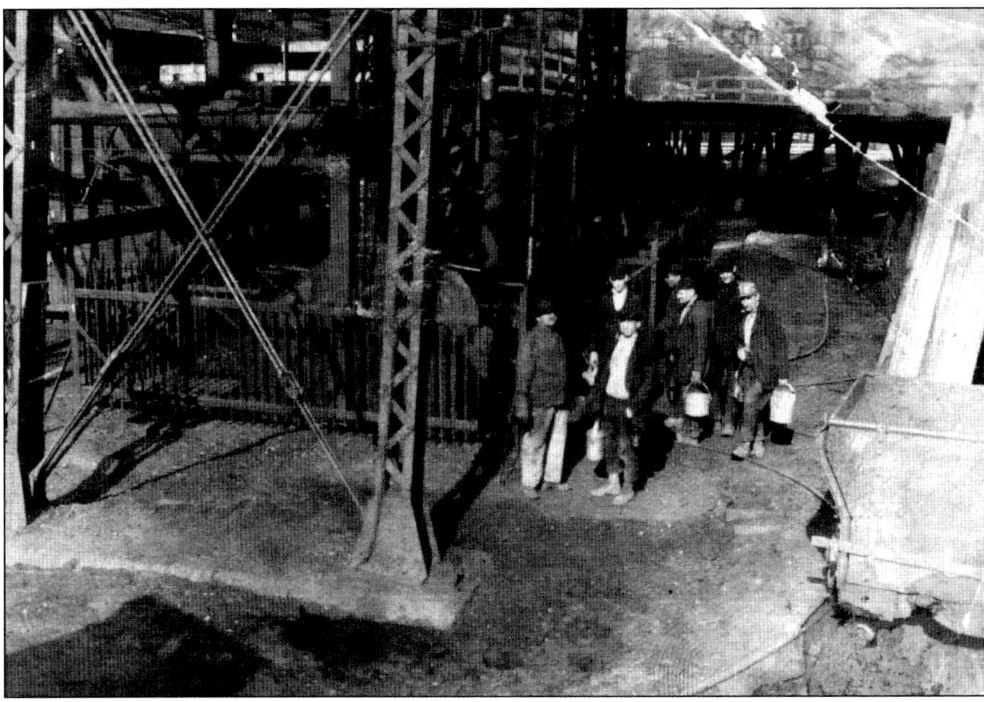

Miners of the western Pennsylvania coal and coke region were hit hard by the Depression. Mines closed, no other work or jobs existed in the area, and families had no money or resources to relocate. Living conditions declined when coal companies no longer kept up the company housing or evicted unemployed miners. Miners who were dependent upon mining for a livelihood had no other skills to transfer into other occupations, and extreme poverty resulted. (Courtesy Valeria Sofranko Wolk.)

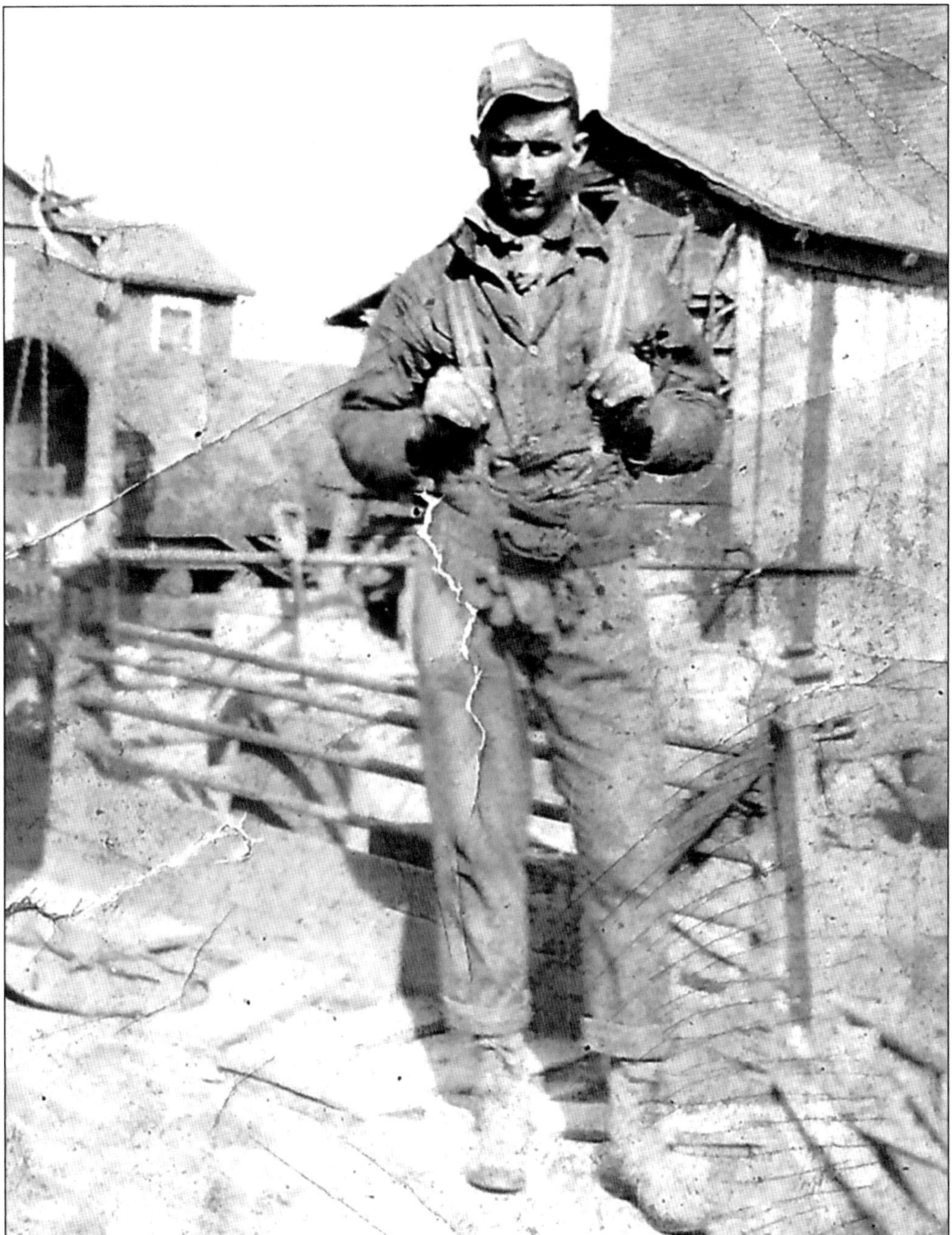

Homesteader Joseph Bann stands outside a mine. Many families lived in houses that were built and owned by the coal companies they worked for, called company houses or coal patches. The homes were typically built close to the mines and coke ovens and were showered by coal and coke ashes from coke ovens that operated 24 hours a day. The houses had no plumbing or running water. Miners came home from work and bathed in the family bathtub, a large tub in the kitchen heated with water boiled on the woodstove. (Courtesy of Helen Bann Stefanek.)

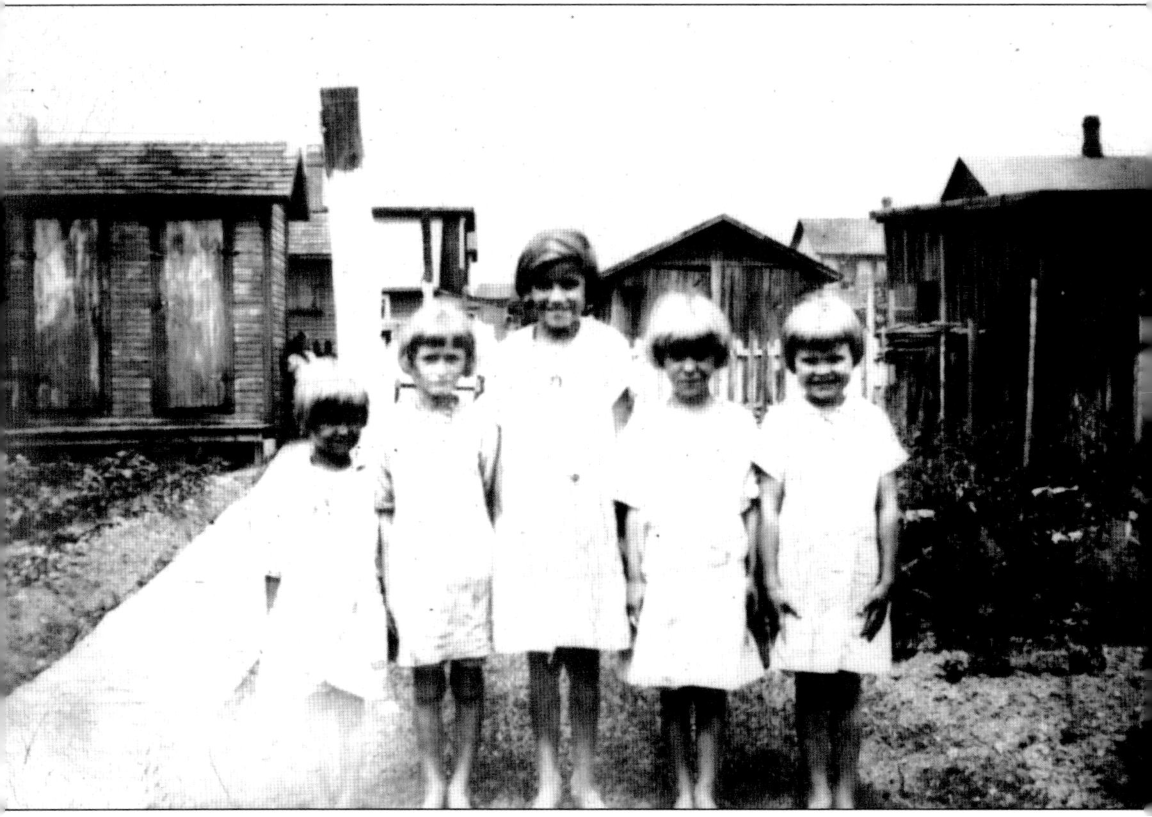

The patch houses had no electricity and residents used kerosene lamps to see at night. Built with little to no insulation, families woke up to frozen water in bowls or glasses left on the kitchen table in the winter. Each home had an outhouse in the backyard that served as a toilet; the odors were difficult to tolerate, especially in the heat of the summer. (Courtesy of Valeria Sofranko Wolk.)

Two

The New Deal's Subsistence Homesteading

Franklin D. Roosevelt ushered in the New Deal to strengthen the economy and create social welfare programs. Under his National Industry Recovery Act, the Division of Subsistence Homesteads was designed to relocate needy families to places where they could live off the land. Subsistence homesteading involved settling families on plots of land where they could grow and raise most of their own food and build and make things they needed, but they would still work in jobs that would be available. President Roosevelt chose Milburn Wilson as the director of the subsistence homesteads. Wilson chose Clarence Pickett, director of the Quaker-sponsored American Friends Service Committee (AFSC), as chief of the Stranded Mining and Industrial Populations Section of the Department of the Interior. The ultimate shape and substance of the homesteads would largely be defined through the efforts of Eleanor Roosevelt and her ally the AFSC, who saw the homesteads as an opportunity to provide people with dignity.

The AFSC had already been working in mining areas of the western Pennsylvania coal region at Herbert Hoover's request in 1931. Teaming up with Eleanor Roosevelt, they put their energies to work and began building a new community, to be called Westmoreland Homesteads.

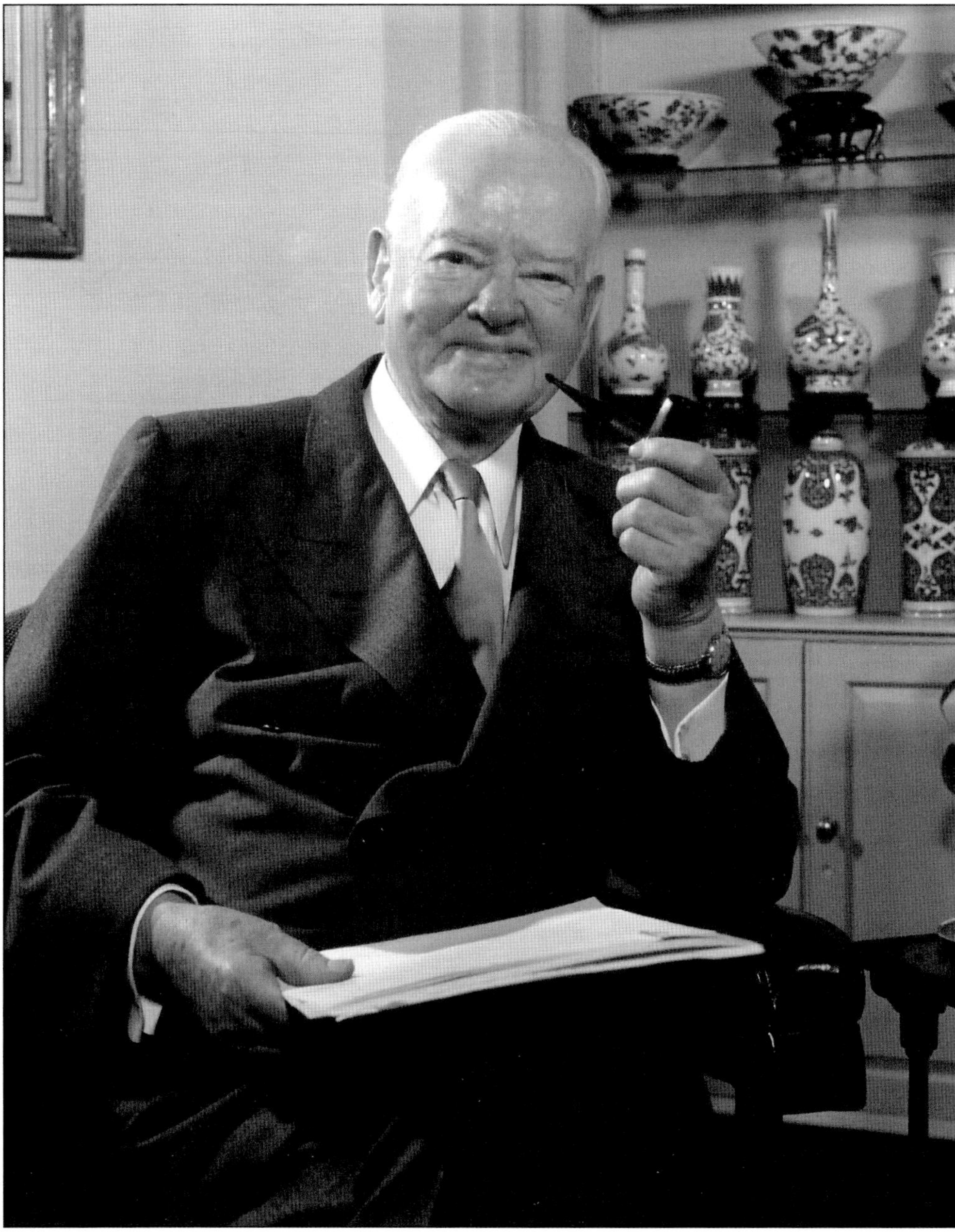

Herbert Hoover, president from 1929 to 1933, was the son of a Quaker blacksmith, Herbert Clark Hoover, and brought to the presidency an unparalleled reputation for public service as an engineer, administrator, and humanitarian. In 1931, he requested the AFSC to start a child-feeding program in the coal-mining region of West Virginia, providing monies through nongovernmental sources. Originally he worked with the AFSC after World War I when, as the head of the American Relief Administration, he used the newly formed AFSC to carry out the logistics of getting food to the millions of starving people in central Europe. Despite criticism, he provided food to postwar Germany and Bolshevik Russia. (Courtesy of the Herbert Hoover Presidential Library.)

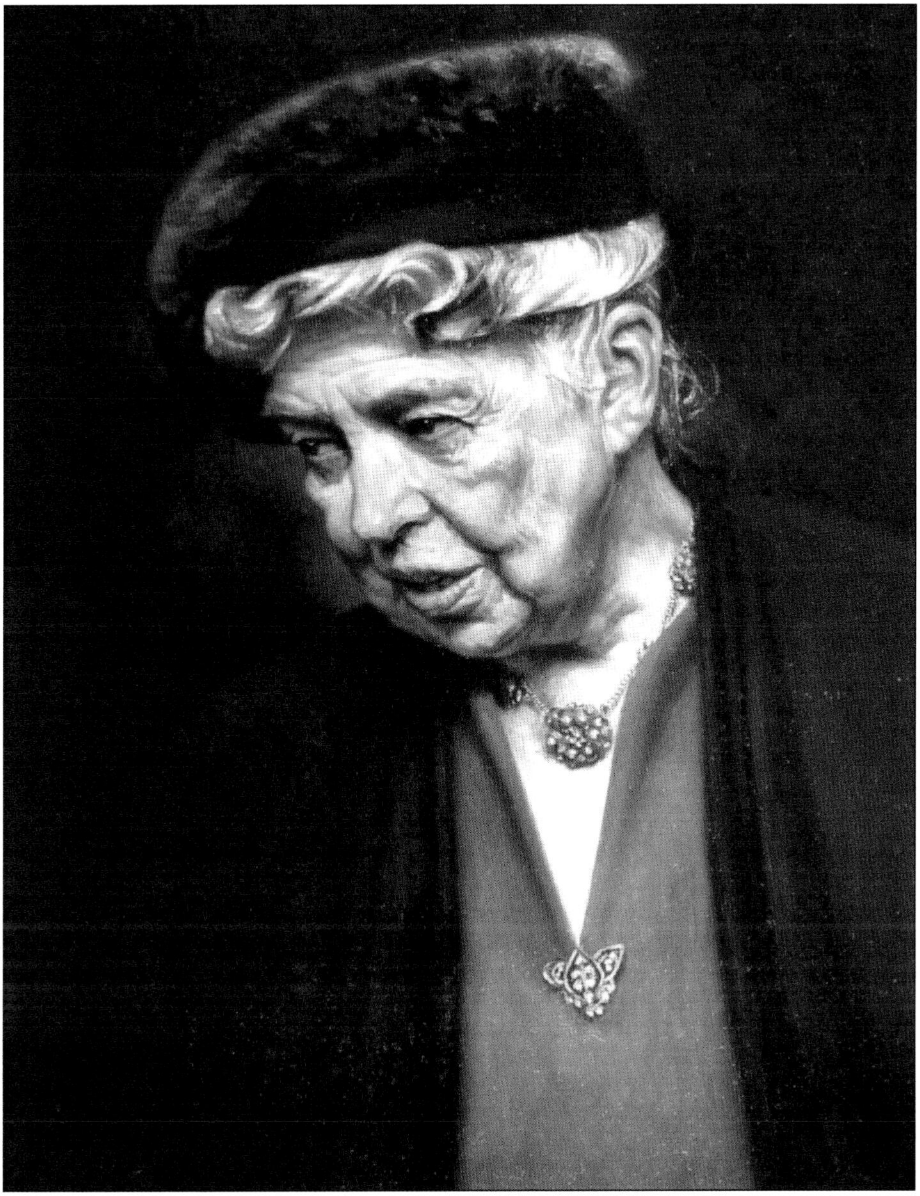

According to the AFSC, Eleanor Roosevelt's association with them began in 1933 when Herbert Hoover was in office. In 1932, the Roosevelts invited Clarence Pickett, the executive secretary of the AFSC, to Hyde Park as an overnight guest. The Roosevelts were aware of the AFSC's work with poverty-stricken miners in West Virginia. They were especially interested in the vocational reeducation and subsistence-living projects AFSC was providing. Eleanor Roosevelt and Pickett had a mutual respect for each other. After Franklin D. Roosevelt became president, Pickett became chief of the Stranded Mining and Industrial Sections of the Department of the Interior. Eleanor Roosevelt was attracted to homesteading for its humanitarian promise of "human dignity" and the opportunity to "develop a sense of mutual responsibility essential to a vital democracy." She came to believe that homesteading would not only "rescue miners from poverty," it would direct them to a "new way of life" according to *Anna Eleanor Roosevelt: The Evolution of a Reformer.* (Courtesy of the Franklin Roosevelt Presidential Library.)

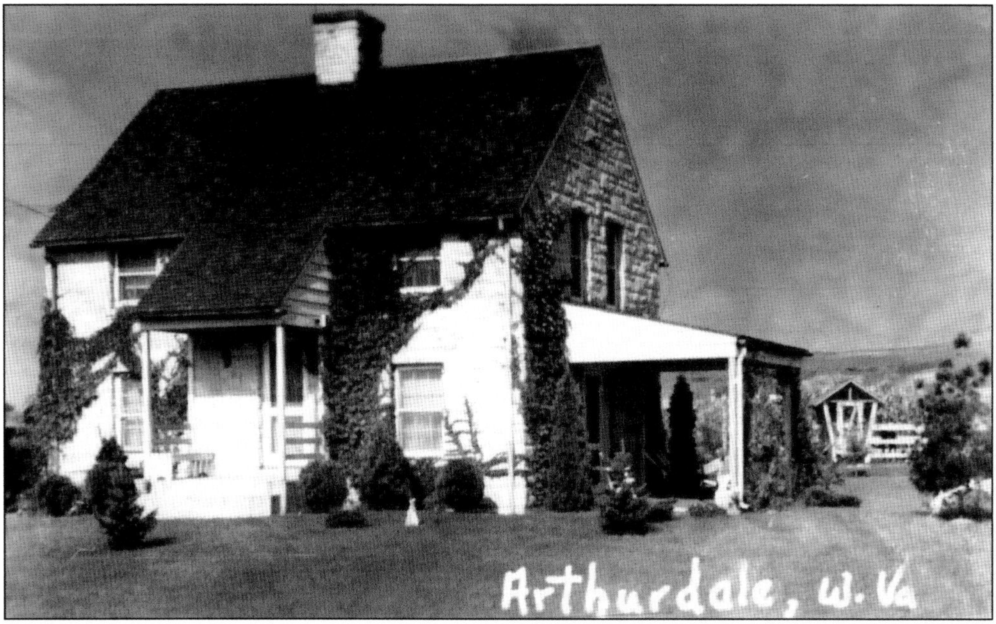

Clarence Pickett had already been working with poverty-stricken miners in western Pennsylvania and West Virginia. The nation's first subsistence homestead project in Arthurdale, West Virginia, established the prototype for all subsequent homestead projects and an array of educational and social programs that would constitute a new way of life for the homesteaders very unlike the one they came from in the coal-mining patches. The house in the above photograph is typical of the Arthurdale home designs. (Courtesy of Virginia Boytim Vahaly and Betty Sue Boytim Mondock.)

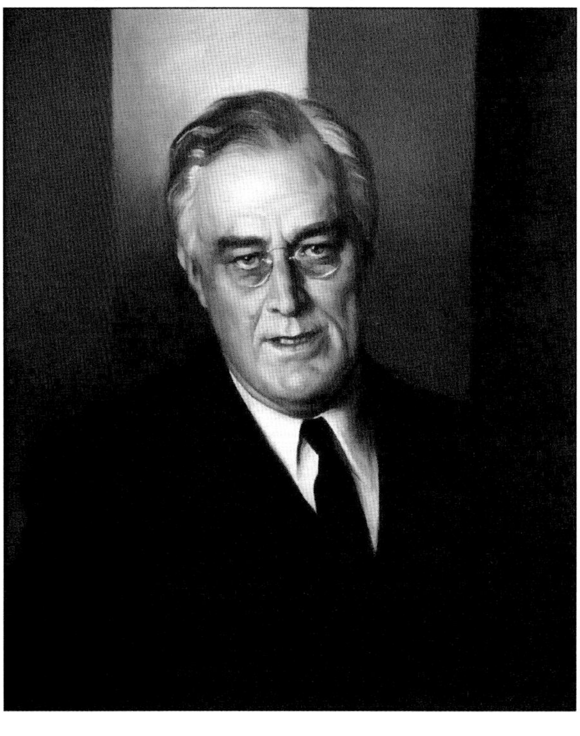

Franklin D. Roosevelt backed Eleanor's project. Eleanor Roosevelt was also attracted to subsistence homesteading because of her love for the land, and she felt that growing one's own food and participating in the construction of one's own home would instill hope and pride in ownership. Her passionate concern for the poor and AFSC's mission and achievement in the field of social justice were a perfect match. (Courtesy of the Franklin Roosevelt Presidential Library.)

Three

The Making of Westmoreland Homesteads

The subsistence homesteads program was soon under way. Mount Pleasant Township in Westmoreland County was selected as the site for the new homesteads. On April 13, 1934, 1,492 acres of land were purchased from the heirs of James P. Hurst. This area was considered to be a "perfect laboratory" for the project with hundreds of miners stranded with no hope of employment in local coal town patches. A total of 772 acres were divided into sections for homesteaders and several acres were reserved for facilities such as barns, chicken houses, athletic fields, a post office, and other community buildings.

In 1934, local architect Paul Bartholomew was hired by the government to design the Westmoreland Homesteads. He designed four-, five-, and six-room homes in the Pennsylvania farmhouse style with dormer windows, shutters, and porches. The homesteaders referred to the style as Cape Cod. The homes would be complete with a basement, running water, bathrooms, and at least 1.6 acres of land. Bartholomew designed the layout of the town to highlight the rolling topography of the former farm, with gently curling roads. Applicants were chosen based upon a point system that included need; size of family; essential skills and work experience needed for the community, like gardening, farming, and carpentry; and ability to participate in building the community. Of the thousands who applied, over 1,850 families were from the local patch towns of Whitney, Weltytown, Calumet, Standard, United, Hecla, Mamoth, and others. Of those, 254 were chosen. The U.S. Department of the Interior mandated that families represent a cross-section of the mining population of western Pennsylvania. A 1940 survey reported that 85 percent were American-born and more than 75 percent were born in Pennsylvania. The average family was composed of 5.5 persons, including 3.3 children, and the average age of the father was 39. The average family earned less than $1,000 per year.

In 1934, under the direction of David Day, the American Field Service Committee set up a summer work camp in Westmoreland Homesteads to get the homesteads rolling. And 55 high school and college students worked 10,000 hours digging a ditch to construct a 260,000-gallon reservoir. A hired workforce, chosen applicants, and Quaker volunteers began to build.

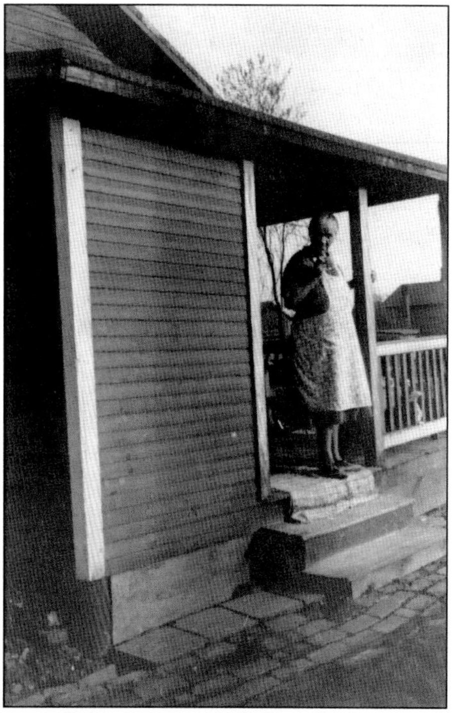

A coal miner's wife stands at the entrance of her patch house. Eleanor Roosevelt had to fight to get this project going. Many people felt the immigrant coal workers and the rural poor were untrainable and unworthy to live in a civilized manner and that Roosevelt's ideas would never work with this class of people. Red scare was prominent and the concept of subsistence homesteading was considered state socialism or a communistic plot led by Eleanor Roosevelt. (Courtesy of Joseph Wolk.)

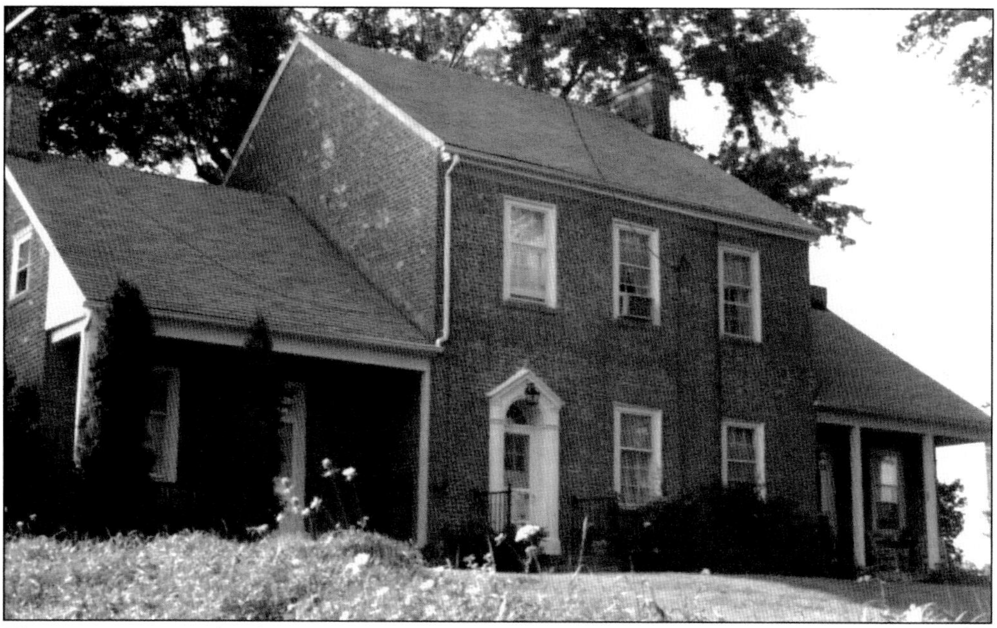

The Hurst House in the above photograph on the Hurst farmland was originally purchased around 1793 by Nathaniel Hurst, a slaveholder from Kentucky who moved into the house accompanied by his slaves. The house later served as an inn and stagecoach stop serving food and drinks. Legend has it that the nicks on the fireplace mantel are from patrons striking their whips. Prior to and during the Civil War, the home served as an underground railroad for runaway slaves with an underground tunnel. The Hurst heirs donated the land to Mount Pleasant Township School District, which later housed Hurst High School. (Courtesy of Jean Andrews Crise.)

At only 29 years of age, David W. Day—pictured here with his wife and children—project manager, Indiana Quaker social worker, and member of AFSC, oversaw the construction of 250 houses. He hired engineers, foremen, and workers. Homesteaders, as required, worked three days of paid work per week, earning $4–5 per day, and two days a week earning credits toward the purchase of their home. Building began in April 1934, and by 1937, all homes were completed. After the credits were accrued, homesteaders moved into their home, paying rent of $12–14 per month, which continued to be counted as credit to the purchase of their home. (Courtesy of Gail Hoffer.)

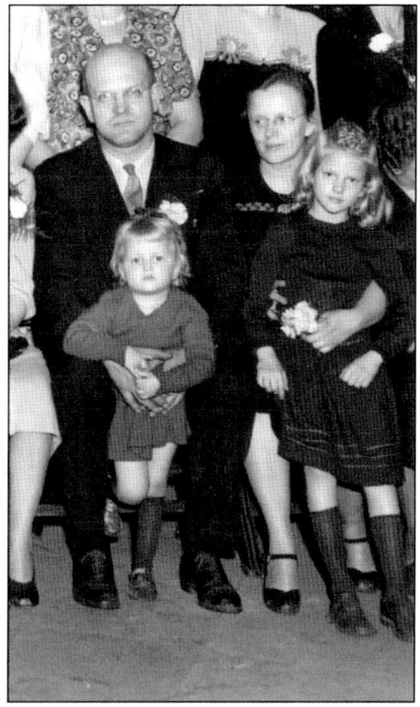

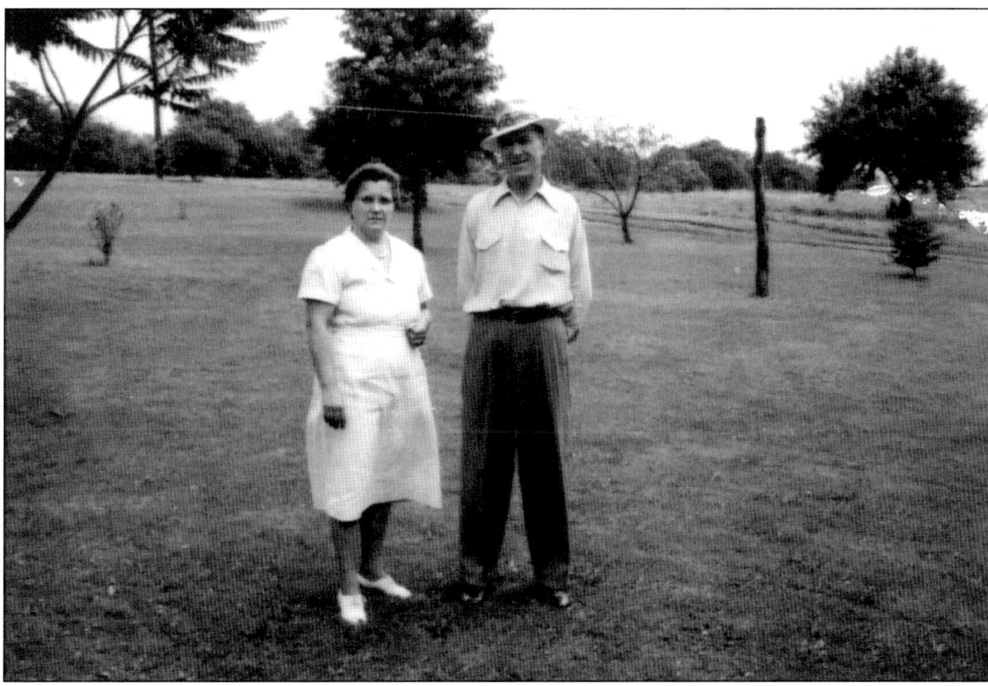

In this photograph, Anthony and Mary Hajduk Wolk stand in their orchard. Like many other original homesteaders, they were transported by the AFSC in a flatbed truck. The AFSC would recruit by driving up and down the streets of local coal towns advertising the new community. They were able to take their children, Florence, Anthony Jr., and Joseph, to see the model homes and lot they would decide upon. Once an application was made, a representative would visit the home of the applicant and interview the family. (Courtesy of Joseph Wolk.)

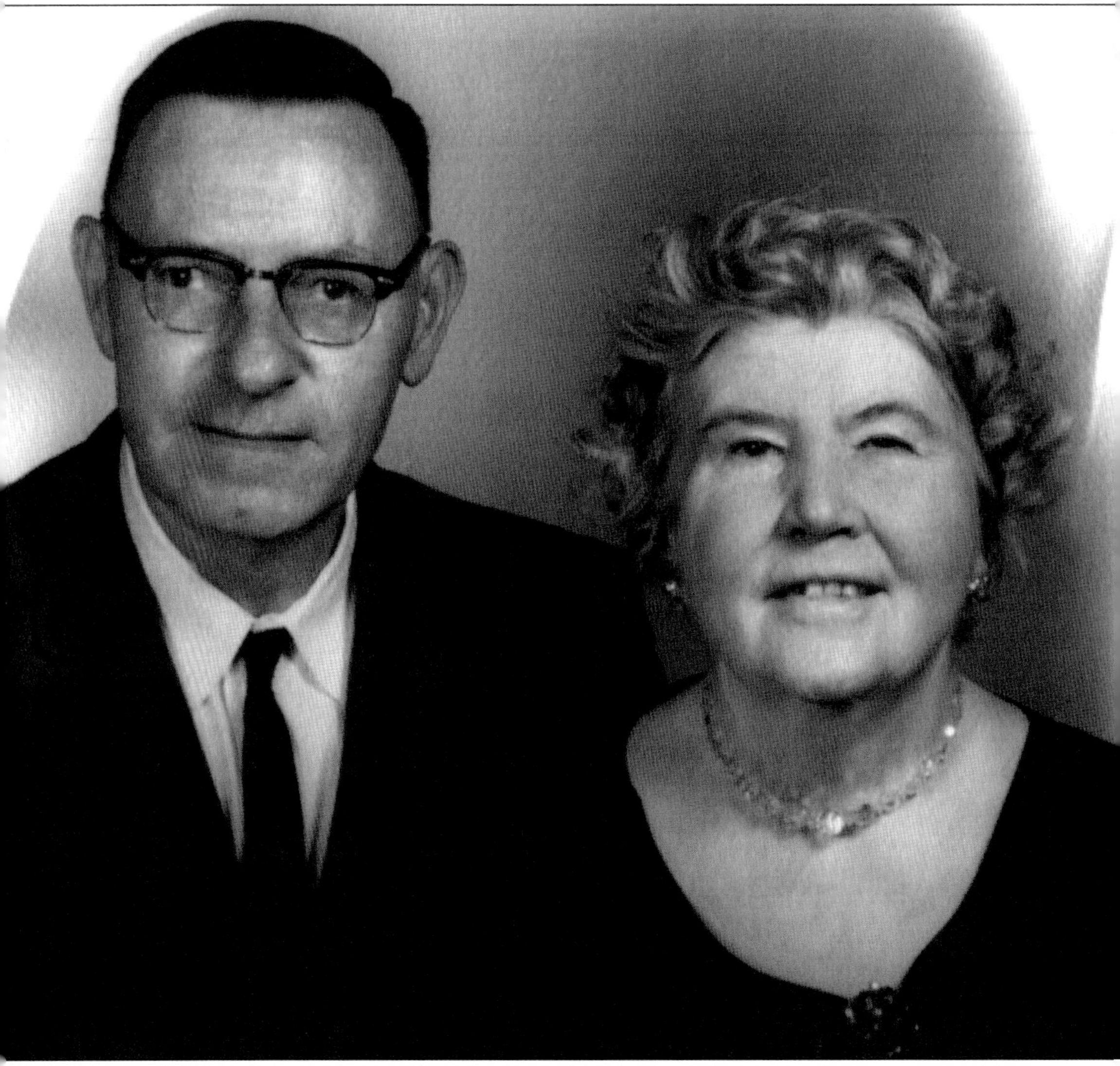

Scotch-Irish Hugh Greer could not catch a break. He took a job picking apples in Virginia where he met and married half Cherokee Evalena Terry in 1923. They began a family during the pre-Depression years. Due to a freak accident, Greer was blinded in one eye. The Greers moved around settling anywhere they could find work. Living in Lorain, Ohio, his five-year-old son was kidnapped. As soon as his son was returned, Greer packed up the family and moved to Lancaster. But things were not working out for him there. He came across an advertisement in the *Grit*, a weekly newspaper, and according to the advertisement, applications were being taken for a new community in Westmoreland County. Hugh Greer applied. His friends and family told him that he was just wasting a 3¢ stamp, and they said, "They will never take someone like you!" His application was accepted, and in 1935, he packed up the family and moved, and there have been Greers in Norvelt ever since. (Courtesy of Rev. David Greer.)

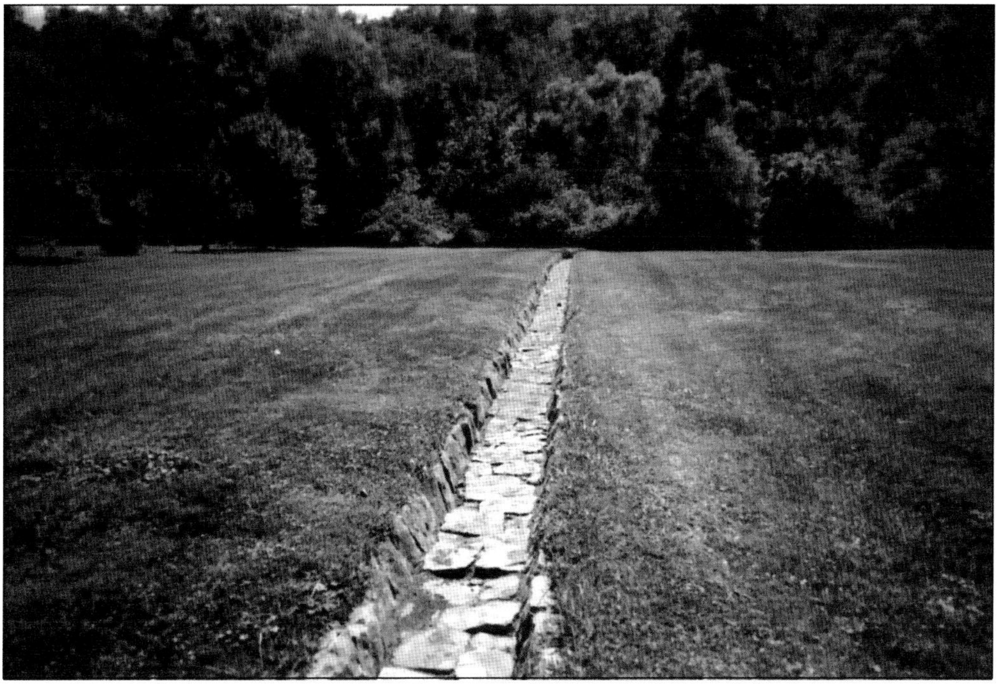

This photograph shows one of many hand-cut stone drainage ditches made by the AFSC volunteers in 1934–1935. Many of the drains are still in perfect condition. (Courtesy of Earl Saville.)

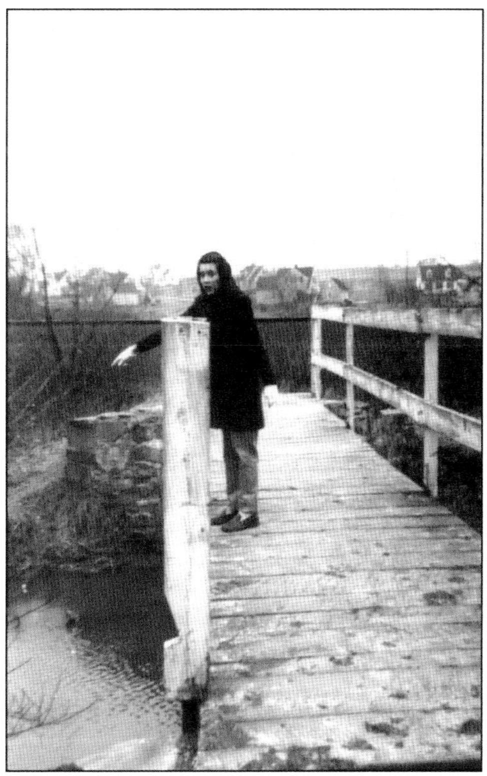

With no bus or streetcar available, this footbridge was made by the AFSC volunteers in the early days of the homestead to permit D section homesteaders to cross the Sewickley Creek to get to the town center and school. Many children crossed this bridge to get to the baseball field and playground by the school. (Courtesy of Patty Ewing Hawse.)

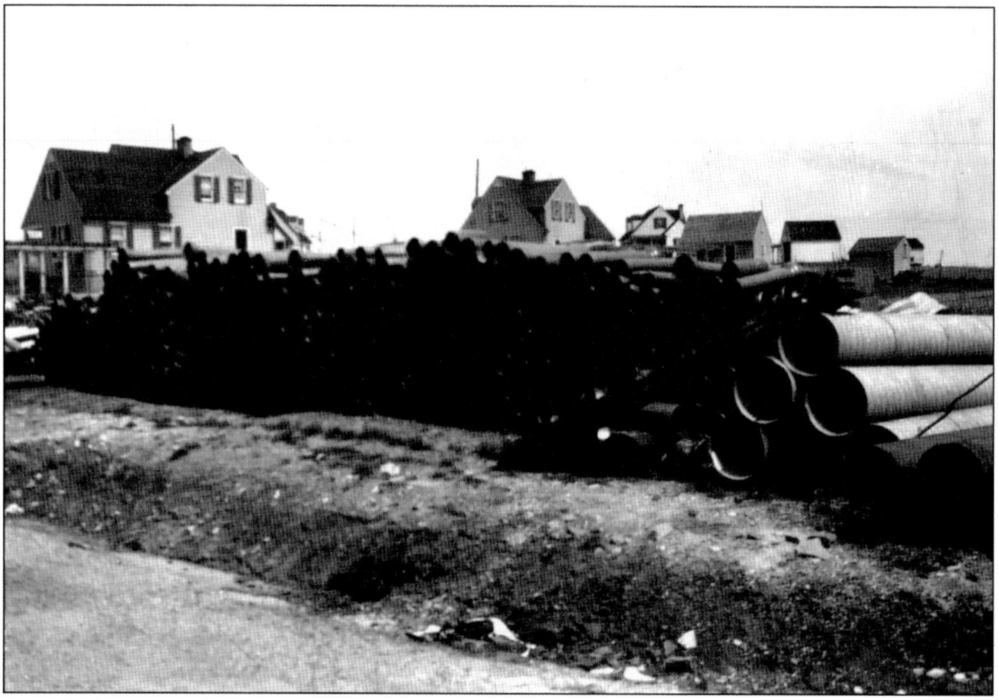

Soon building supplies arrived and construction began. This photograph shows one of the many piles of building supplies needed for the completion of the homes. (Courtesy of Kimberly Sulzer.)

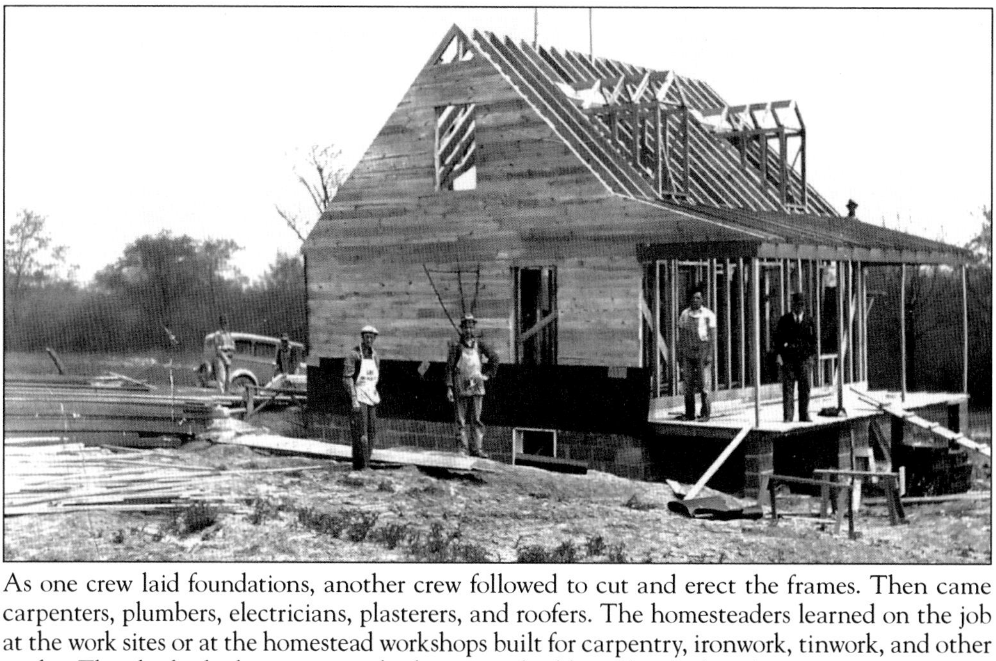

As one crew laid foundations, another crew followed to cut and erect the frames. Then came carpenters, plumbers, electricians, plasterers, and roofers. The homesteaders learned on the job at the work sites or at the homestead workshops built for carpentry, ironwork, tinwork, and other trades. They built chicken coops and other co-op buildings for the hog farm, poultry farm, and beef and dairy farm. (Courtesy of Andrea Dominick.)

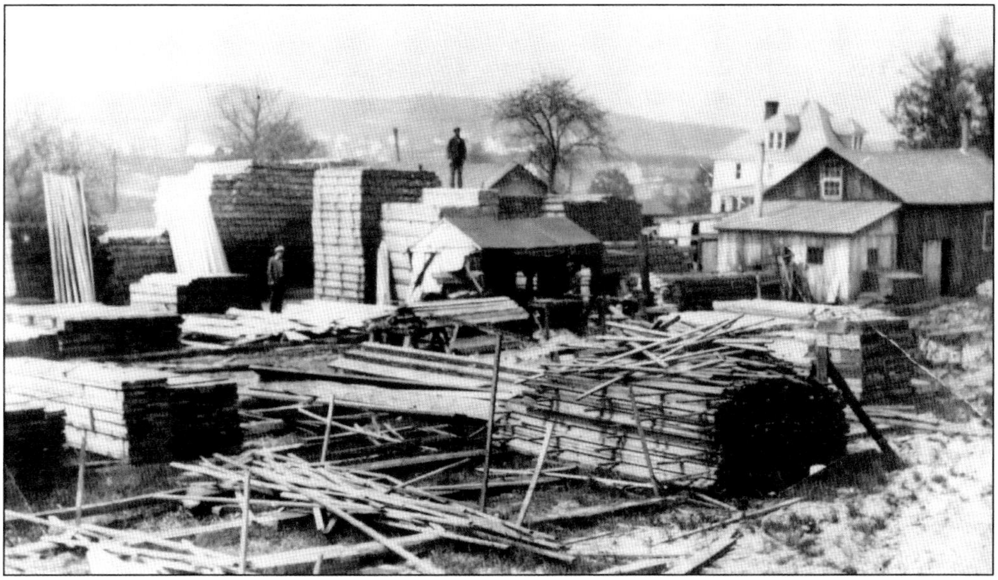

AFSC instructors taught residents how to operate machinery such as jigsaws to make their own furniture, make housing repairs, and so on. The community had a craft shed with tools residents were welcome to use to make crafts and home furnishings. Basements were hand dug, framing was cut in a workshop near the railroad or a workshop behind the construction office of what is now Hoffer's Funeral Home. A chain-driven truck would haul the wood to the house sites. The photograph above shows, from left to right, homesteaders Floyd Allison, Tony Wolk, and John Kennedy near the construction office organizing lumber deliveries for new home construction. (Courtesy of Joe Kennedy.)

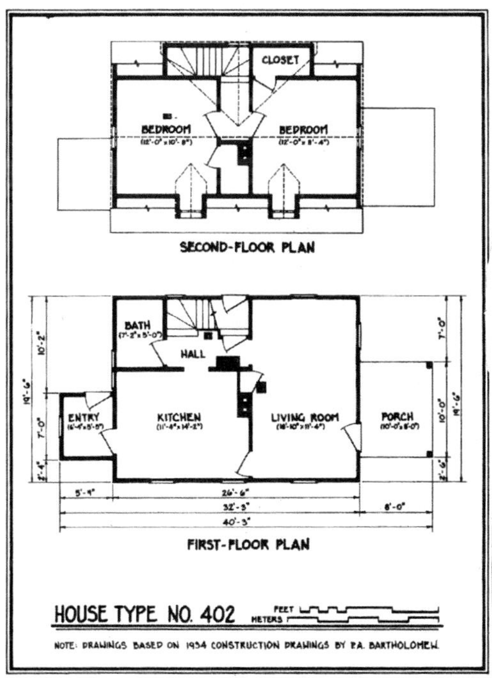

Figure 10 Plans of Type 402 house. Delineator: Isabel C. Yang, HABS.

This is one of six different house plans available in Westmoreland Homesteads, designed by Paul Bartholomew. All basic plans included one-and-a-half-story frame houses. Westmoreland Homesteads was developed into five sections; each section was identified by a letter from A to F. Each homestead would be numbered and referred to as A-1, A-2, and so on. (Courtesy of Norvelt and Penn-Craft, Pennsylvania.)

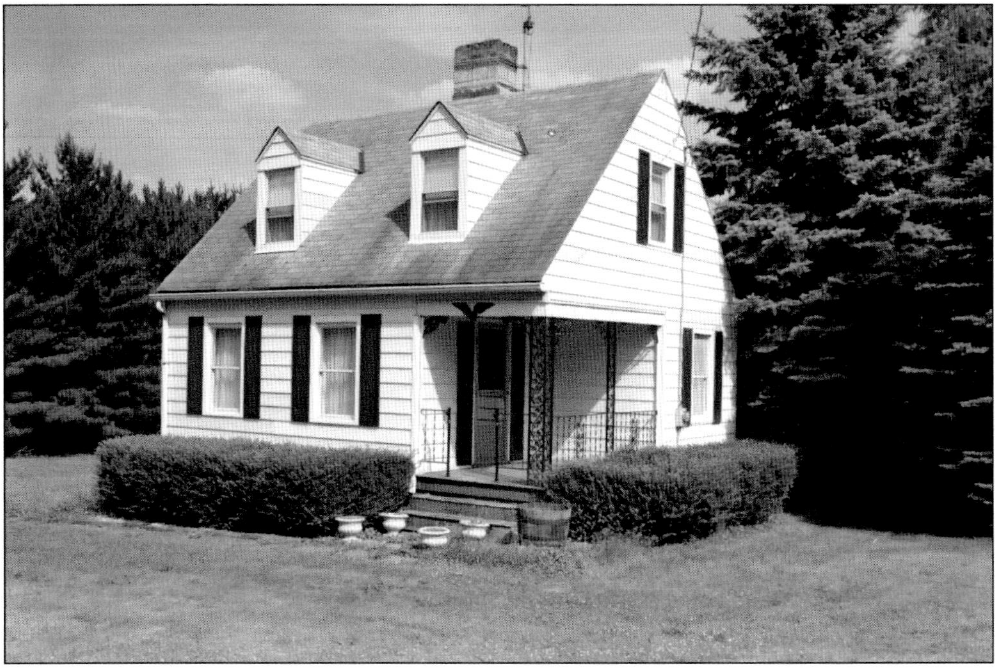

Workers were required to participate in the construction of their houses, and a man's labor was treated as equity, reducing the cost of the home and land. Working three days a week, a worker earned $4–5 for one day of work and credit toward the purchase of the home for two days of work. This photograph displays a home plan, 601 R in B section. (Courtesy of the Library of Congress.)

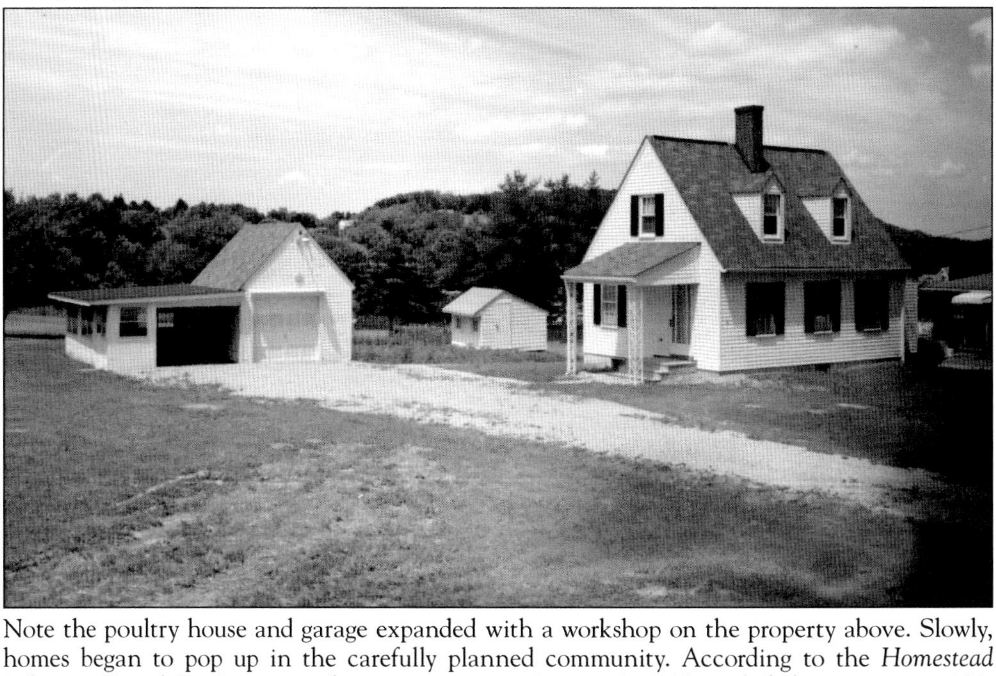

Note the poultry house and garage expanded with a workshop on the property above. Slowly, homes began to pop up in the carefully planned community. According to the *Homestead Informer*, David Day's report of construction on August 8, 1935, included excavations, 130; foundation walls, 93; houses raised, 93; interiors finished, 69; and occupied to date, 52. (Courtesy of the Library of Congress.)

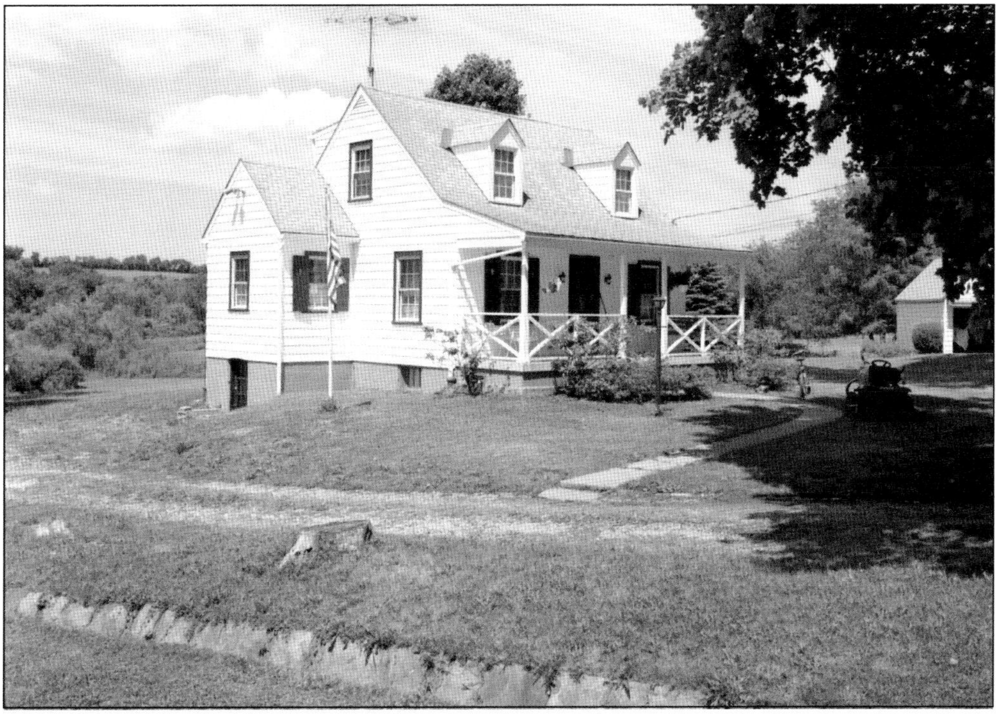

This photograph shows house plan 503 R in E section. This is a five-room home with one bath, garage, coop, and grape arbor. (Courtesy of the Library of Congress.)

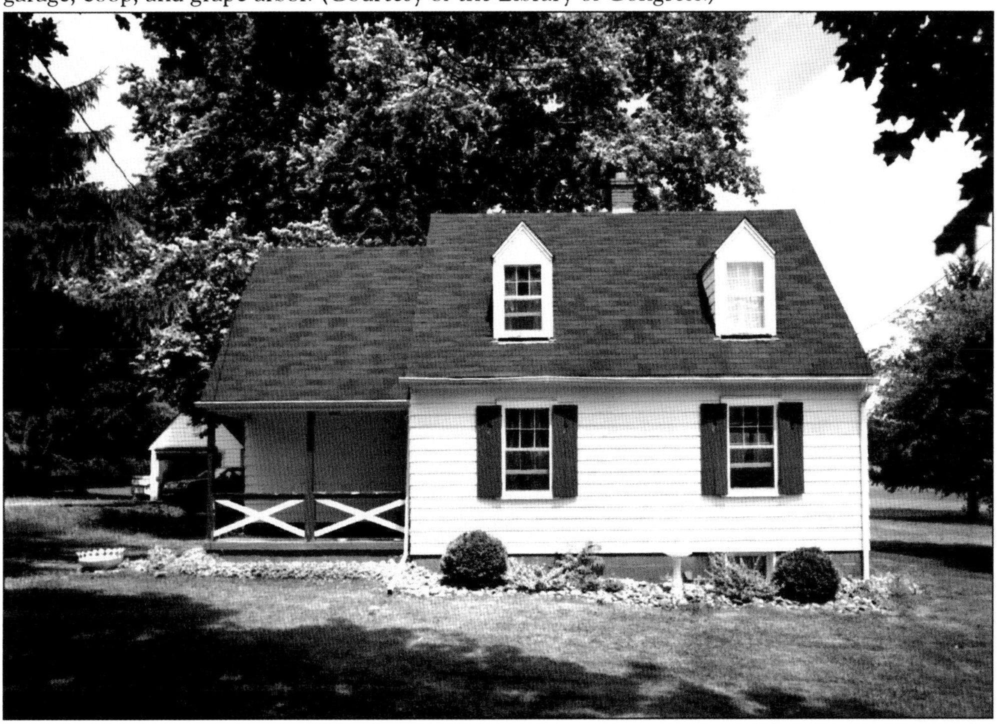

This photograph shows house plan 601 R in B section, which had one bath, garage, coop, and grape arbor. (Courtesy of the Library of Congress.)

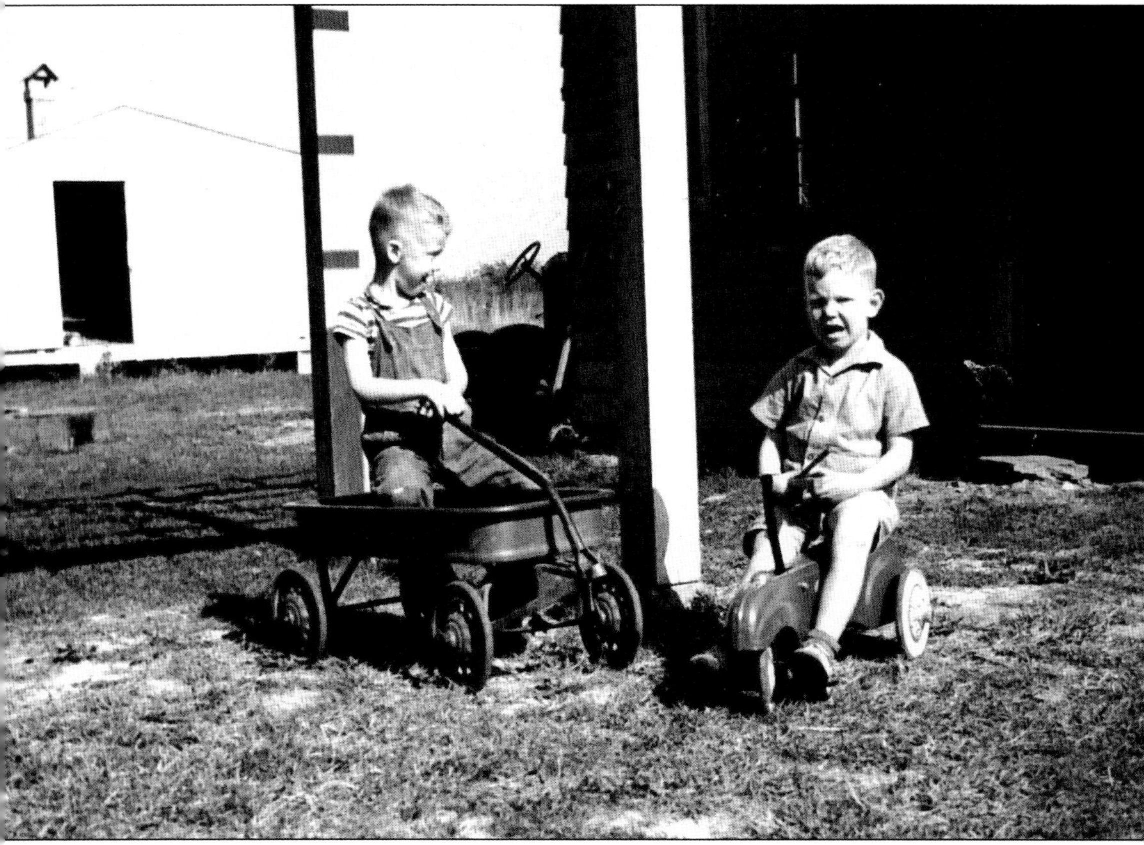

As the building proceeded, families waited in expectation to get their homestead completed and move into their new homes. Having to work five days per week on their home, many fathers had to walk two to five miles or more per day to get to the work site in Norvelt. Explained as an experimental community, future homesteaders could only imagine the dream of having their own home fulfilled. After just moving into their new homes in B section, the two boys in this photograph, Joseph Kennedy (left) and Chuck Goulding, are enjoying what their parents worked hard for. (Courtesy of Joseph Kennedy.)

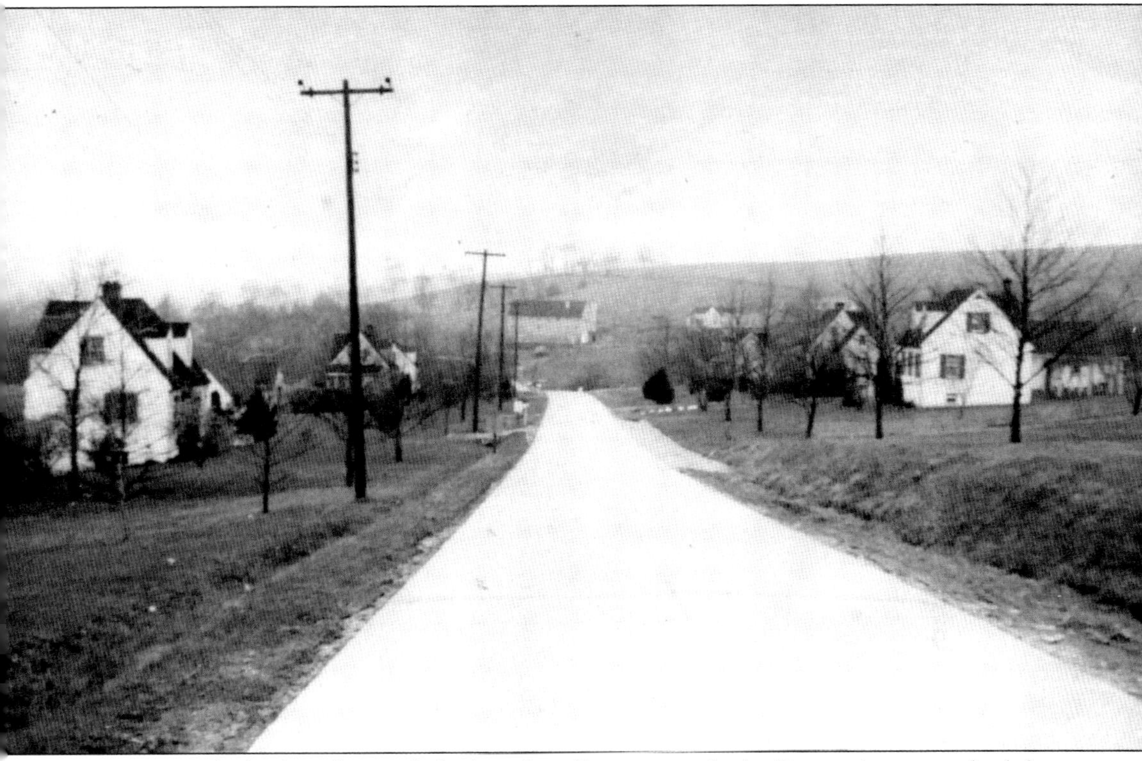

This photograph displays the newly laid road on F section with the Pastore home on the left, followed by the Ludwig home, and the Yanda home on the right, followed by the Pavick home. The Andrews farmhouse is in the background. Norway maple trees were provided for the sides of the property. Roads were made using red dog, waste material from coke ovens. (Courtesy of Ann Riggen.)

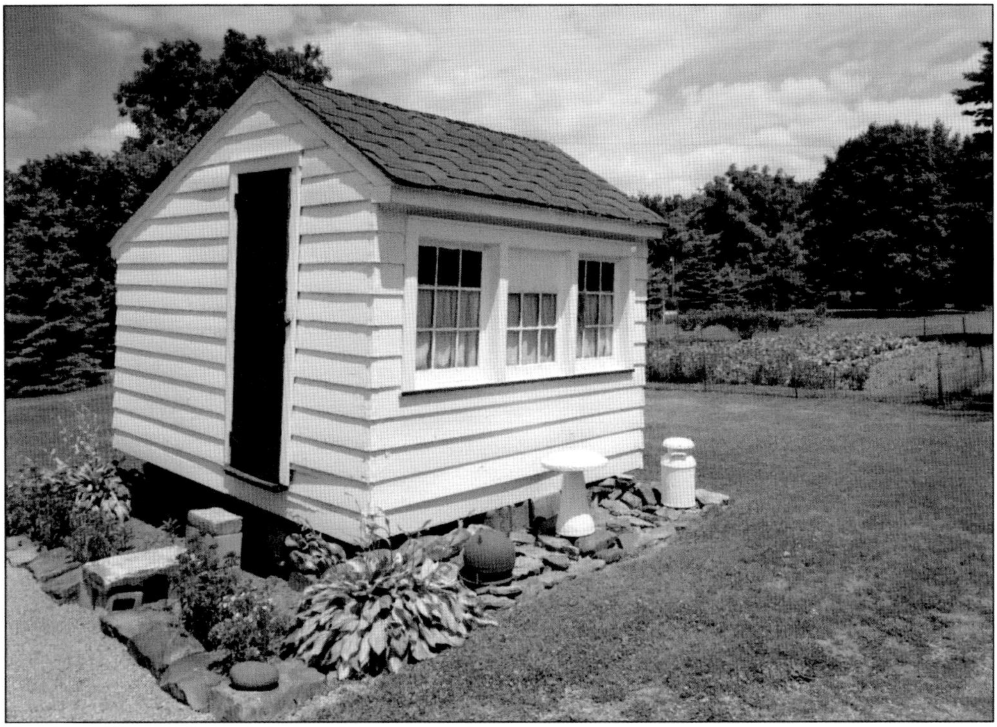

A poultry house—chicken coop, as many homesteaders called it—was built on each lot so homesteaders could raise chickens for eggs and meat. (Courtesy of the Library of Congress.)

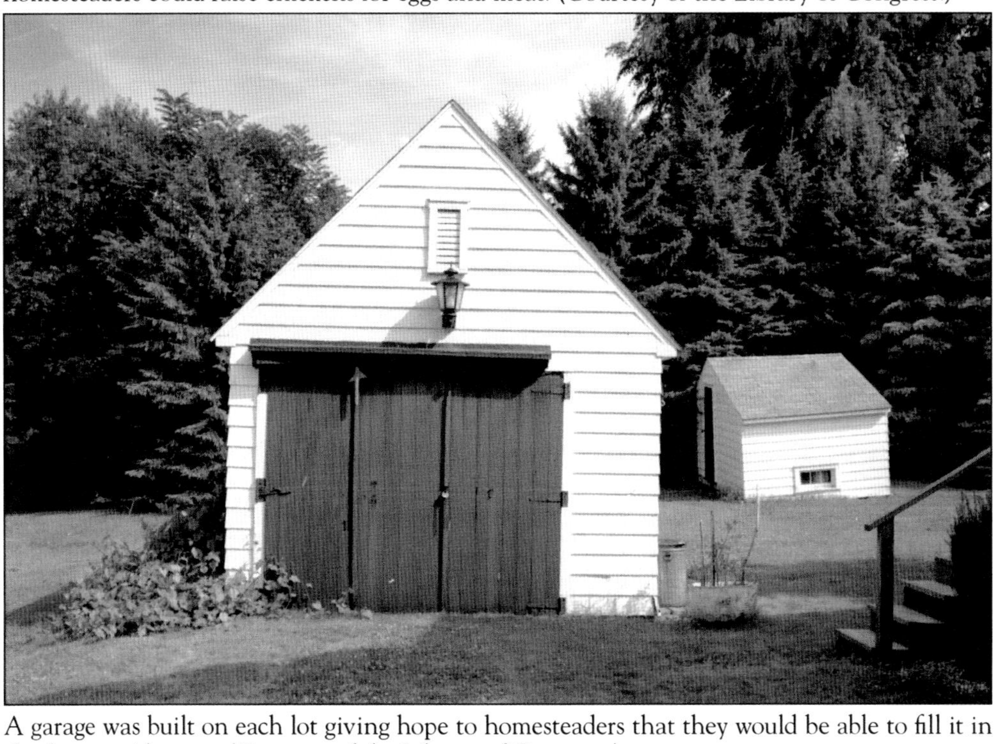

A garage was built on each lot giving hope to homesteaders that they would be able to fill it in the future with a car. (Courtesy of the Library of Congress.)

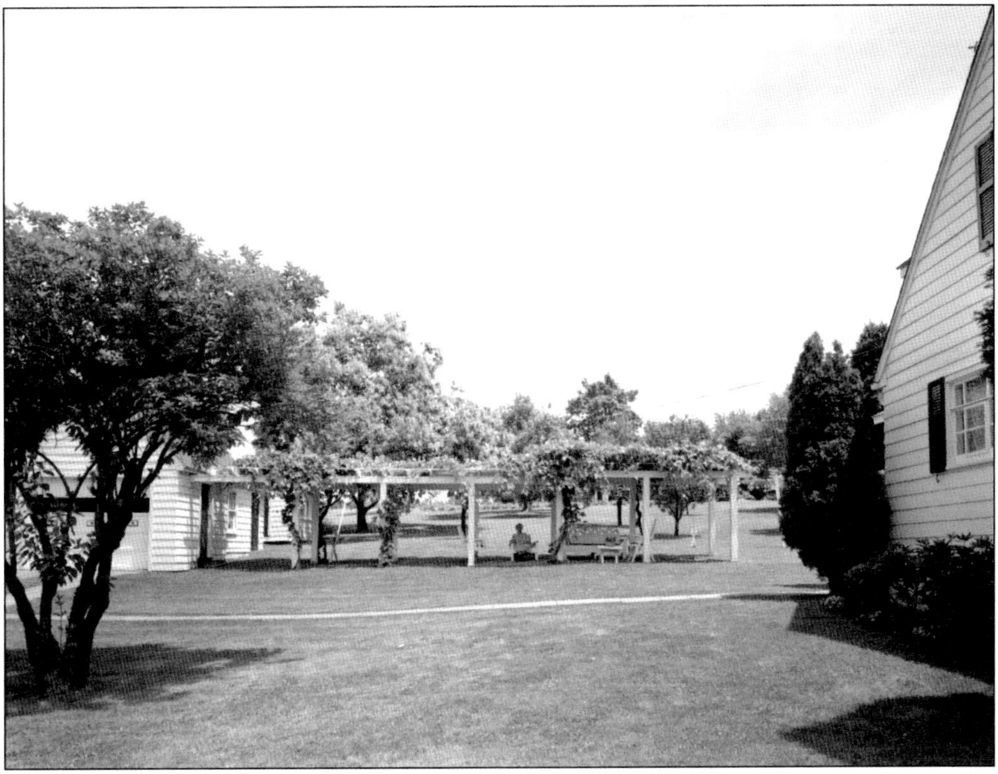

Each home site was provided a grape arbor for production of jellies, juices, wines, and pies. This photograph of Mary Wolk, original homesteader, sitting in a chair under her grape arbor shows a common site. (Courtesy of the Library of Congress.)

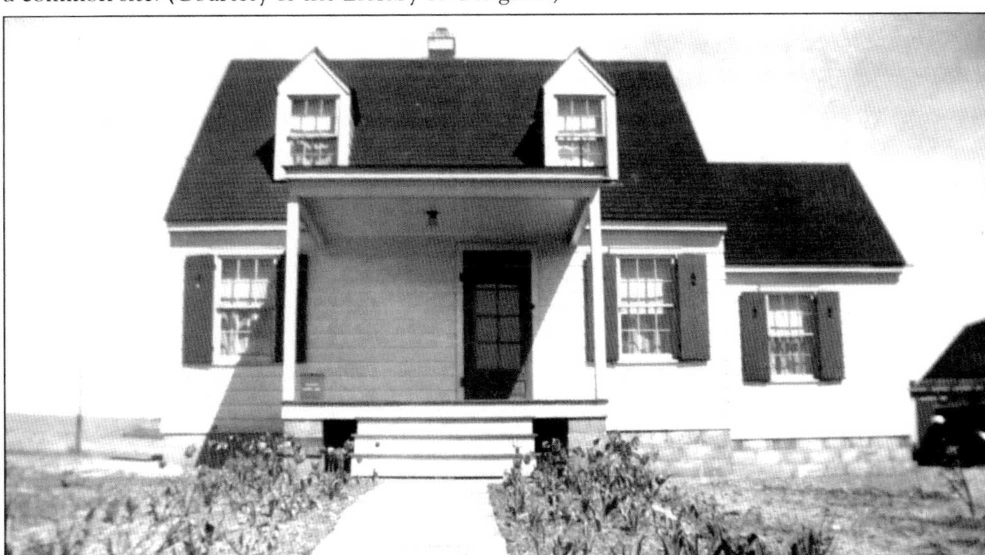

Each home was designed with an eat-in kitchen and living room on the first floor with a utility room or hallway. Five- and six-room homes had a bedroom on the first floor and a bathroom and two bedrooms on the second floor. Six-room homes had a small child's room accessed through one of the bedrooms. (Courtesy of Helen Bann Stefanek.)

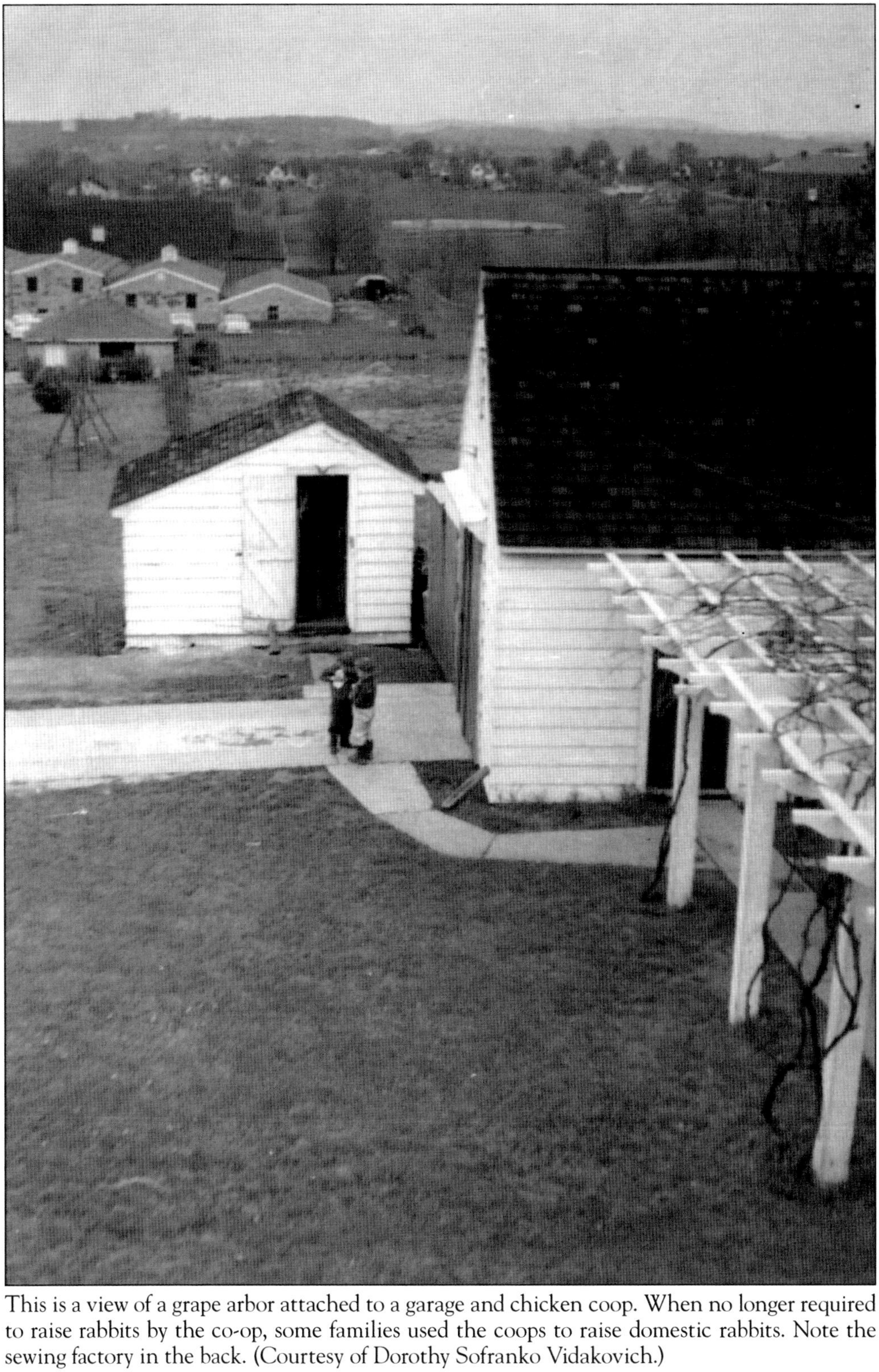

This is a view of a grape arbor attached to a garage and chicken coop. When no longer required to raise rabbits by the co-op, some families used the coops to raise domestic rabbits. Note the sewing factory in the back. (Courtesy of Dorothy Sofranko Vidakovich.)

Four

The Cooperative Back-to-the-Land Movement

The economic depression of the 1930s "fomented diverse intellectual unrest," according to *Back to the Land! Pennsylvania: New Deal Era Communities*. Many people questioned the effects of industrial development on the U.S. economy. Many thought it created dependencies upon one and, at the same time, spawned a propertyless proletariat. Upon seeing the harsh living conditions of the West Virginia miners, Eleanor Roosevelt expressed concern that the conditions of poverty were ripe for a revolution. Thomas Jefferson's agrarian economy was seen as a panacea among some intellectual circles who cried for a return to the land. The subsistence homesteads were viewed as a solution to the economic and social woes. As part of the subsistence homesteading movement and in keeping with the back-to-the-land sentiment, a cooperative organization was formed in 1935 under the leadership of David Day and the AFSC and operated by the homesteaders with a loan of $370,000. The loan from the federal government was to pay for the construction of the homes and other facilities. The community was provided with a chicken barn, incubator, a large dairy farm with milking cows for meat and dairy products, a pig farm, and vegetable garden. The co-op formed the Westmoreland Community Enterprises to operate the 600-acre co-op farm.

David Day encouraged subsistence gardening, industrial development, and formation of cooperative associations as a means of helping the homesteaders become self sufficient. He organized study groups for homesteaders to learn theory and practice of cooperatives. The co-op established a credit union and encouraged residents to buy from the co-op. The meat and dairy products from the farm were sold to outside firms and at the co-op store. Proceeds were returned to the farm for maintenance. In 1936, the garment factory and brick community center and trade center were built and included the co-op store, a lunch counter with a soda fountain, barbershop, beauty parlor, doctor, and dentist offices. Health care was provided by the federal government, and a community nurse was hired and lived in one of the homesteads. AFSC provided self-help counseling, and volunteers gave instruction in cooking, sewing, canning, carpentry, health, personal hygiene, dancing, art, music, and horticulture for all homesteaders. David Day started and edited the biweekly newsletter that kept everyone abreast of activities and happenings. He worked hard to get the homestead project started and kept the community together through his editorials, articles, and words of wisdom.

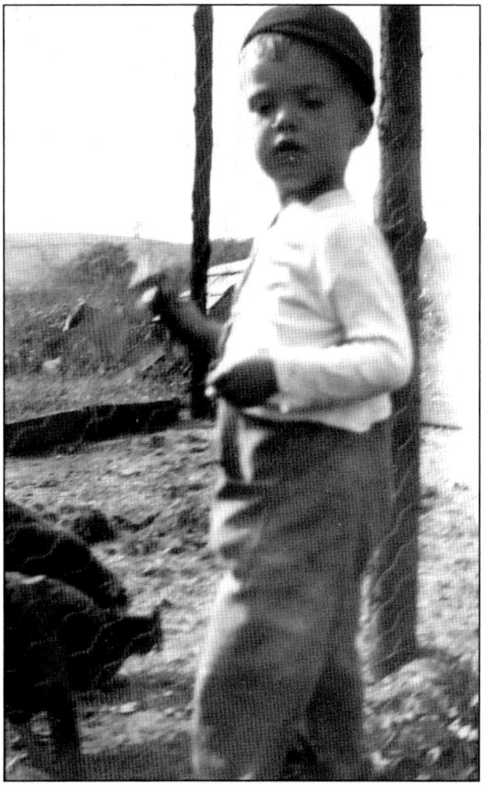

As the community began to develop, even children became involved; even the youngest got enjoyment from the new surroundings. In this photograph, a Pavick boy, a son of Mr. Pavick who ran the pig farm, is feeding the pigs. (Courtesy of Patty Pavick Kelly.)

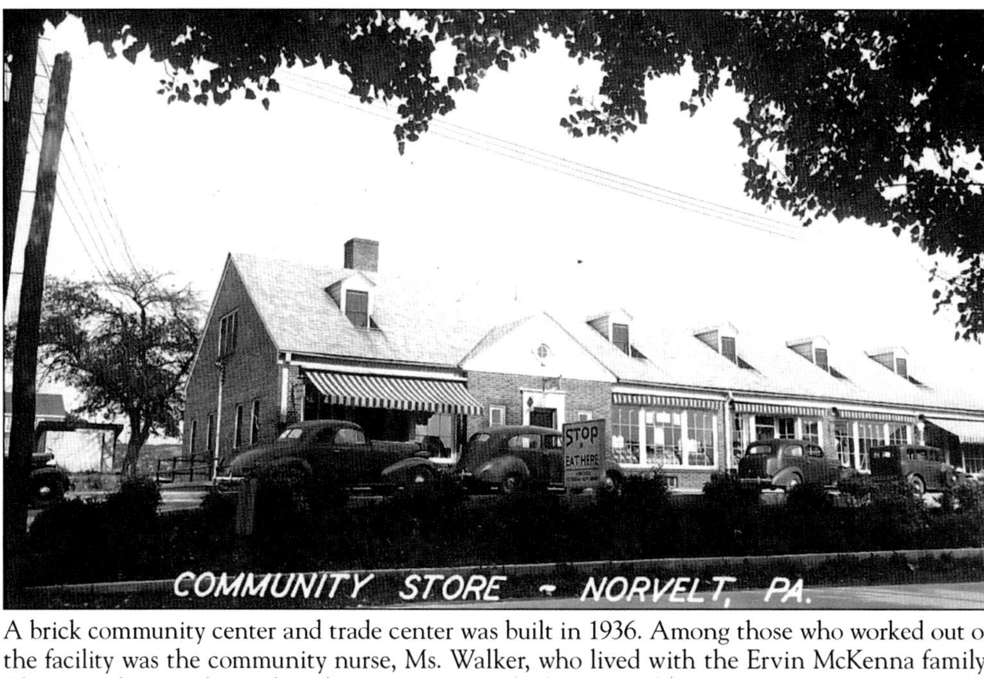

A brick community center and trade center was built in 1936. Among those who worked out of the facility was the community nurse, Ms. Walker, who lived with the Ervin McKenna family. The store that was located in the center reported a business of $2,543.74 in June 1936. On the basis of 170 families in residence, this represented an average patronage of just under $15 per family, which was described as commendable by David Day. (Courtesy of Andrea Dominick.)

This is a photograph of Ray Faust, store manager, standing in front of the trade center, which housed government offices and Westmoreland Homestead Community offices on the top floor. C. B. Somers, a homesteader and general manager of Westmoreland Community Enterprises, had his office on the second floor. The shoe shop was in the basement, operated by Luigi "Louis" Pastore. Barbershop, beauty shop, dairy bar, and general store run by manager Ray Faust were on the first floor. The *Homestead Informer* announced that earnings of the co-op store for June 1937 were $8,861.07, significantly more than the previous year. (Courtesy of Betty Sue Boytim Mondock and Virginia Boytim Vahaly.)

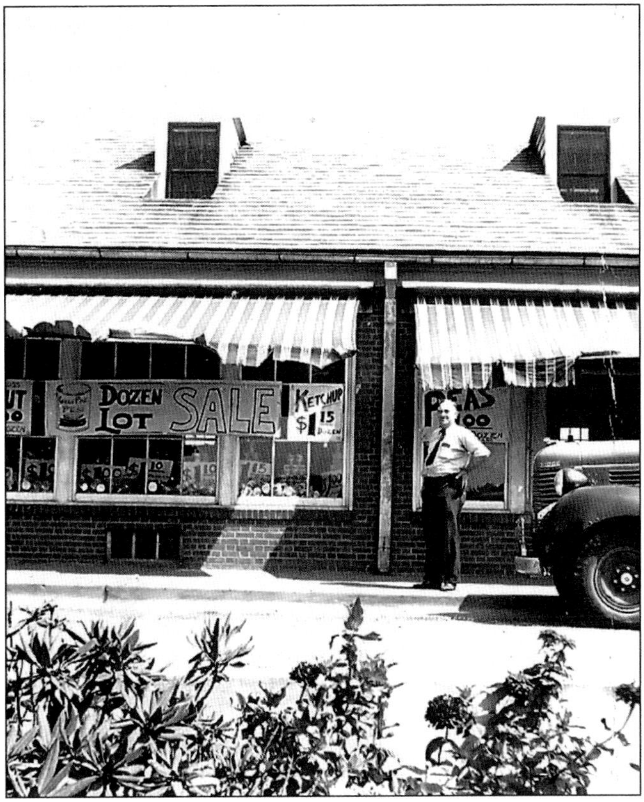

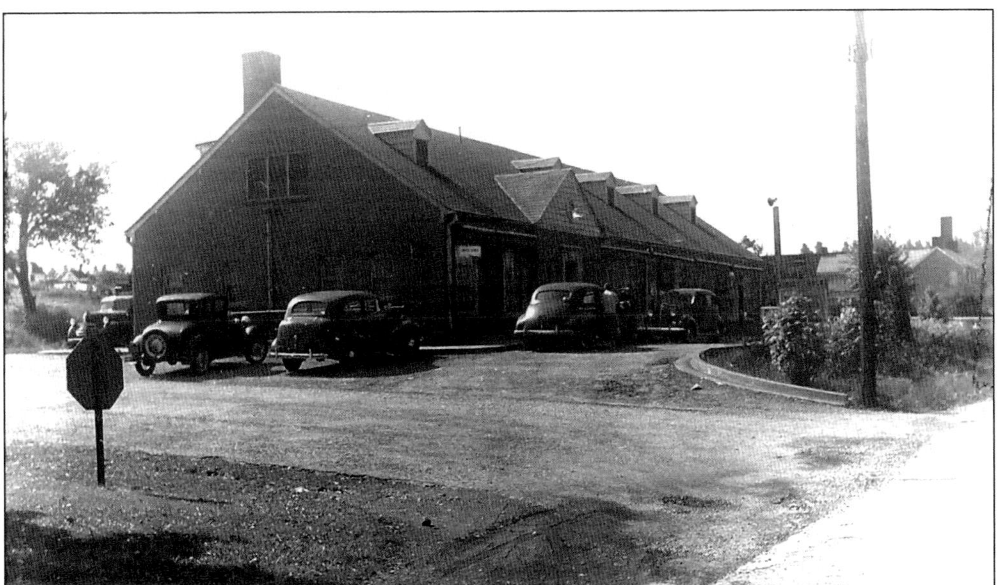

This community center and trade center held the offices of the physician and public-health nurse. Both used the trade center as a medical office and both visited the homesteaders in their homes when needed. The building also housed the Post Office, run by Postmistress Agnes Whisdosh, and a barbershop run by Wallace Hoffer. To the left of the community center was Weibel's dairy barn. (Courtesy of Sally Puskar.)

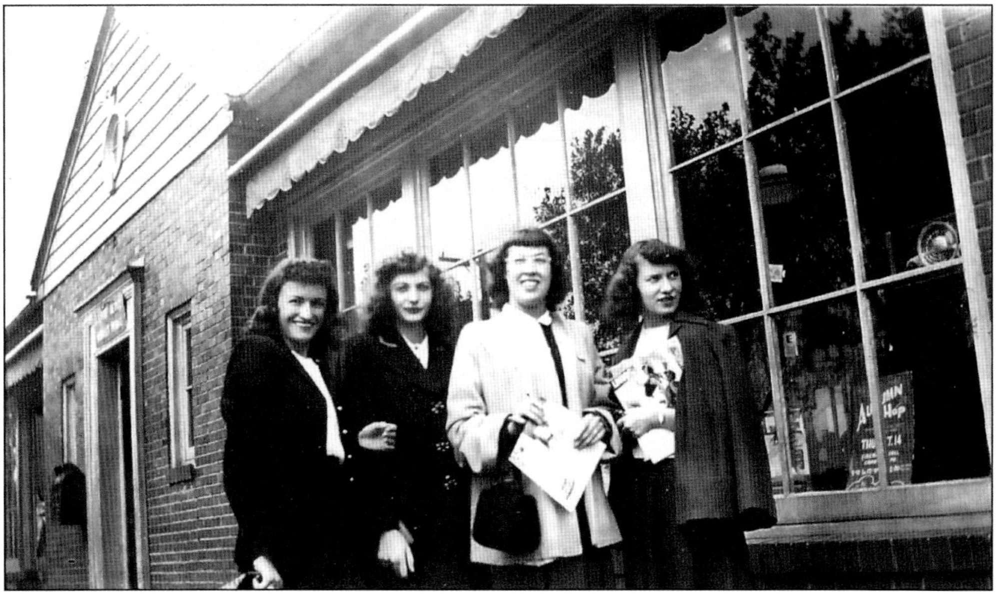

The young women in this photograph are standing in front of the community store. It was a popular spot to meet, shop, and enjoy sodas in Weibel's Dairy Bar. The first addition of the *Homestead Informer* on August 8, 1935, announced that the cooperative store and dairy bar "belongs to the community" and were counting on their support. Pictured from left to right are Virginia Vahaly, Jennie Testa Snyder, Fanny Eicholtz Shirey, and Mildred Johnson Kennedy. (Courtesy of Valeria Sofranko Wolk.)

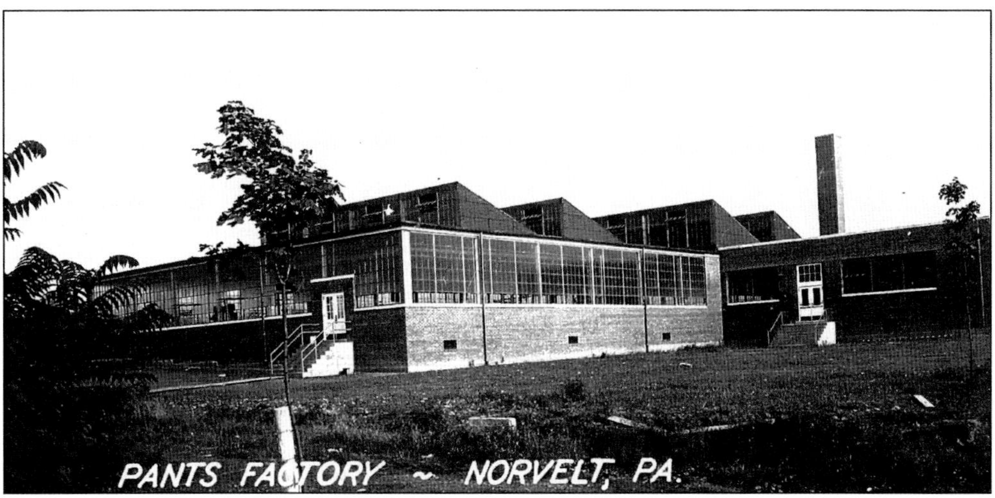

The *Homestead Informer*'s May 1937 issue reported a rumor being circulated that the government might build a factory at Westmoreland: "And if our luck is good it may be that eventually we will get a factory here. In the meantime, don't pass up any good jobs in order to hold yourselves open for one in that factory." The photograph above was taken shortly after the factory opened. (Courtesy of Betty Sue Boytim Mondock and Virginia Boytim Vahaly.)

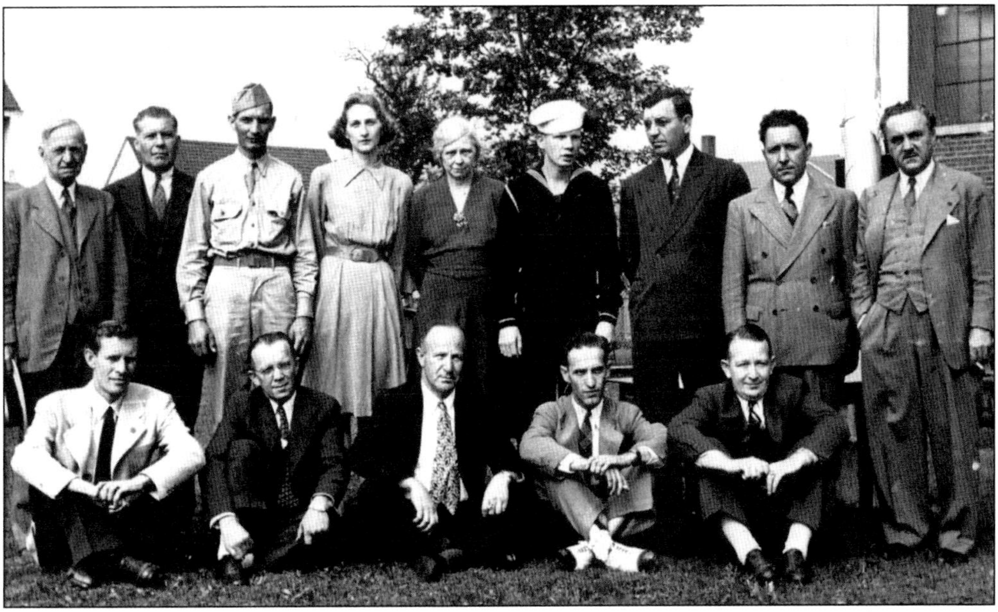

The homesteaders' hopes were answered when the garment factory was erected in 1939. It employed many workers over the years and made pants and chevrons for the military in the 1940s during World War II. In later years, it made bulletproof vests for soldiers in Operation Desert Storm and the war in Iraq. The owners of the factory in the above photograph pose with a soldier and sailor during World War II to display the uniforms made at the factory. (Courtesy of Betty Sue Boytim Mondock and Virginia Boytim Vahaly.)

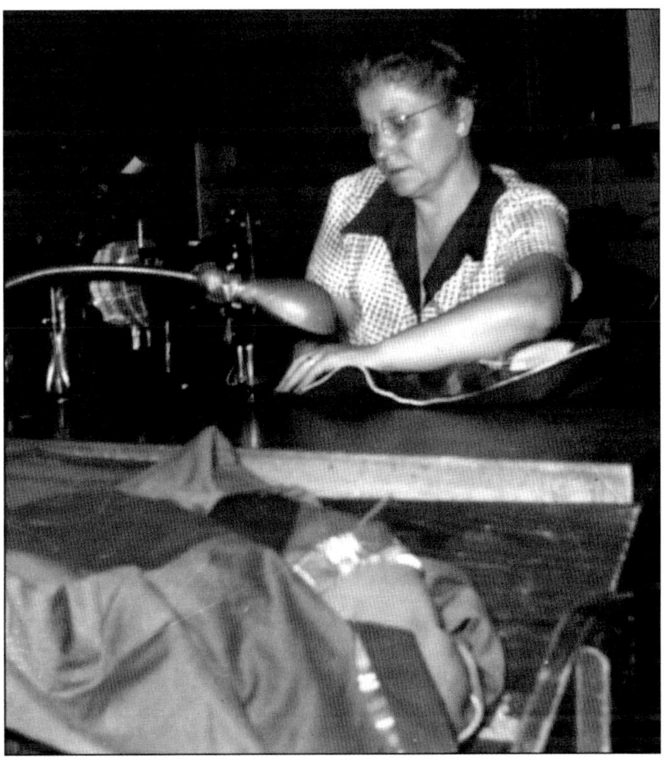

Seen in this photograph, Mary Hajduk Wolk, a "pocket girl," worked at the factory nearly all of her years in Norvelt, until her retirement in 1969. In later years, the garment factory made ladies' jackets and coats and men's sport coats and suits. (Courtesy of Valeria Sofranko Wolk.)

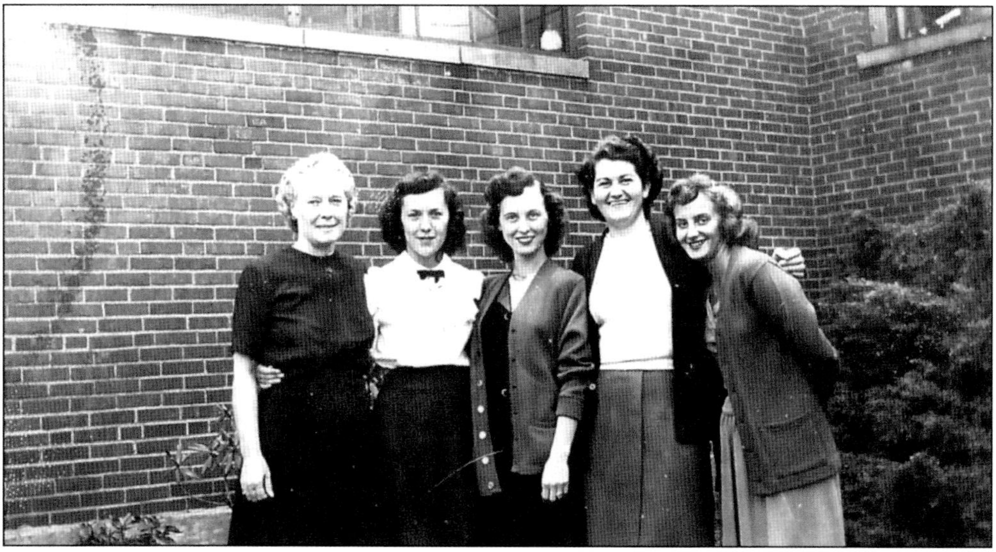

Many friendships were forged among workers at the garment factory. Pictured from left to right, office personnel in the early 1940s were Eva Patterson; Josephine Emerick Curci; Valeria Sofranko Wolk; Flora, a New York employee; and Gen Garsteck. Often, high school students would work evenings, especially during World War II, when production was increased to make uniforms for the military. The sewing machine operators would wonder if their sons or boyfriends would be wearing the uniform they made. (Courtesy of Valeria Sofranko Wolk.)

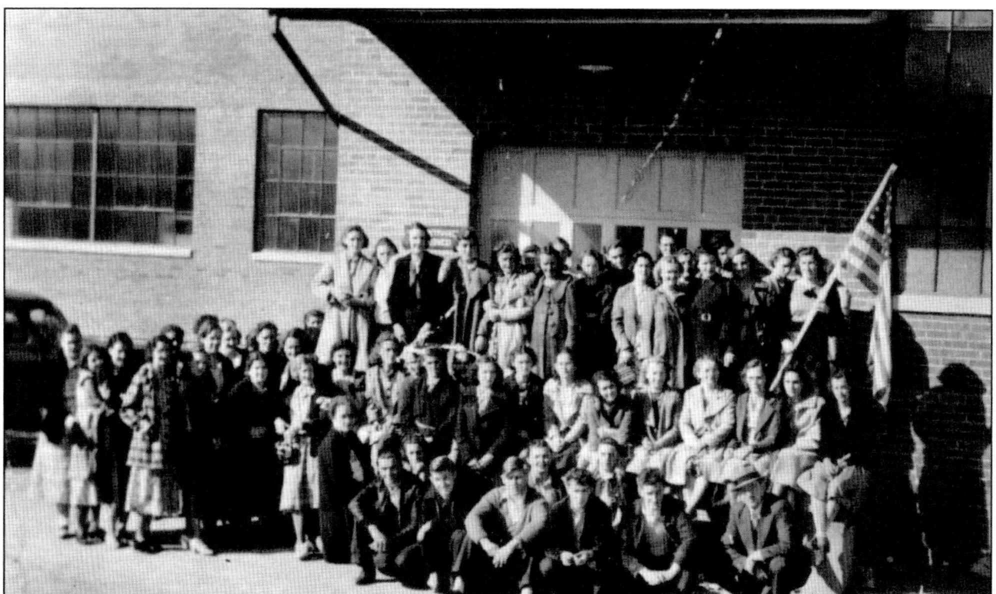

This group photograph was taken at the garment factory during World War II. Nearly everyone working in the pants factory knew someone in harm's way. The workers would schedule times to honor them. (Courtesy of Gail Hoffer.)

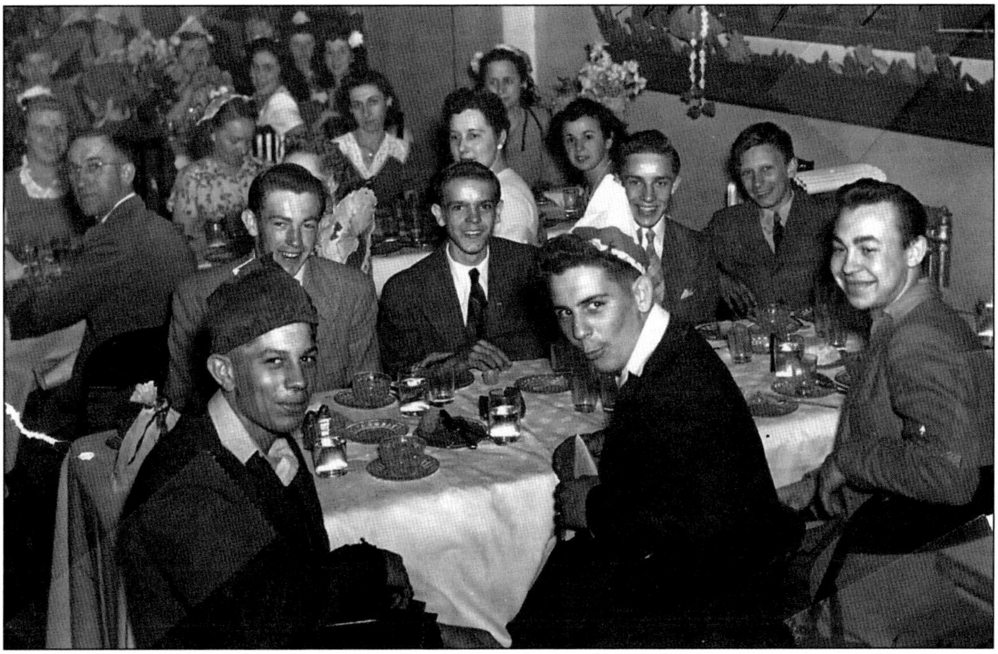

Workers in this photograph enjoy a Christmas party in the mid-1940s. The company was called Washington Sales and later AMCO of Norvelt. Everyone in Norvelt seemed to refer to it as "the pants factory." Pictured at the table from left to right are (first row) Andy Karinchak, Alex Delynko, and Tom Horechoff; (second row) Regis Kelley and Art Hunter. (Courtesy of Kathleen Kelley.)

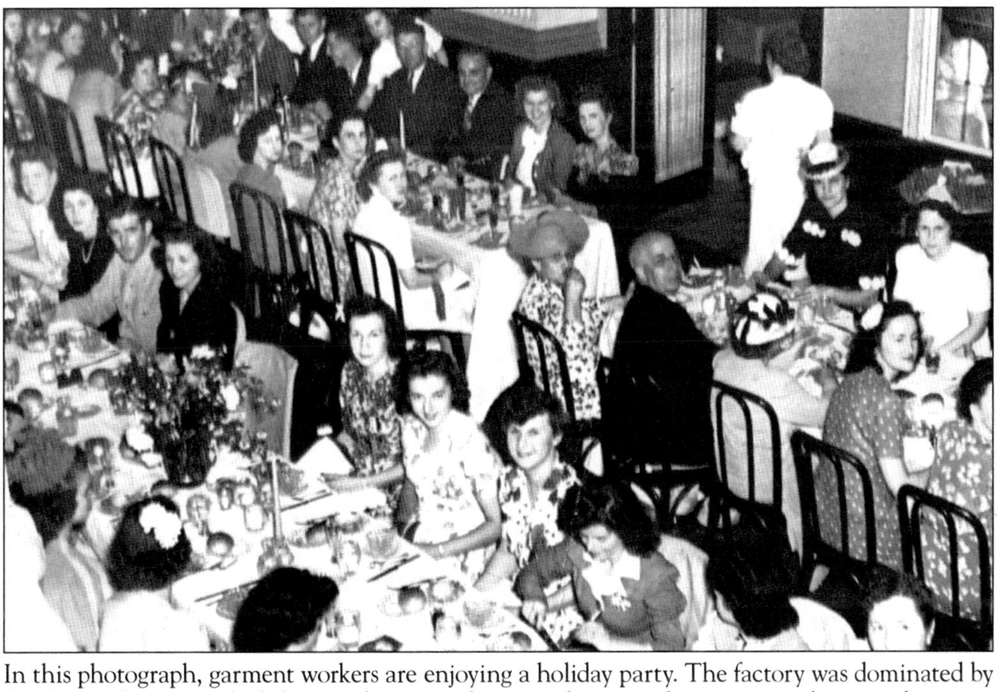

In this photograph, garment workers are enjoying a holiday party. The factory was dominated by female employees, and while most homesteaders were happy to have any employer in the town, many critics of the homestead movement complained that the government was encouraging a low-paying sweat shop. Most men found work outside of the co-op. (Courtesy of Kathleen Kelley.)

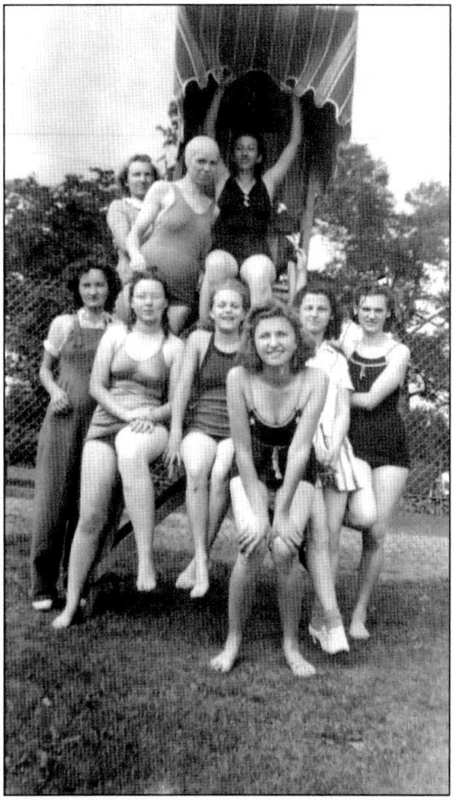

The garment factory served as a social network for homesteaders during their high school years and later. The photograph at left shows girls at a local swimming pool socializing after work. (Courtesy of Valeria Sofranko Wolk.)

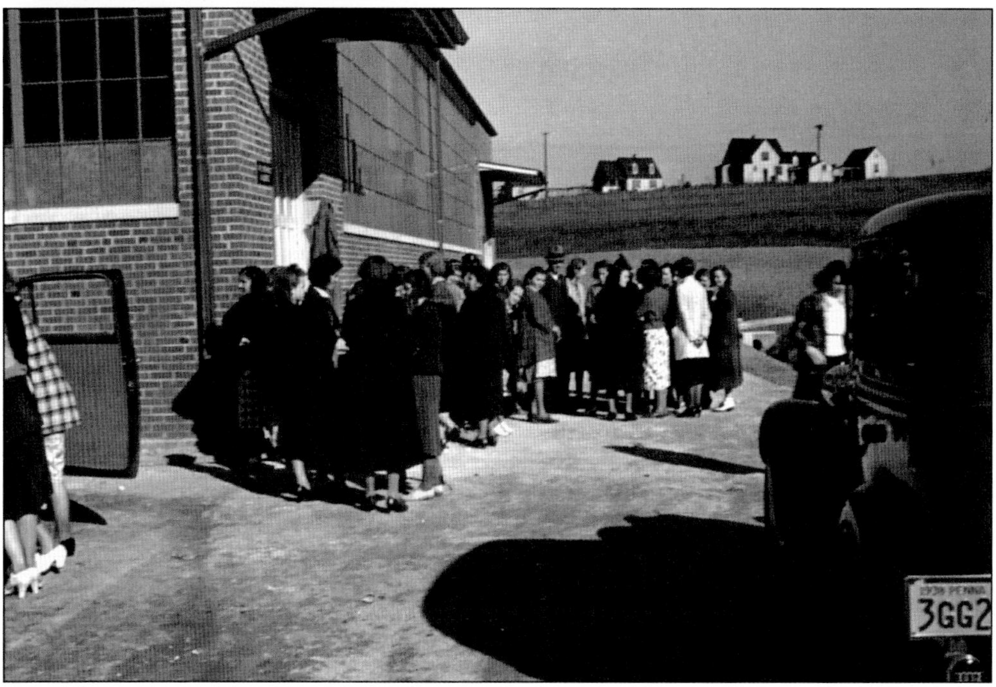

Sewing factory workers gather outside awaiting the start of a workday in 1939. (Courtesy of Patting Ewing Hawse.)

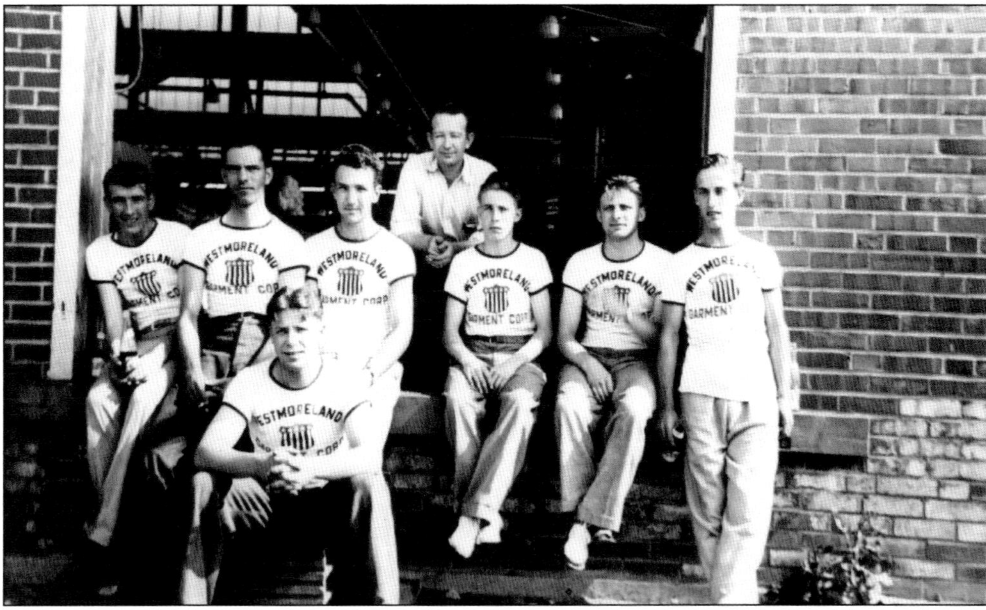

These young men, cutters at the garment factory, wear their Westmoreland Garment Company baseball team T-shirts. Every summer the factory had a baseball team, and many young homesteaders who worked at the factory played on the team. (Courtesy of Sharon Smith.)

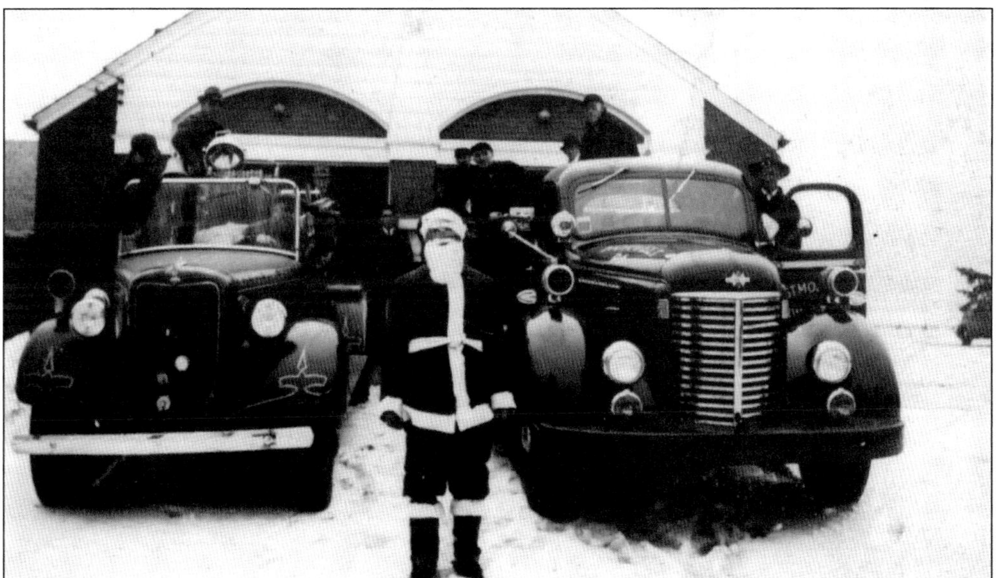

One of the most important developments in Westmoreland Homesteads was the creation of the Westmoreland Homestead Volunteer Fire Department. Early on, the firemen worked hard to establish a top-notch station. In one of the first meetings, on June 1, 1936, they met at the schoolhouse to review the public alarm system. Each section in Norvelt was given a special blast. Five blasts of the siren meant a special firemen's meeting was to be held; three blasts was a general fire alarm and all firemen were to report to the Dillon barn immediately. Here the firemen are preparing for their annual Christmas "door to door" drive through the community to deliver candy to the children. (Courtesy of Steve Viazanko.)

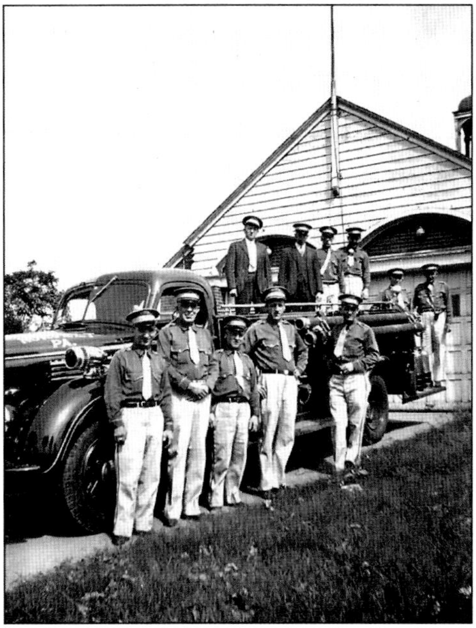

On August 19, 1936, a new Ford V-8 chassis was purchased as a first step in securing a fire truck. It was turned over to the Westmoreland Homesteads fire department on August 31, 1936. The firemen worked hard to raise money to purchase the needed parts to complete the fire truck. (Courtesy of Steve Vizanko.)

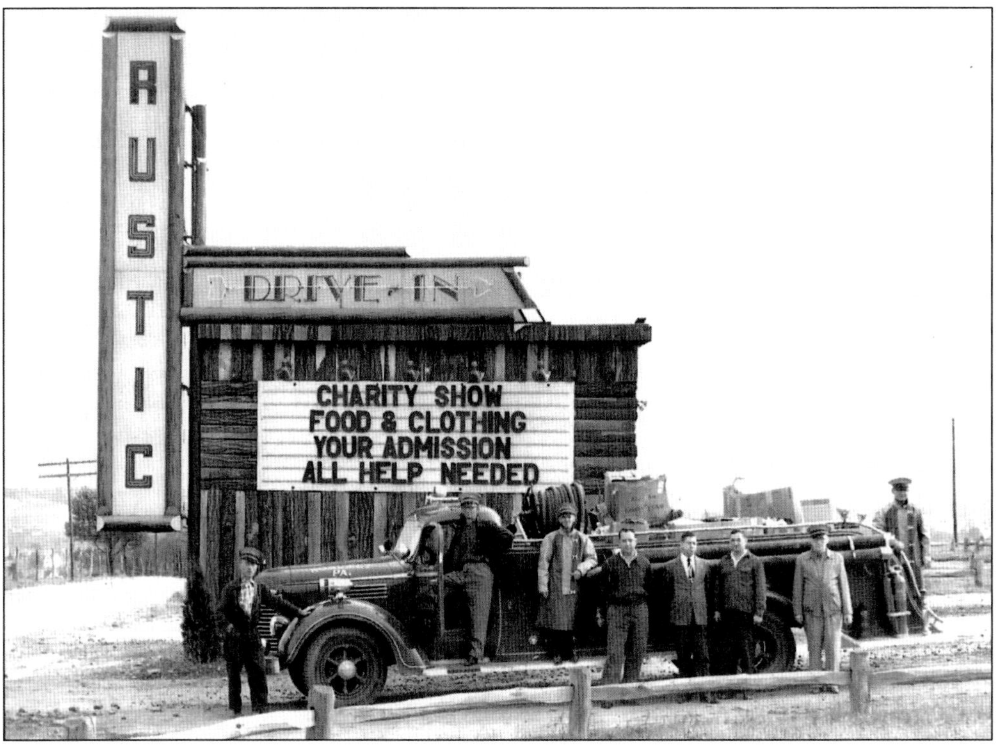

On September 2, 1936, Paul Schlingman, James Hatcher, Elmer Linden, Homer Fillmore, and Jake Lowther began to take up collections to help build the fire truck after they received their Ford V-8 chassis, but it would not be ready for fighting fires until they raised $500–600 to buy the body and get the vehicle road-ready. The above photograph shows the firemen on a typical fund drive. George Dzambo, fire chief, is standing on the running board next to the driver's seat. (Courtesy of Geraldine Dzambo Mizikar.)

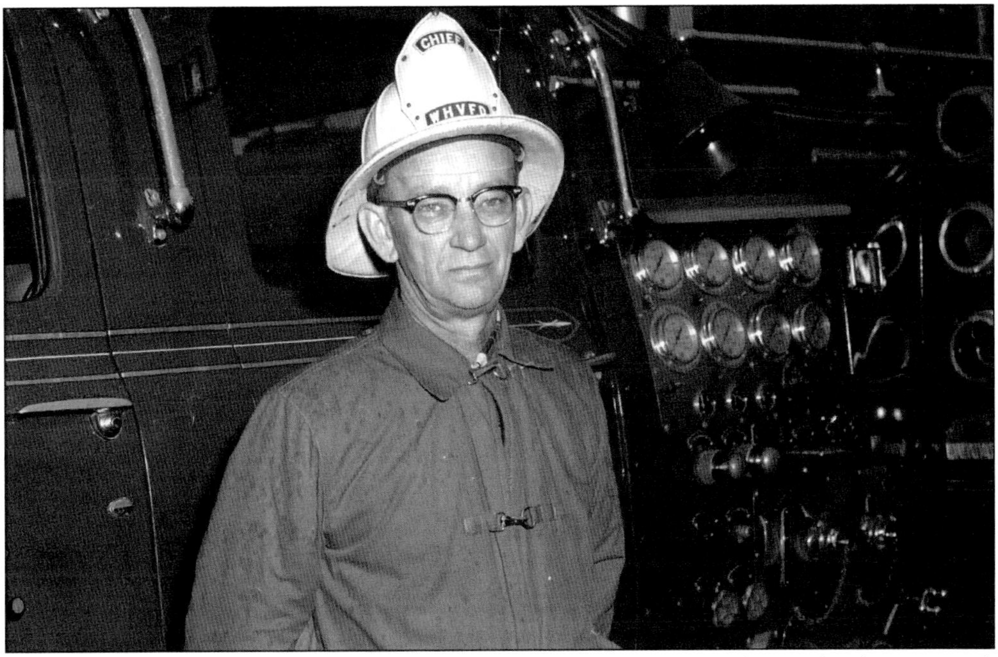

George Dzambo, fire chief of 15 years, stands in front of the completed fire truck. The new truck had been outfitted by the Callow Company of Mount Pleasant and was finished except for hoses, spotlights, and a few other necessities. Badges for all members were purchased, but there still was not enough money to buy coats for the firemen. (Courtesy of Geraldine Dzambo Mizikar.)

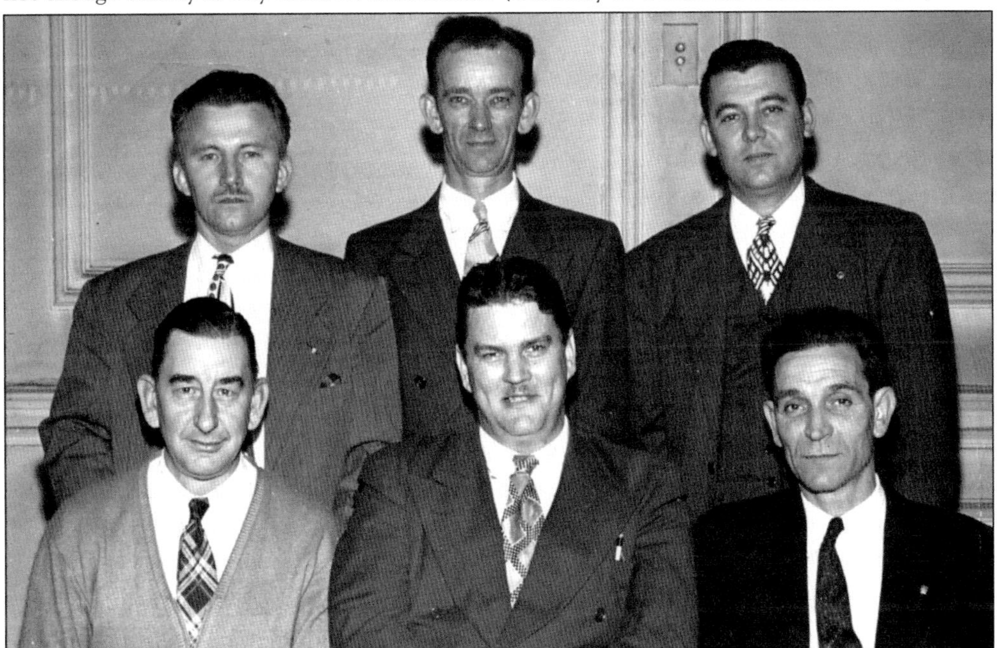

This photograph of Westmoreland Homesteads Volunteer Fire Department officers includes, from left to right, (first row) Paul Schlingman, John May, and Robert Coking; (second row) unknown, George Dzambo, and George Raishart. (Courtesy of Geraldine Dzambo Mizikar.)

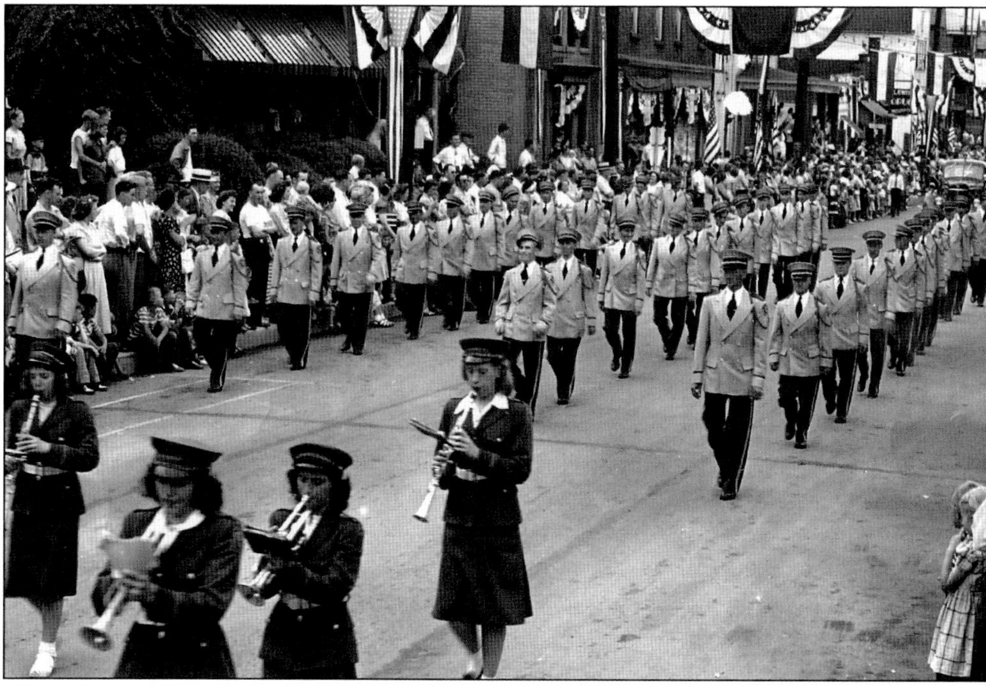

The volunteer fire department grew, and by 1949, the firemen did have badges and uniforms, and many members proudly marched in parades representing the Westmoreland Homestead Volunteer Fire Department. This photograph shows the firemen marching in the Mount Pleasant parade behind the Mount Pleasant all girls' band. (Courtesy of Geraldine Dzambo Mizikar.)

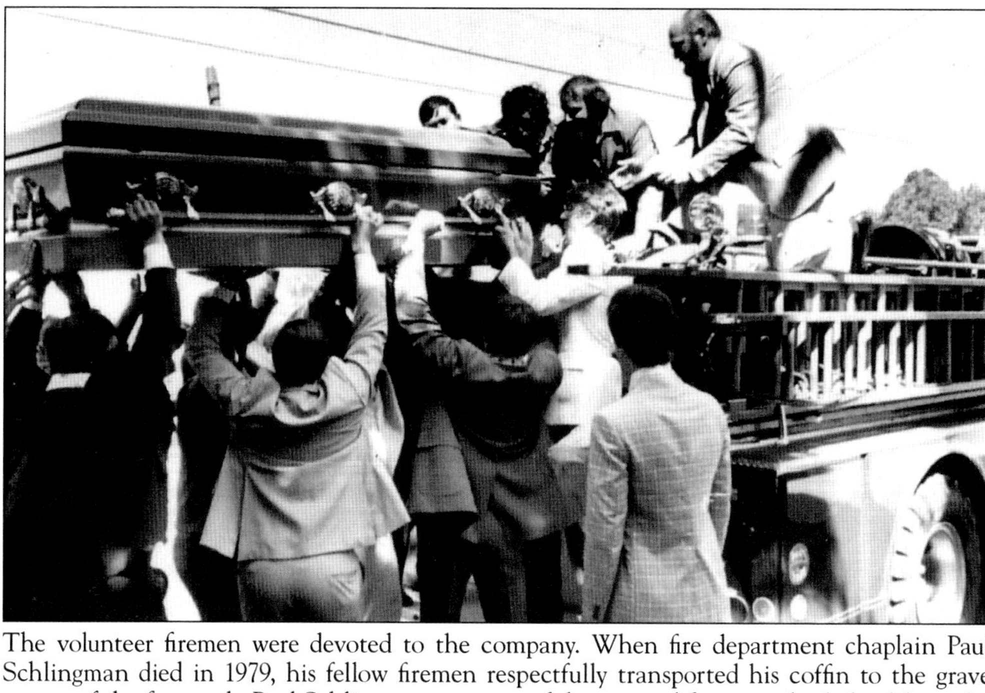

The volunteer firemen were devoted to the company. When fire department chaplain Paul Schlingman died in 1979, his fellow firemen respectfully transported his coffin to the grave on top of the fire truck. Paul Schlingman was one of the original firemen who helped form the company, which was chartered in 1938. (Courtesy of Lois Schlingman Weyandt.)

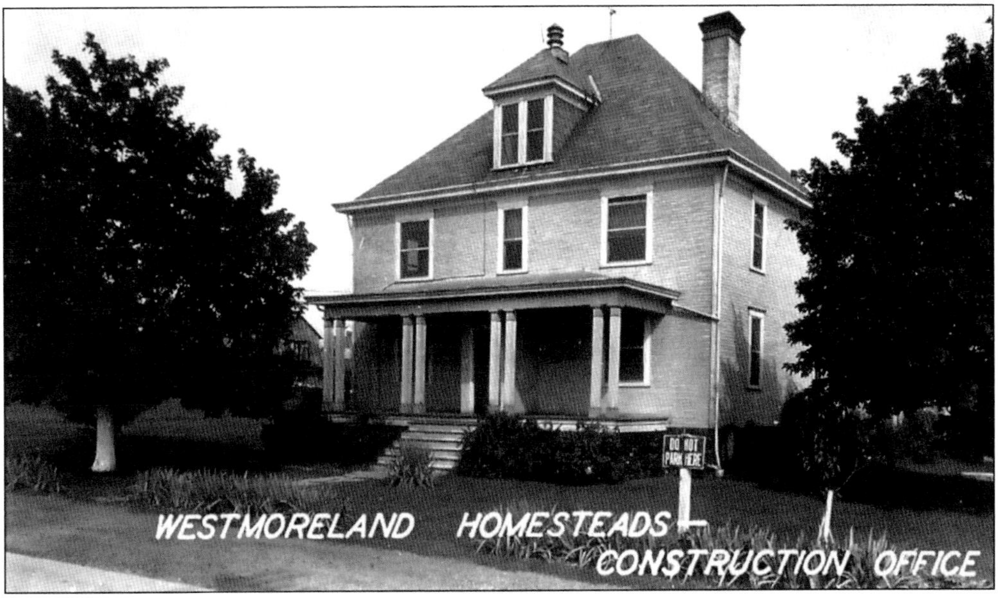

The above Westmoreland Homesteads Construction Office served many functions. Initially it was the administrative office building of the homestead, as well as the post office and an art classroom. When it was sold, it became a funeral home. (Courtesy of Sally Puskar.)

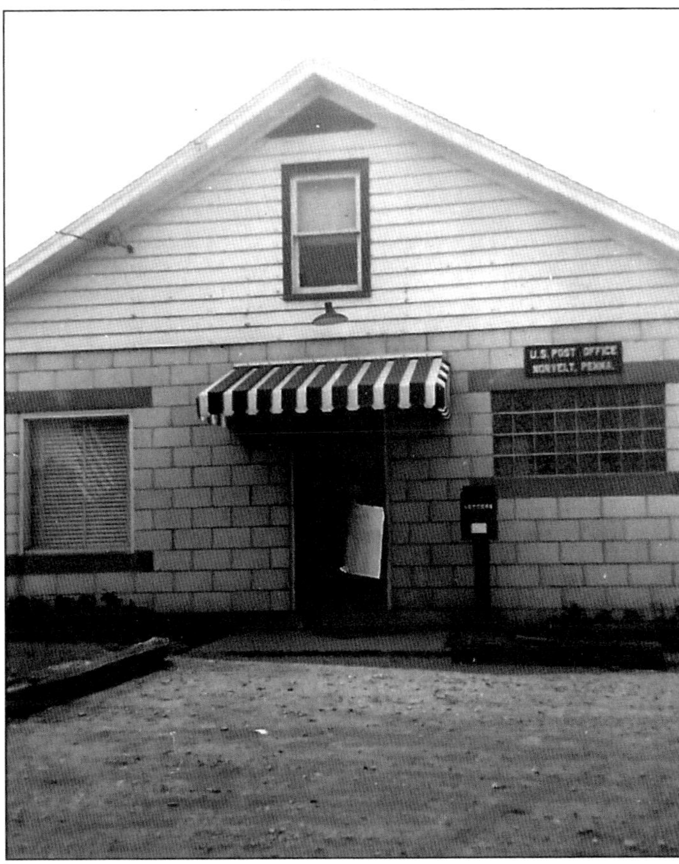

The mail delivery was moved to the co-op office in the former Fisher house and was addressed rural delivery No. 1, Mount Pleasant. On June 15, 1937, homesteader H. Ellis White wrote an article in the *Homestead Informer* called "The Flag" about the thrill of seeing the American flag raised at a recent meeting and District Representative Allon's closing remarks that Westmoreland Homesteads was to have a post office and the name chosen for the town would be Norvelt, a name suggested by homesteader Addah White, after a request made by the *Informer* a few months before. The Norvelt Post Office is pictured here. (Courtesy of Stephen Whisdosh.)

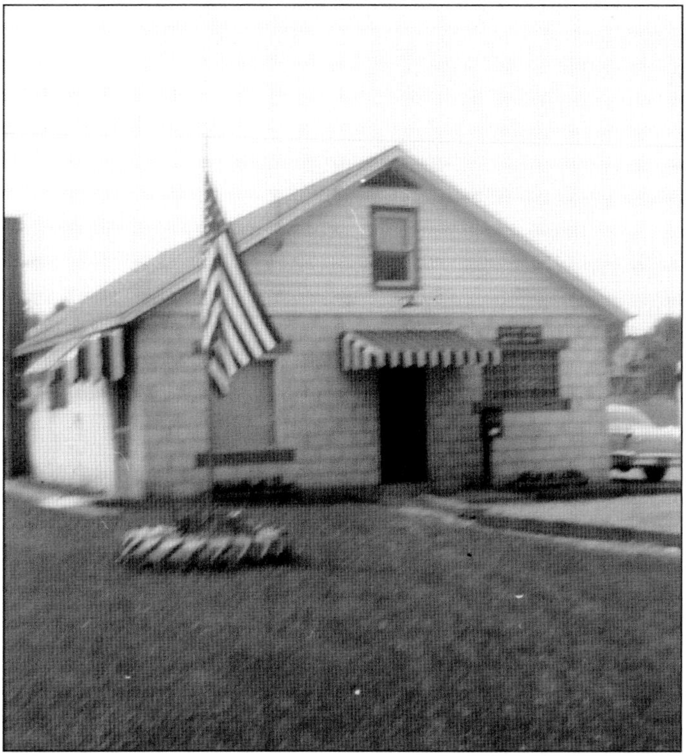

The Westmoreland Homesteads post office was built in 1937 in the center of the town on its main street, Mount Pleasant Road. Agnes Whisdosh was the first postmistress, and her son Stephen was her assistant and later became the postmaster. His wife Ann worked as his helper until they both retired. (Courtesy of Stephen Whisdosh.)

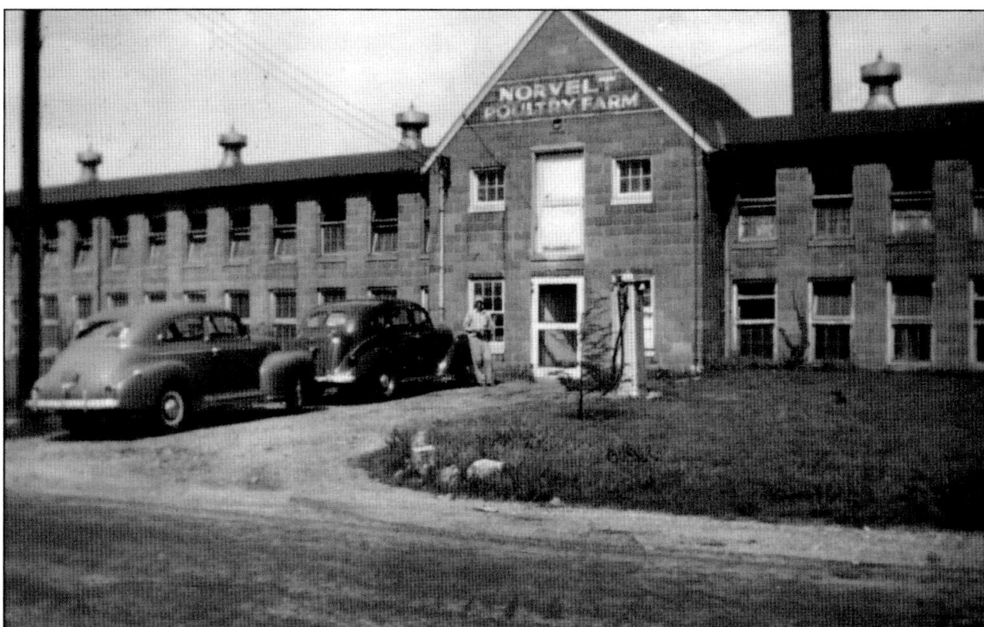

The co-op's poultry business was to be a major source of income. Chicks were purchased from New England. They had been bred for vitality and productive ability in Vermont and New Hampshire over a period of years. The flocks were accredited and guaranteed free from diseases that can easily destroy a poultry business. This photograph shows the front of the Norvelt Poultry Farm. (Courtesy of Virginia Boytim Vahaly and Betty Sue Boytim Mondock.)

On February 24, 1936, Washington approved the poultry project. Incubators and equipment were ordered on February 27, and on March 9, 1936, the first 8,000 eggs were placed into the incubators. By April 1, 1936, the *Homestead Informer* announced that 8,000 chicks hatched. The co-op was set up and regulated the brooder stoves and instructed the various homesteaders in handling. (Courtesy of Betty Sue Boytim Mondock and Virginia Boytim Vahaly.)

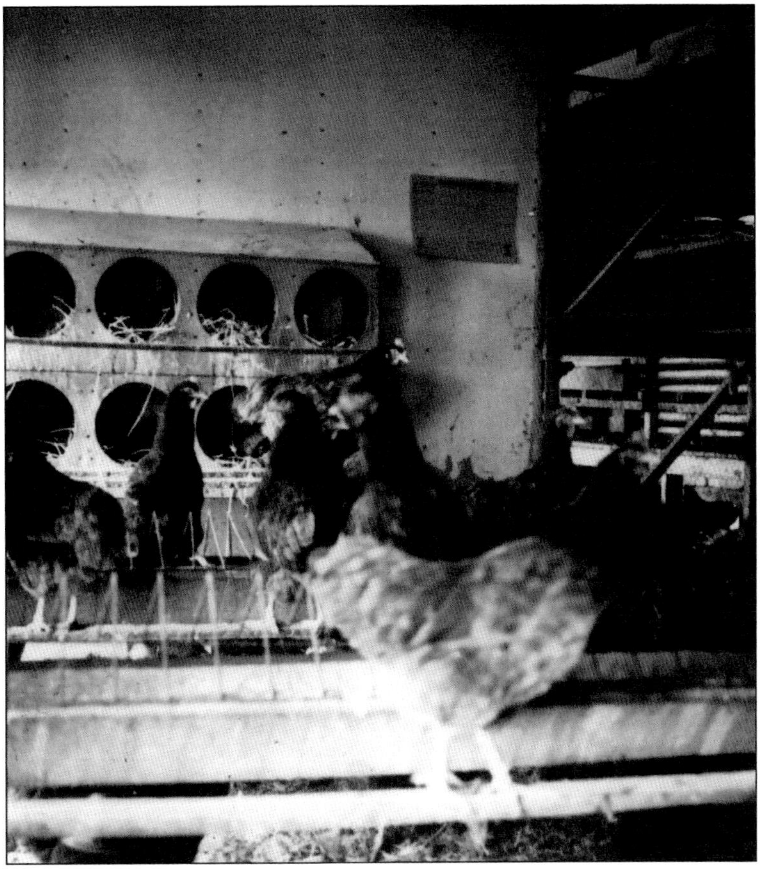

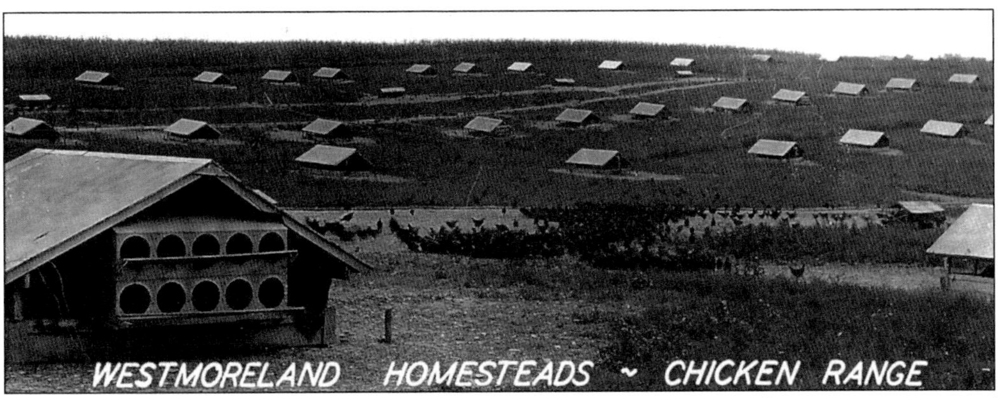

On August 1, 1936, the Pennsylvania Bureau of Markets began a regular testing program of diseases in all flocks, regardless of ownership, costing 8¢ per bird. One-half of the cost was carried by the cooperative association and the other half by the Pennsylvania Farms Hatchery at Lewistown, which the co-op had contracted for the sale of all surplus hatching eggs in 1936–1937. (Courtesy of Betty Sue Boytim Mondock and Virginia Boytim Vahaly.)

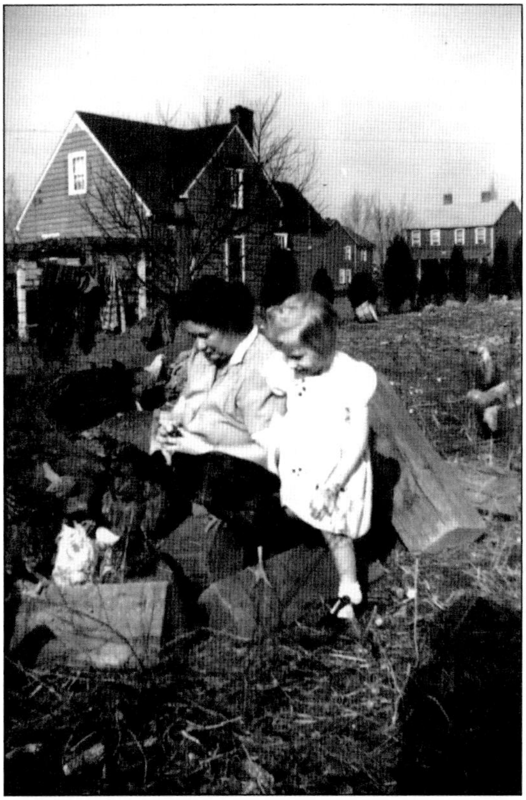

This photograph shows Agnes Whisdosh, postmistress, with her niece Josey Whisdosh Walton feeding chickens in their backyard. Individually the homesteaders raised their own chickens for themselves or the co-op, where food would be exchanged. (Courtesy of Stephen Whisdosh.)

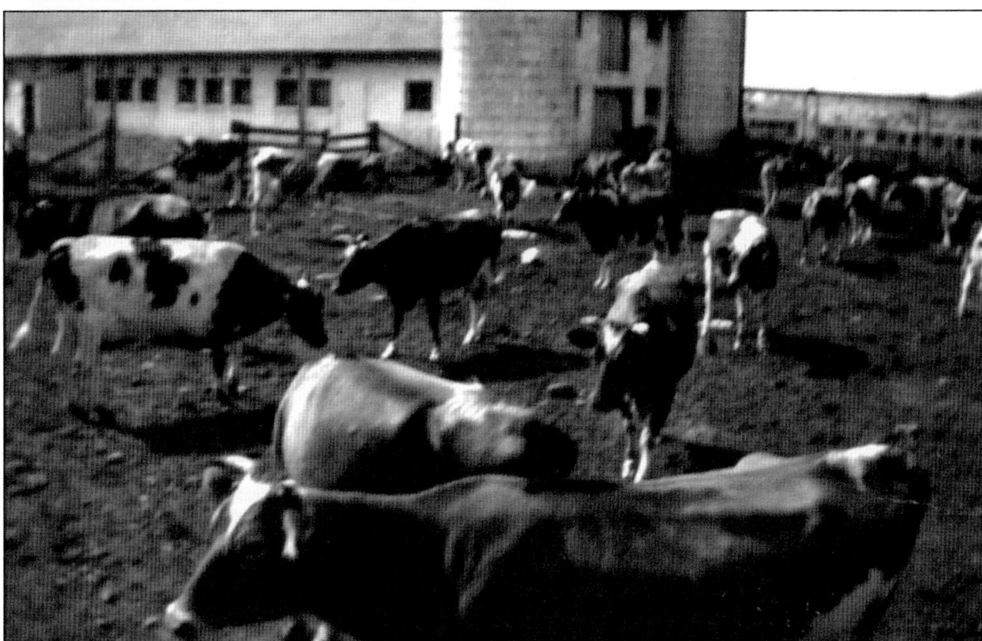

The dairy barn along Kecksburg Road housed the new herd of Guernsey cows purchased by the co-op to furnish milk for the homesteaders. The barn contained 26 stanchions and eight box stalls. (Courtesy of Betty Sue Boytim Mondock and Virginia Boytim Vahaly.)

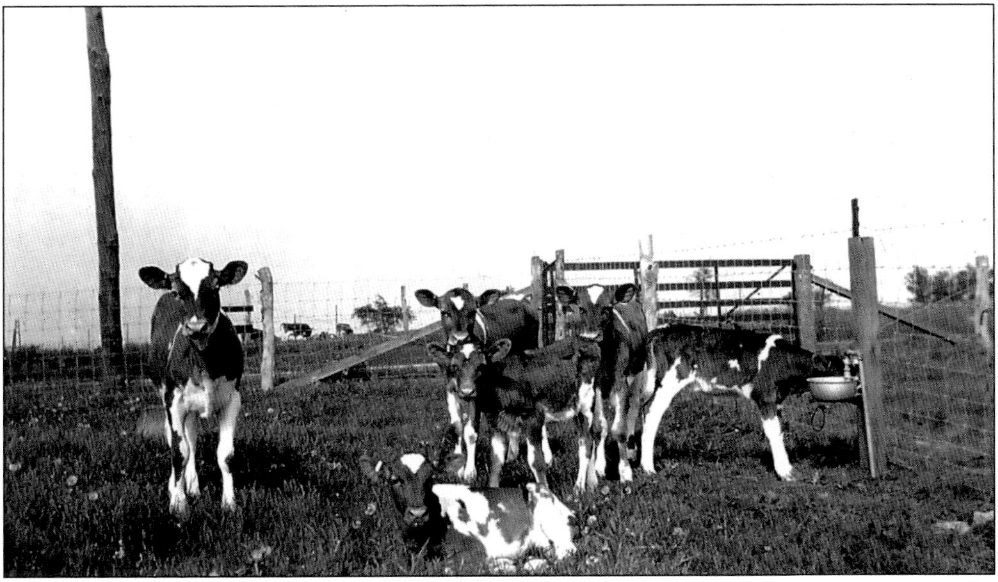

The Bash farm was hired by the co-op to pasteurize, bottle, and deliver co-op milk to the doors of homesteaders because it was more economical than using co-op labor and trucks. The farm was managed by Elmer Linden. (Courtesy of Betty Sue Boytim Mondock and Virginia Boytim Vahaly.)

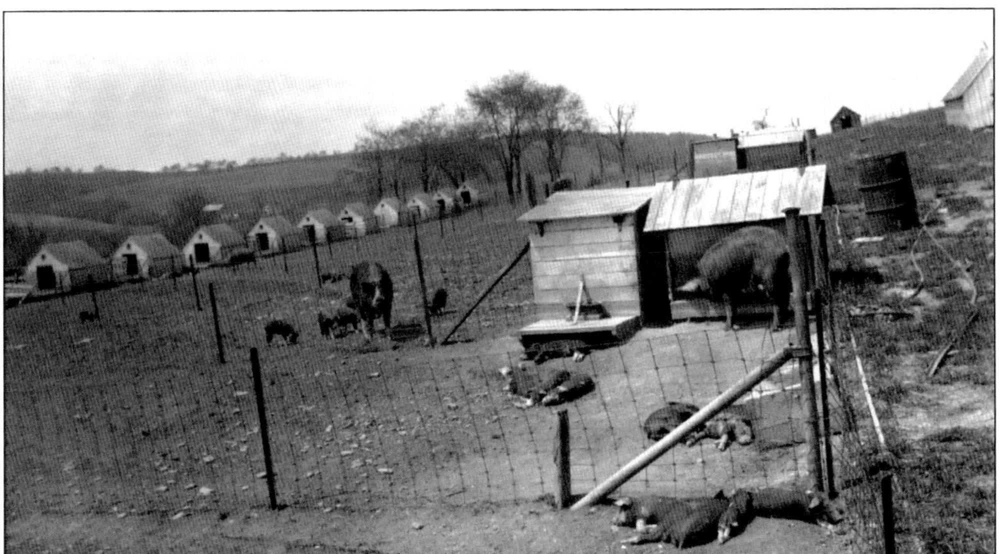

Hogs were raised on the Kuhn Farm. The original purpose was to raise the pigs for home consumption. However, because of overpopulation, the homestead had to dispose of at least 50 of the hogs that weighed 200–250 pounds. Additionally, 10 brood sows, weighing around 500 pounds each, had to be sold at a price of 10¢ per pound. (Courtesy of Earl Saville.)

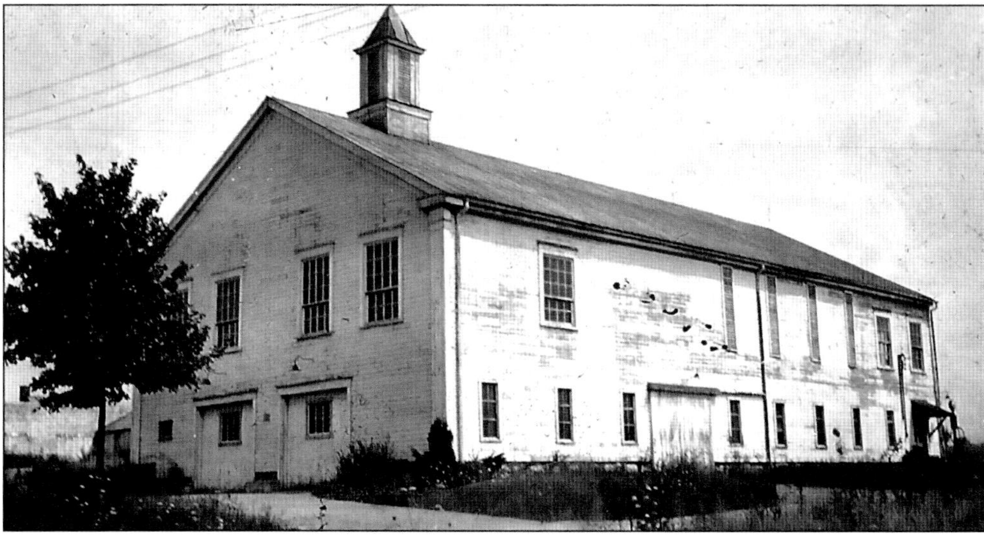

This barn was part of the Fisher Farm and was used by the homesteaders for the storage of supplies; it later stood empty until it was used as an auction barn. It is the current home of Johnson True Value and Heating Store. (Courtesy of the Library of Congress.)

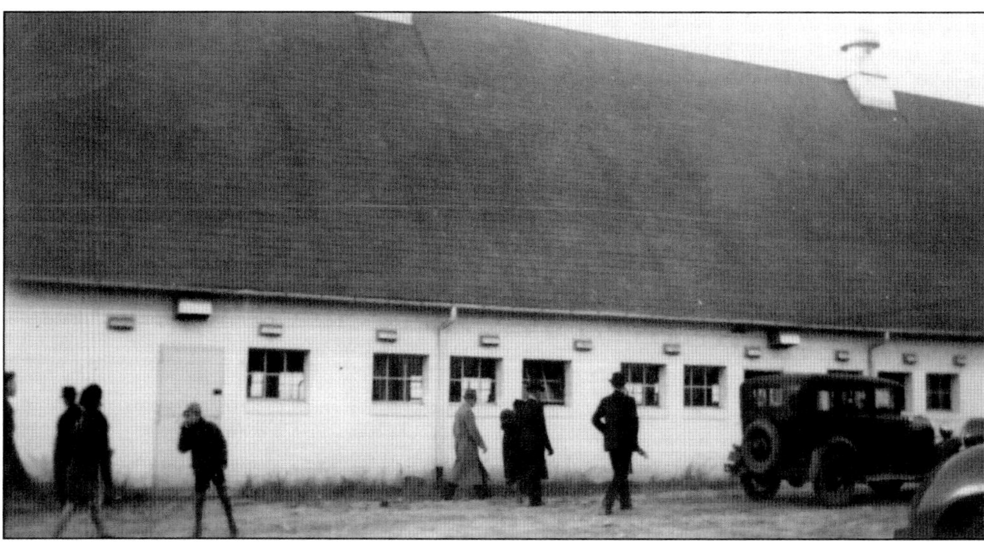

This photograph shows work crews heading to the community dairy barn for work. (Courtesy of Sharon Smith.)

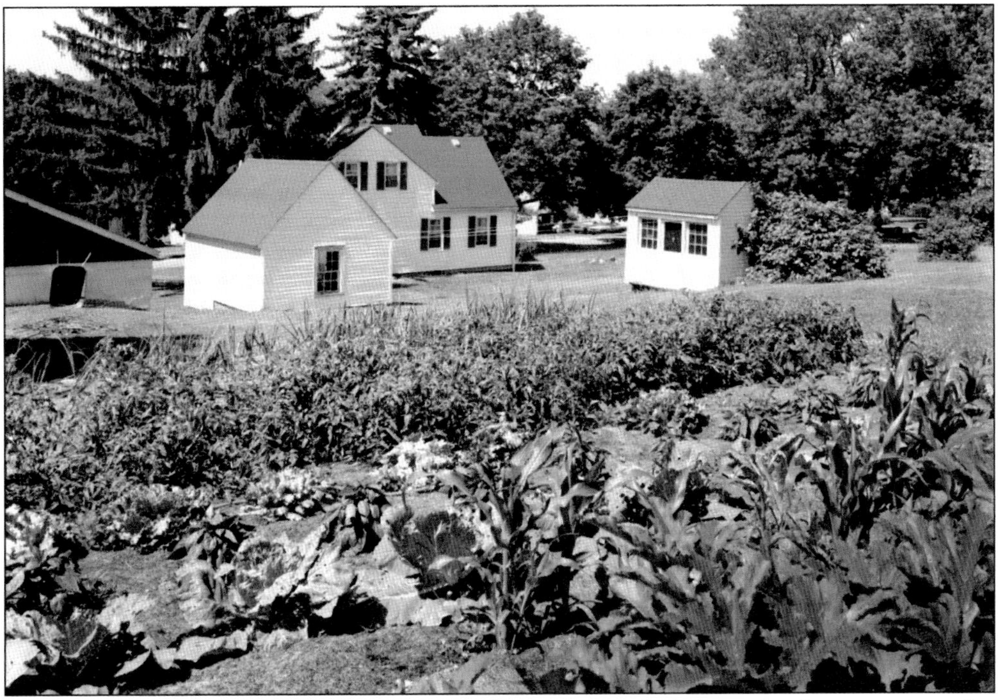

This photograph shows a home in E section with a garage on the left, poultry house on the right, and vegetable garden in the front. The co-op required that all homes have a vegetable garden. The government and AFSC provided agricultural instruction on topics such as fall plowing, hotbed growing, tree planting, lawn care, grass seeding, pruning fruit trees, care of septic tanks, shrubbery, use of poultry litter as a fertilizer in gardens, and the use of canning equipment. (Courtesy of Library of Congress.)

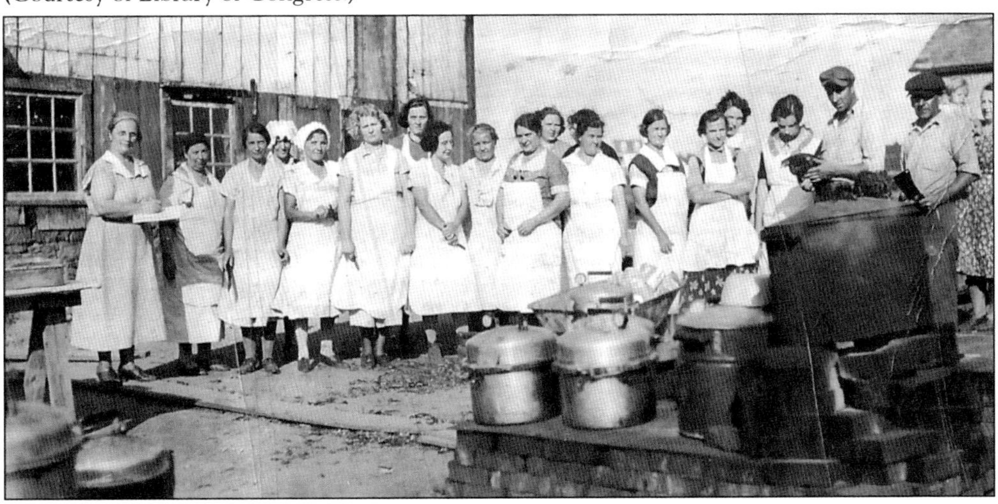

Addah White, a homesteader, was appointed under the Federal Emergency Educational Programs as an instructor in canning and other home economic activities. She conducted classes in different homes in the community and offered sewing and cooking instruction as well. The above photograph shows local women attending a canning class. The women received one third of the total amount of canned goods for their labor, or an average of one can per hour worked or three cans. Residents would work together to can vegetables. (Courtesy of Joseph Wolk.)

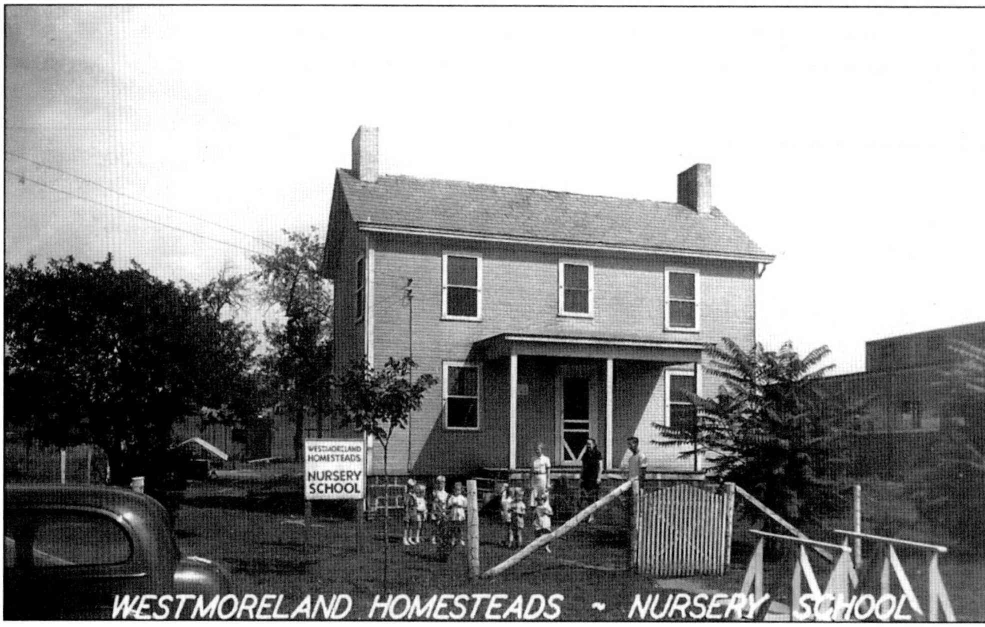

The nursery school, manned by Quakers of AFSC, provided a day care program for children whose parents worked. It opened on May 25, 1936, with nine children enrolled the first day, including Lowell Briercheck, Billy Trump, Charles Goulding, Anna Katherine McKelvey, John Kennedy, Francis Gray, Mary Louise Sompol, Dorothy Jane Sofranko, and Dolores Joan Klosky. Children continued to be enrolled until the class reached a total of 30. (Courtesy of the Library of Congress.)

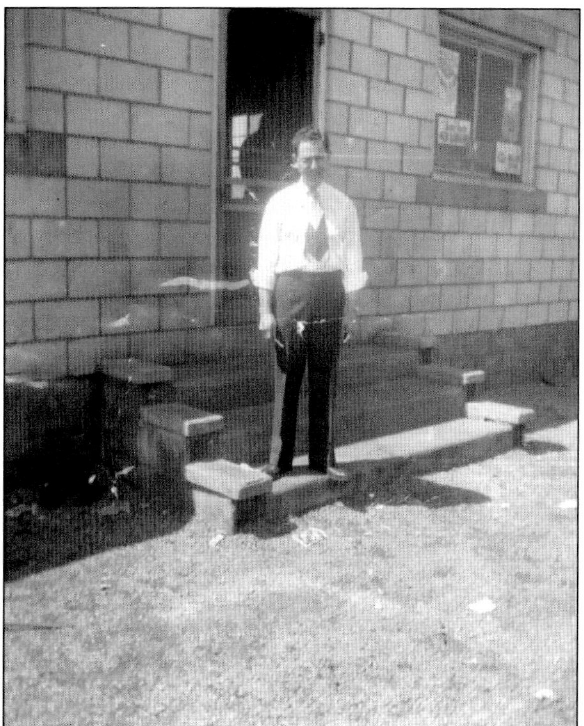

Stephen Whisdosh ran a small store by his home selling bread, milk, and other grocery items. Whisdosh is shown here at the front of the store. (Courtesy of the Library of Congress.)

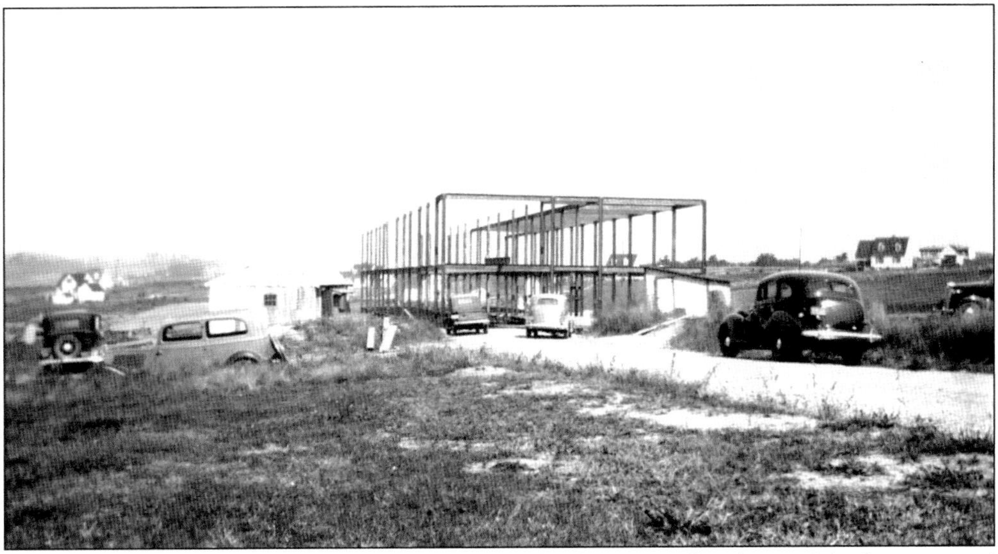

This photograph shows the building progress shortly after groundbreaking of the long-awaited Norvelt Elementary School. Its design was borrowed from Independence Hall in Philadelphia. (Courtesy of Sharon Smith.)

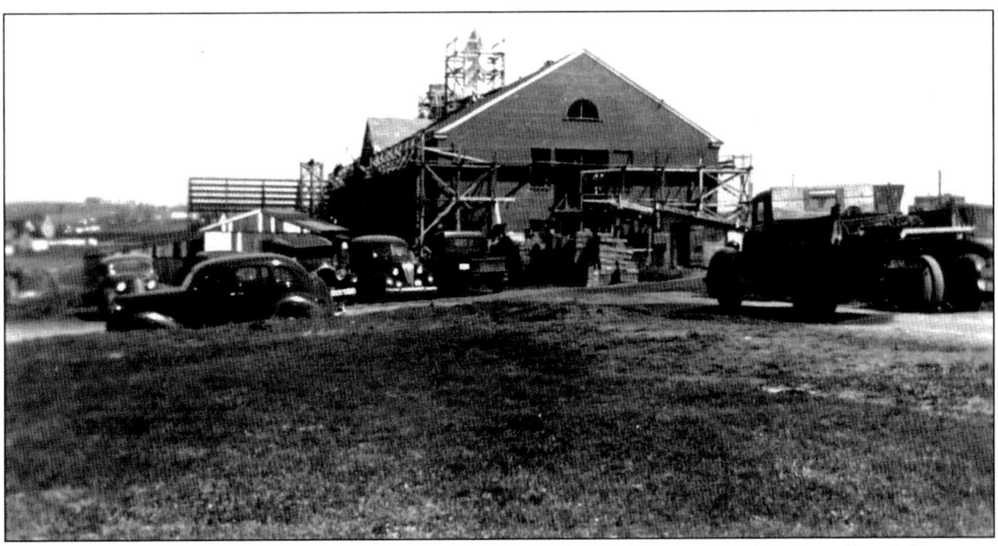

This photograph shows the Norvelt school taking on form. (Courtesy of Sharon Smith.)

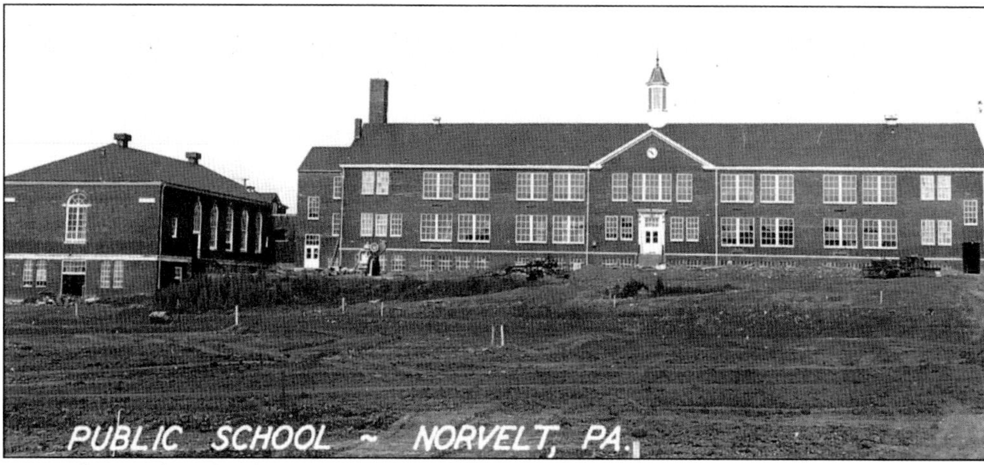

In April 1936, the school prepared to accommodate 50–60 new pupils and bring the enrollment to 260. Half sessions were held until the completion of new rooms for sixth, seventh, and eighth grades. In the meantime, it was running at full speed with a boy's ball team playing against nearby United and Hecla schools. In June 1936, grades one through four marked the end of the year with an operetta and grade five presented a Memorial Day play written and staged by the class. The school was completed in 1939. (Courtesy of the Library of Congress.)

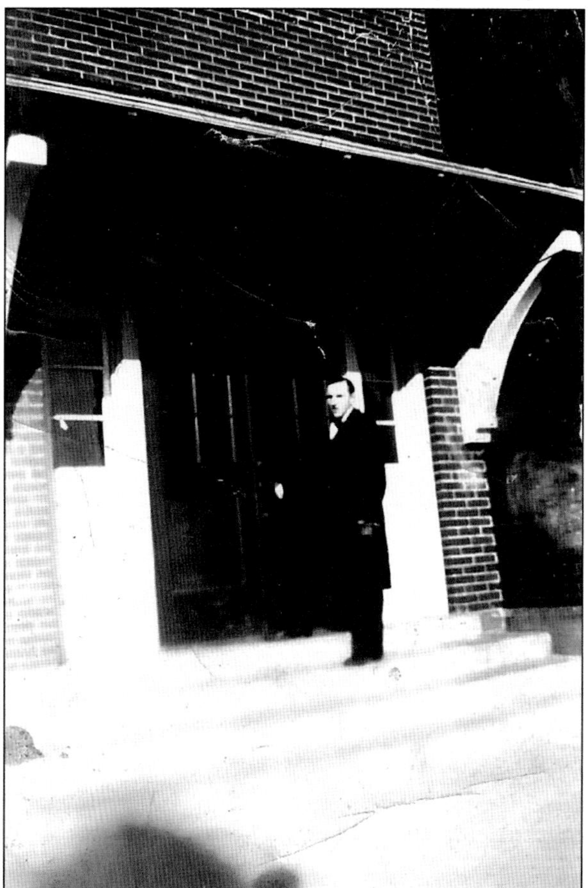

Grades 9–10 attended Hurst High School, in the photograph at left, part of the Mount Pleasant Township schools. Superintendent of schools Mr. Rumbaugh also served as a speaker for the homestead Sunday-evening meetings. In this photograph, homesteader John Whisdosh is entering Hurst High for the first time as a freshman. (Courtesy of Josey Walton.)

The photograph at right is Dr. Wright at his private practice in Pleasant Unity, where he treated many homesteaders. (Courtesy of Josey Walton.)

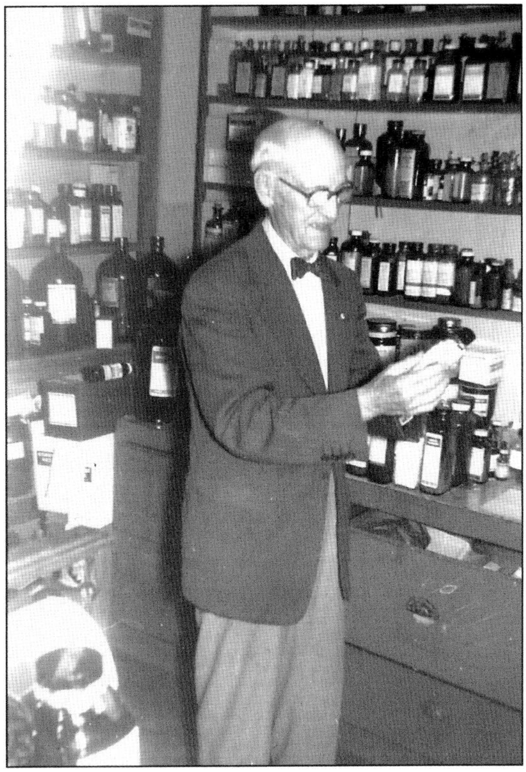

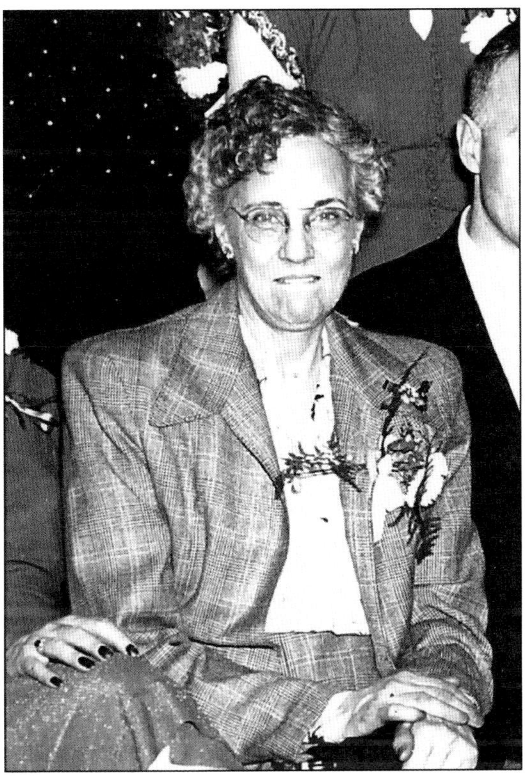

Miss Walker was the public health nurse provided to the homesteads under the Resettlement Administration. She resided in the B-1 home of the Ervin McKenna family. Her duties were to assist in consulting relationships with any and all health problems in the community. She wrote many articles for the *Homestead Informer* giving advice regarding wellness, preventing infections, and dealing with sickness. She provided this recipe to "build red corpuscles: Creamed Liver: Drop liver in salted boiling water for 5 to 10 minutes then dice, melt 2 tbsp of fat, add 3 tbsp flour, 4/3 tsp. salt, dash pepper and milk. Stir until smooth. Add 2 cups diced liver, 1 tbsp minced onion, and 1 tbsp green pepper. Serve on toast." (Courtesy of Gail Hoffer.)

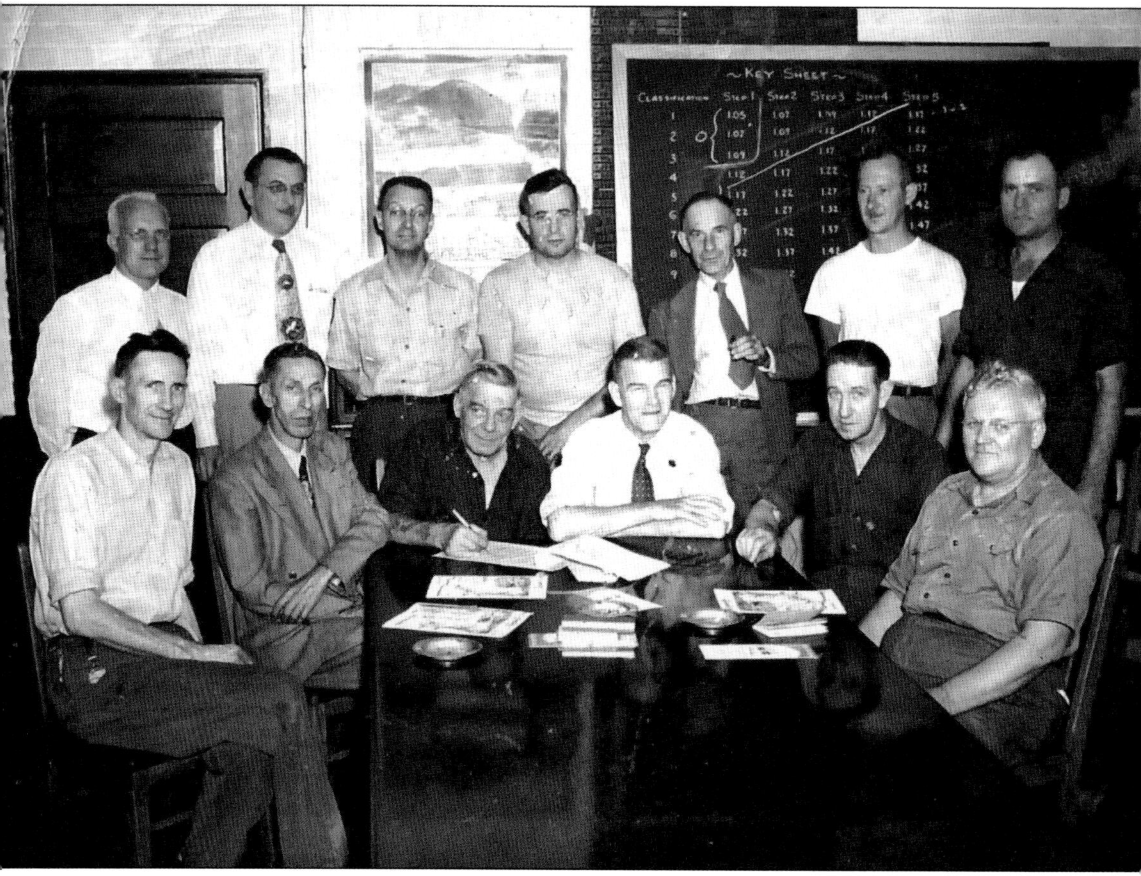

This photograph shows homesteaders attending one of many meetings needed in running the co-op. Their hard work and cooperation was fostered by David Day's encouragement and guidance to become self sufficient. As described in *The Homesteader* in October 1936, basic cooperative ideas were: 1. Open voluntary membership, 2. Democratic voting, 3. Patronage dividends (surplus rebates), 4. Limited interest on invested capital, 5. Sales for cash at market, 6. Neutrality of race, religion, and politics, 7. Constant education, and 8. Continuous expansion. (Courtesy of Sharon Smith.)

Five

BUILDING A COMMUNITY

Eleanor Roosevelt and the AFSC believed that to make the residents independent, functioning members of the community, they needed exposure and participation in the arts. People living in coal towns, farms, and rural areas had little, if any, previous opportunity to experience the arts, theater, crafting, and social and cultural venues.

From the start, social and cultural activities played a pivotal role in Norvelt, and all residents were encouraged to partake. The town greeted a host of lecturers. Speakers like George Fichenor, editor and publisher of *Our New World*, talked about cooperatives, wholesales, and associations. Other speakers included the local school superintendent Mr. Rumbaugh and Dr. Sheots, a professor of English in a Presbyterian college in India who spoke on "Education in India." Discussion groups met regularly. Agricultural meetings were held with speakers, like F. M. Bronton, who spoke on planting and growing. Sunday-evening meetings provided speakers such as Sina Stanton of Washington, D.C., on August 11, 1935, who "is a closer observer of affairs at our nation's capitol and will bring news of interest to all" and a nurse from the AFSC camp spoke on hygiene, nursing, and "the advantage we have over the people in large cities."

The *Homestead Informer* was an important component in building the community and was first published on August 8, 1935, by David Day, the homesteads' site administrator. As envisioned by Eleanor Roosevelt, the writing and publication of the *Homestead Informer* was soon taken over by the homesteaders themselves. Subsequent issues of the newsletter document the educational foundation of the community and the AFSC's efforts in implementing homesteaders' participation in all phases of community life. A "homestead calendar" was filled with activities for homesteaders. The May 1936 issue described weekly meetings scheduled for the health and child study group, community forum, glee club, Boy Scouts, firemen, baseball team, and musical committee. The July 8, 1936, issue described a fall festival music program and a ladies' Bible class making a friendship quilt. The June 1937 issue announced the Little Mothers Sewing Club publication of a sample sewing book to "get children interested in sewing" and a Mother's Day program held by the health and child study group for homestead mothers who "are becoming increasingly conscious of their work as a profession." A girls' teen club hosted speakers from Seton Hill College who organized plays.

The community also had a strong interest in world events. As a precursor to war, citizens were warned in the June 1936 *Homestead Informer* that no other country has as many fascist organizations as Japan that work in public advocating the abolition of the parliamentary system and the establishment of a dictatorship. In October 1936, the *Homestead Informer* kept the homesteaders aware of international events: discussing the unrest in Europe, announcing that the 1940 Olympic Games would be held in pugnacious militarism of Japan, and letting readers know that South America was beginning to join in the armament race, urged on by "reactionary and chauvinistic press" with Argentina, Brazil, Chile, and Peru adding heavily to their budgets while their citizens lacked decent housing, sanitation, employment, and food. On October 14, 1936, it was reported that German cooperatives and businesses were being wiped out by Nazis, and the League of Nations recommended to all countries to re-examine their history books and warn school children about unjust prejudices against other countries.

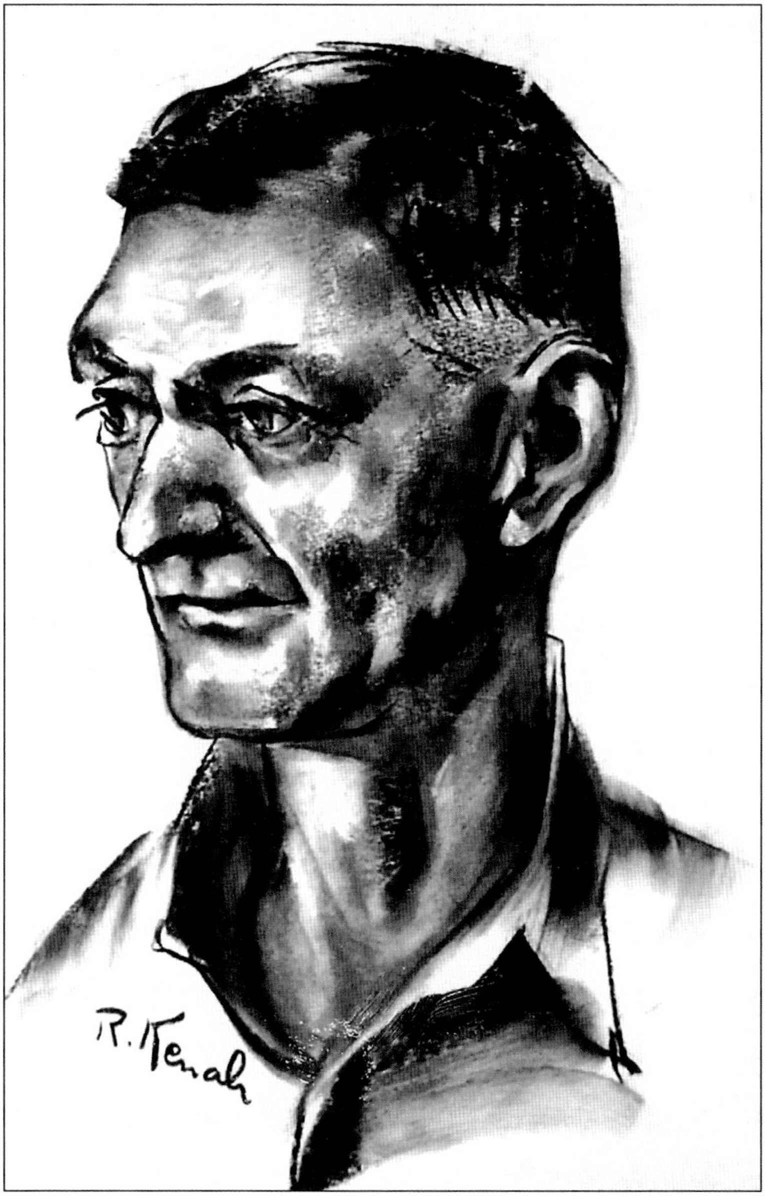

From 1935 to 1943, Franklin D. Roosevelt's $5 billion work-relief program, the WPA's Federal Art Project (FAP), provided employment for artists during the Depression. Richard Hay Kenah—seen here in his self portrait—an unemployed artist from New Brighton, found work through the WPA as Westmoreland Homesteads's artist-in-residence where he taught art, illustrated for and edited the *Homestead Informer*, and helped organize outings and programs for homesteaders. His lasting contribution to the community was a mural commissioned by Adrian Dornbush, Kenah's FSA supervisor in Washington, D.C. During World War II, Kenah worked for the Army Quartermaster Corps as an illustrator and poster maker. He then became chief illustrator for the U.S. Geological Survey in charge of the exhibit division. He was commissioned to complete three post office murals in Bridgeport, Ohio; Bluefield, West Virginia; and Louisburg, North Carolina; and a three-panel mural depicting the history of the Harmony Society for the auditorium of the old Ambridge High School. That mural is now in Old Economy Village. (Courtesy of Gail Hoffer.)

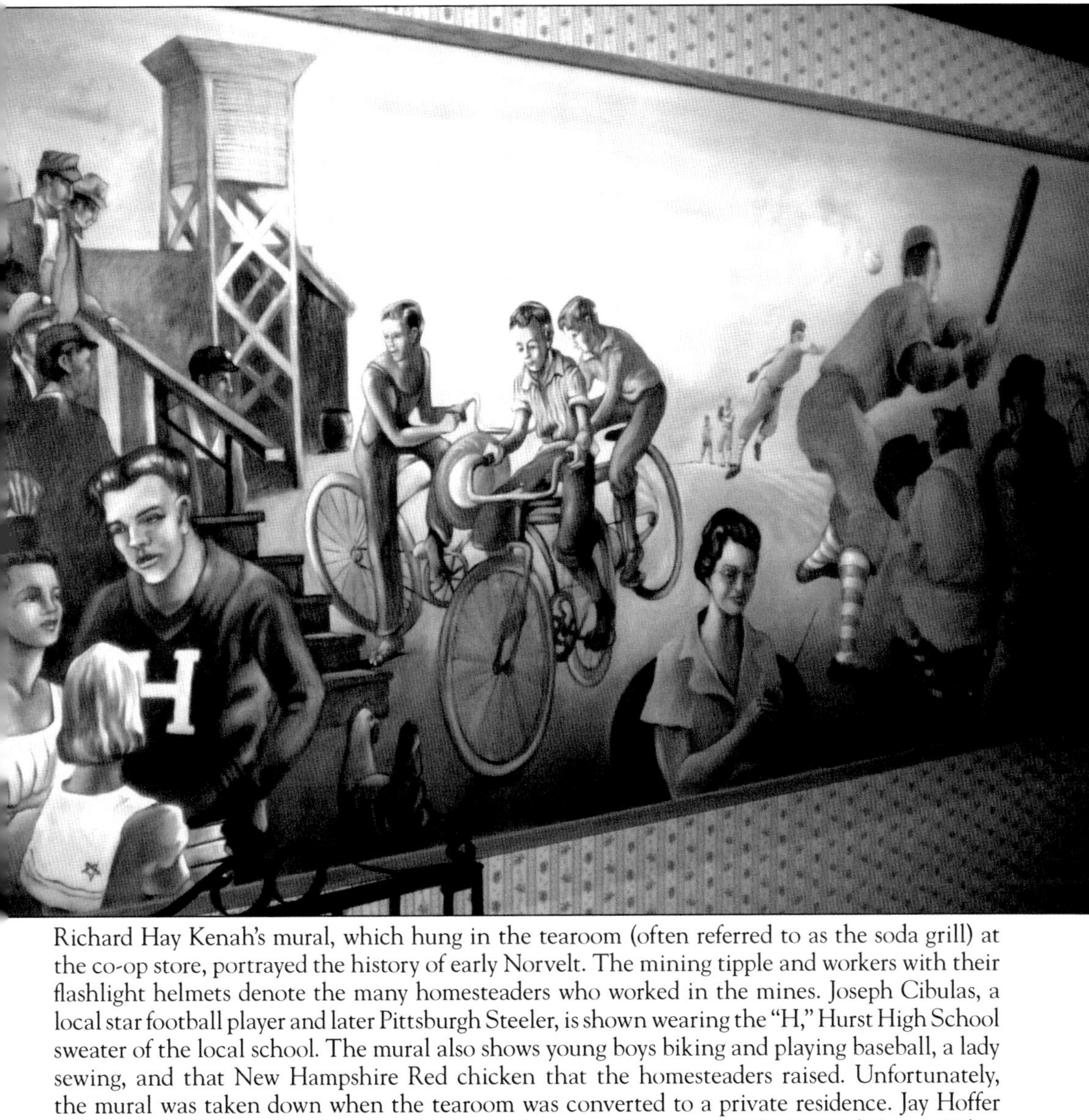

Richard Hay Kenah's mural, which hung in the tearoom (often referred to as the soda grill) at the co-op store, portrayed the history of early Norvelt. The mining tipple and workers with their flashlight helmets denote the many homesteaders who worked in the mines. Joseph Cibulas, a local star football player and later Pittsburgh Steeler, is shown wearing the "H," Hurst High School sweater of the local school. The mural also shows young boys biking and playing baseball, a lady sewing, and that New Hampshire Red chicken that the homesteaders raised. Unfortunately, the mural was taken down when the tearoom was converted to a private residence. Jay Hoffer had one panel restored and it is on display in the entry of the Jay Hoffer Funeral Home. What happened to the other panels remains a mystery. (Courtesy of Gail Hoffer.)

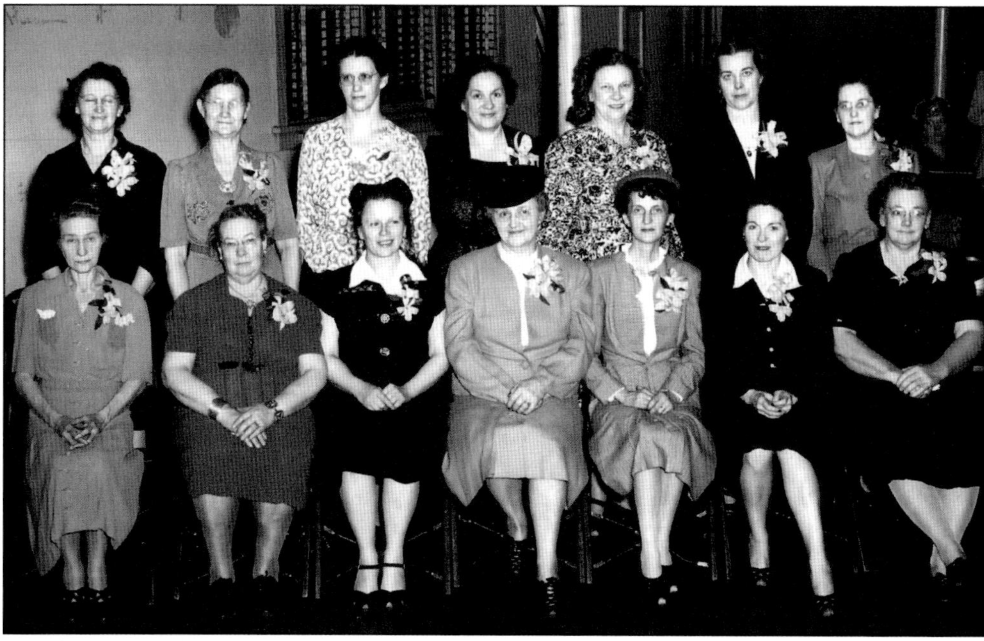

The first issue of the *Homestead Informer* revealed a sense of excitement as the community slowly came to life. Announcements were made of the opening of the tearoom on June 8, 1935, led by the efforts of the mothers with plans for lunches and dinners to be served and as a place where homesteader clubs, such as the Kiwanis, would meet. This is an early photograph of the Homestead Mothers, organized in March 1935. Eventually the club became known as the Mother's Club and continues to exist today. Of the 12 current members, 9 are original homesteaders. (Courtesy of Gail Hoffer.)

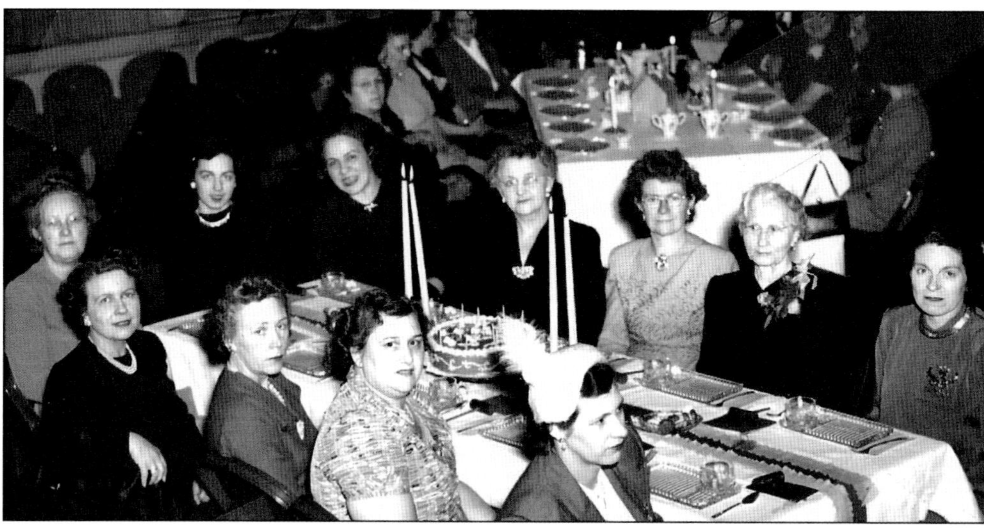

In this group photograph, the Mother's Club is celebrating at a local restaurant. Eleanor Roosevelt was very conscious of the fragility of the family and the need to bolster family life. The March 18, 1936, issue of the *Homestead Informer* reviewed member Brook Hatcher's description of mothers as being "increasingly conscious of their work as a profession noting that the woman who chooses motherhood as her form of service to the world should study it as carefully as a lawyer or physician." (Courtesy of Gail Hoffer.)

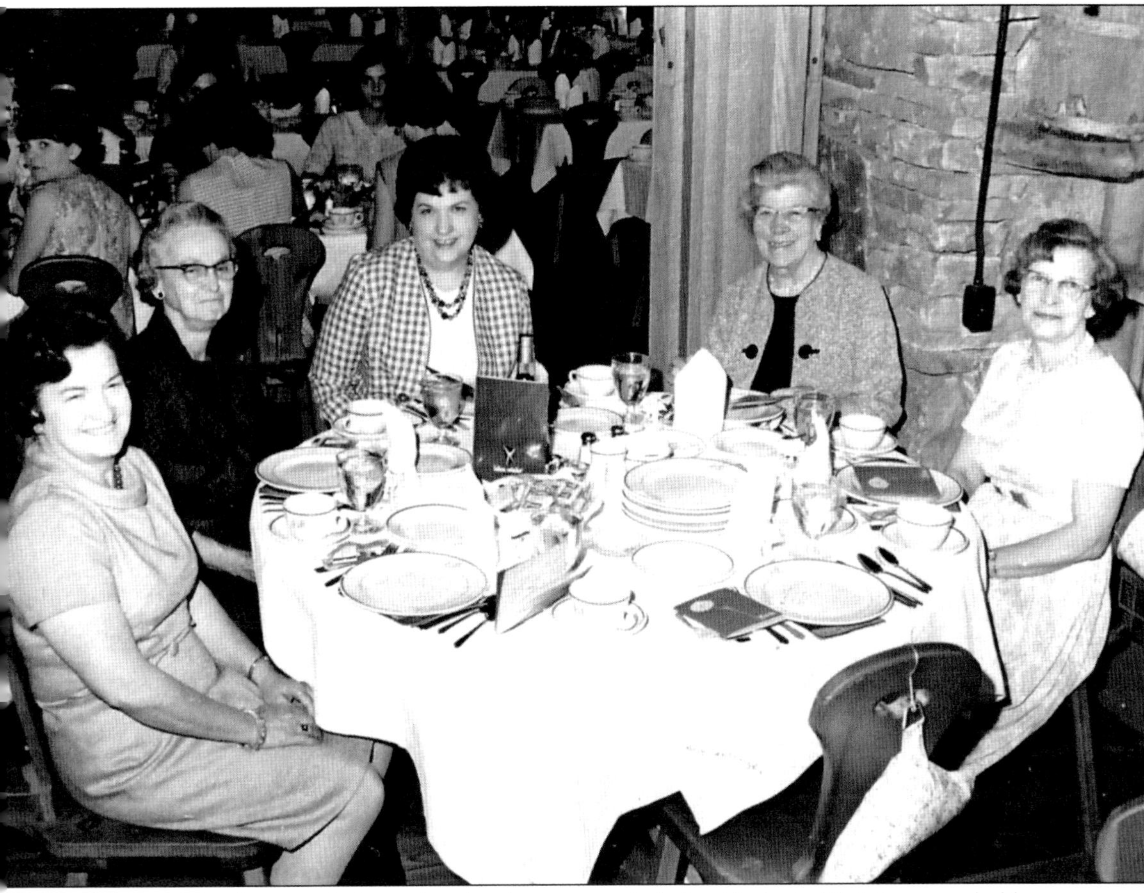

Members of the Jones and Davis family, above, attended the Mother's Club banquet held at Seven Springs Resort in Champion, Pennsylvania. Pictured from left to right are Iona Jones, Mrs. Hoke, Donna Howard, Emma Jones, and Jean Davis. (Courtesy of Shirley Jones Rusinko.)

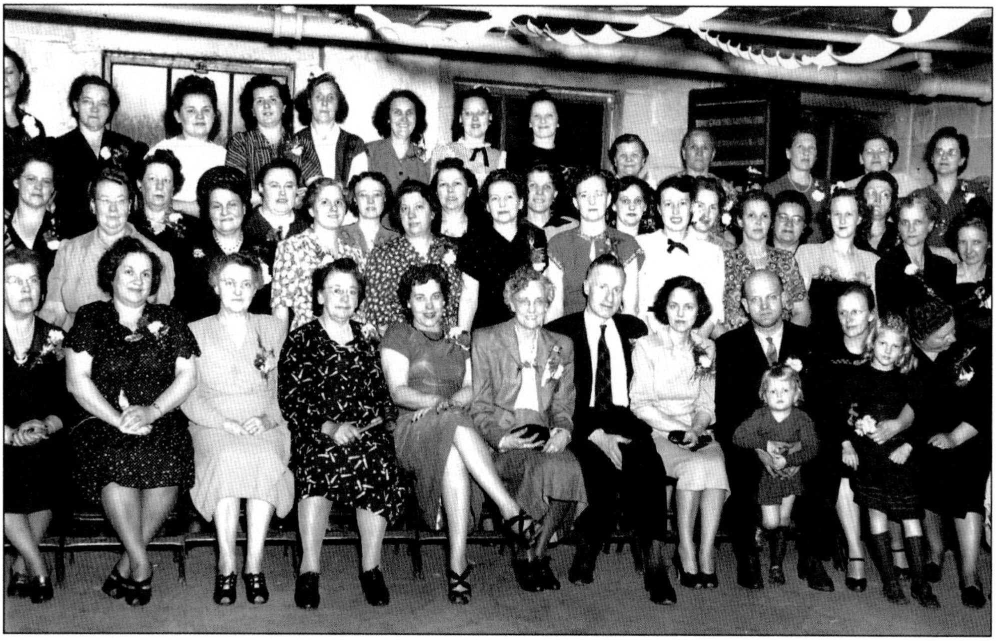

This group photograph was taken in the early days of the homestead. In the first row, David Day, AFSC site manager, and his wife, Olive, each holding a daughter, are present. Living in the community in a homestead house, they participated in social activities. Olive Day was very active in the Ladies Bible Study and Mother's Club. Residents enjoyed their community activities. (Courtesy of Gail Hoffer.)

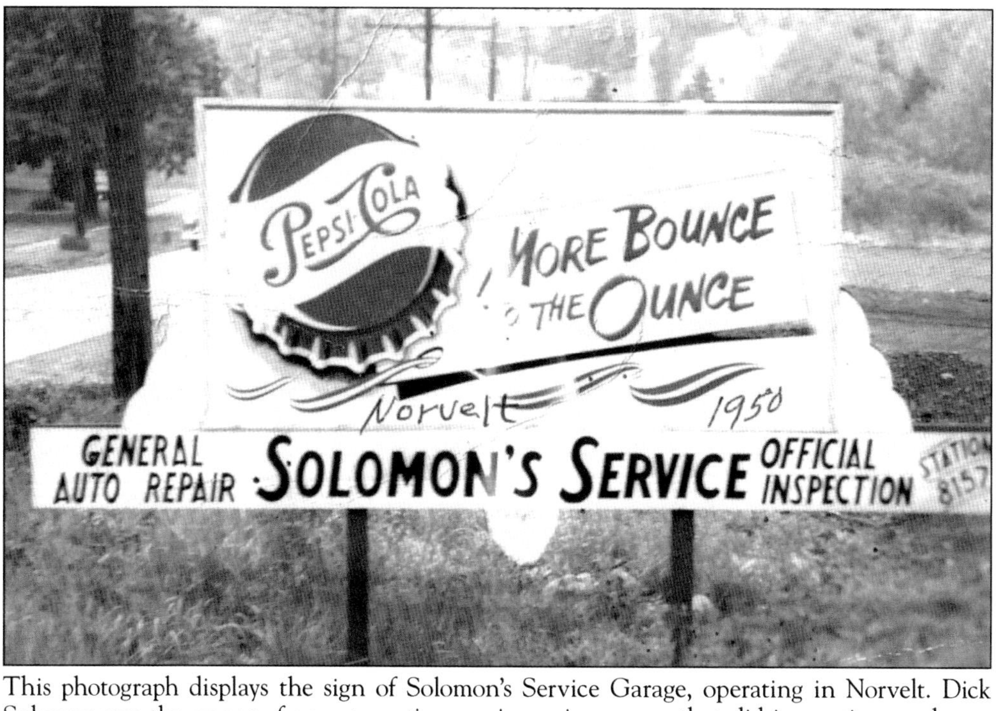

This photograph displays the sign of Solomon's Service Garage, operating in Norvelt. Dick Solomon was the owner of an automotive repair service garage that did inspections and auto parts sales. (Courtesy of Dick Solomon.)

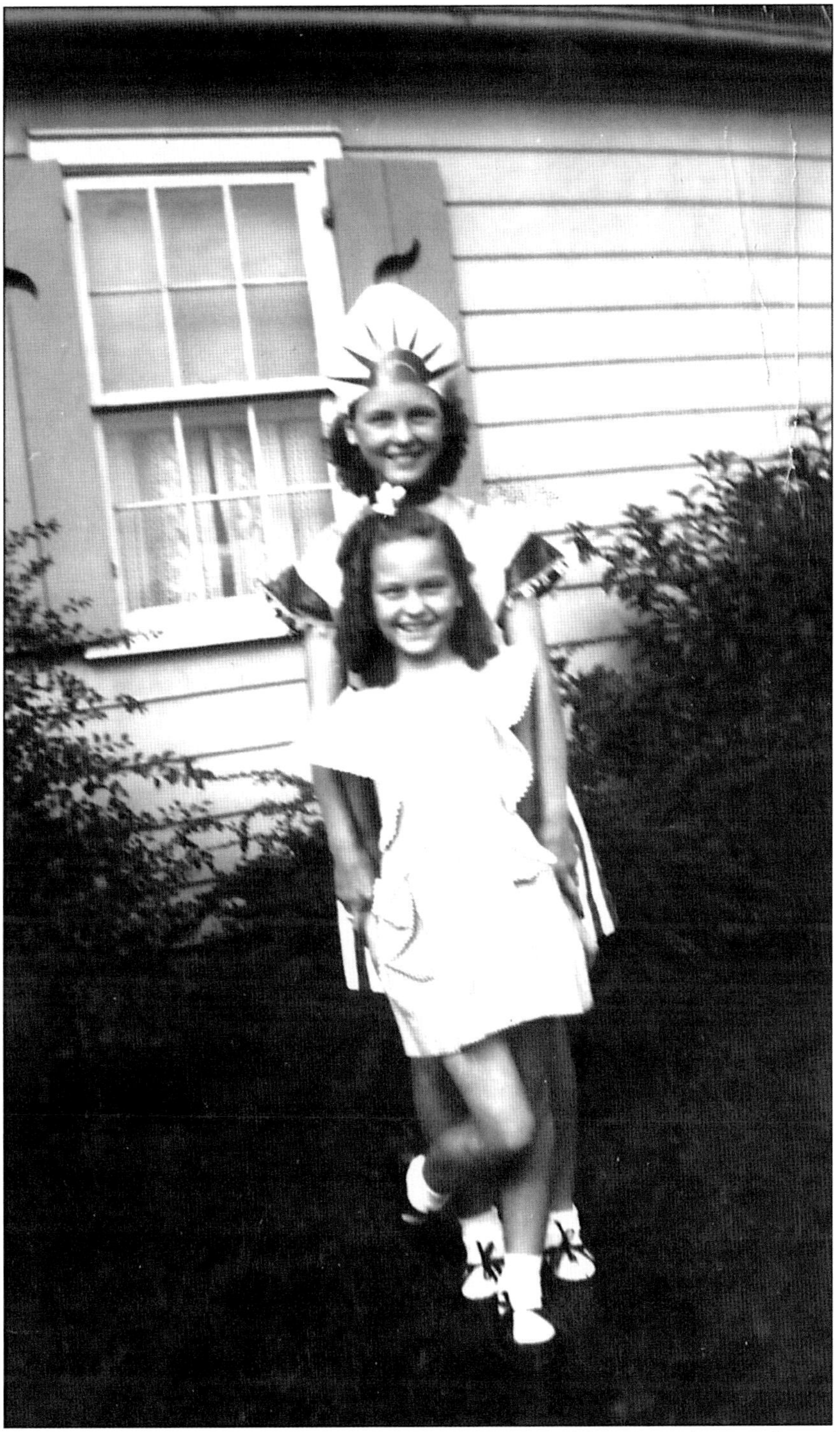

The current Norvelt Elementary School's auditorium was used for plays, dances, dance lessons, stage shows, and musicals hosted and conducted by local citizens. In this photograph, Valeria Sofranko Wolk and her younger sister Dorothy Sofranko Vidakovich pose before their tap-dancing recital. (Courtesy Valeria Sofranko Wolk.)

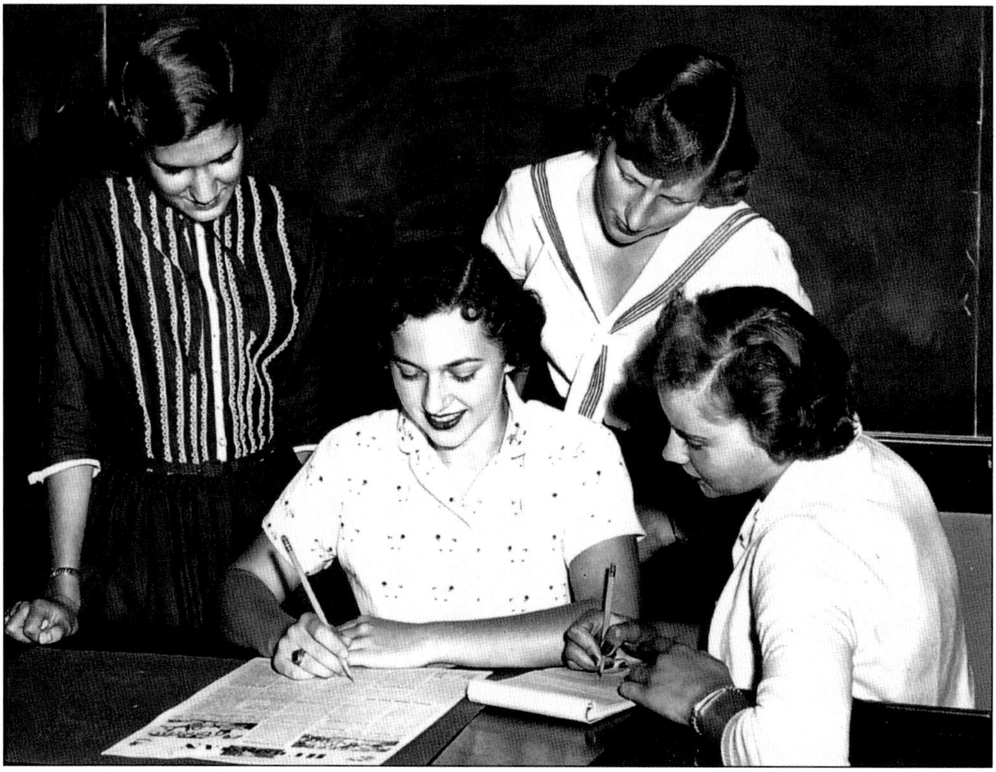

Many homestead youth got their first journalism experiences working on the *Homestead Informer*. In this photograph, from left to right, high school students Patty Craig, Josey Whisdosh, Mary Gonda, and Donna Wadsworth work on their school newspaper at Hurst High School. (Courtesy Shirley Jones Rusinko.)

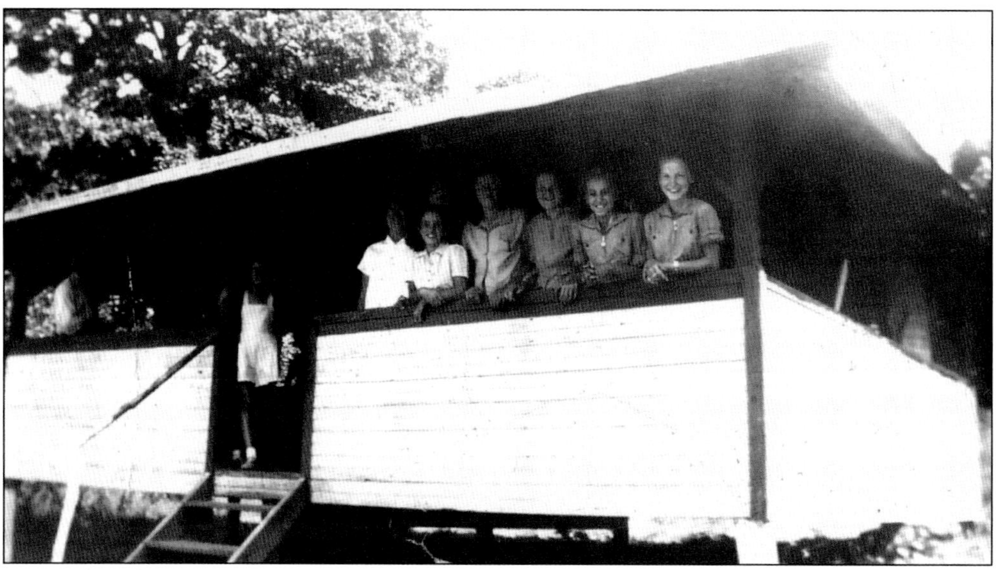

Boy and Girl Scout troops were formed in 1936 and remain popular in Norvelt today. This photograph shows the local Girl Scout troop posing on its annual camping trip at Camp WESCO. (Courtesy of Valeria Sofranko Wolk.)

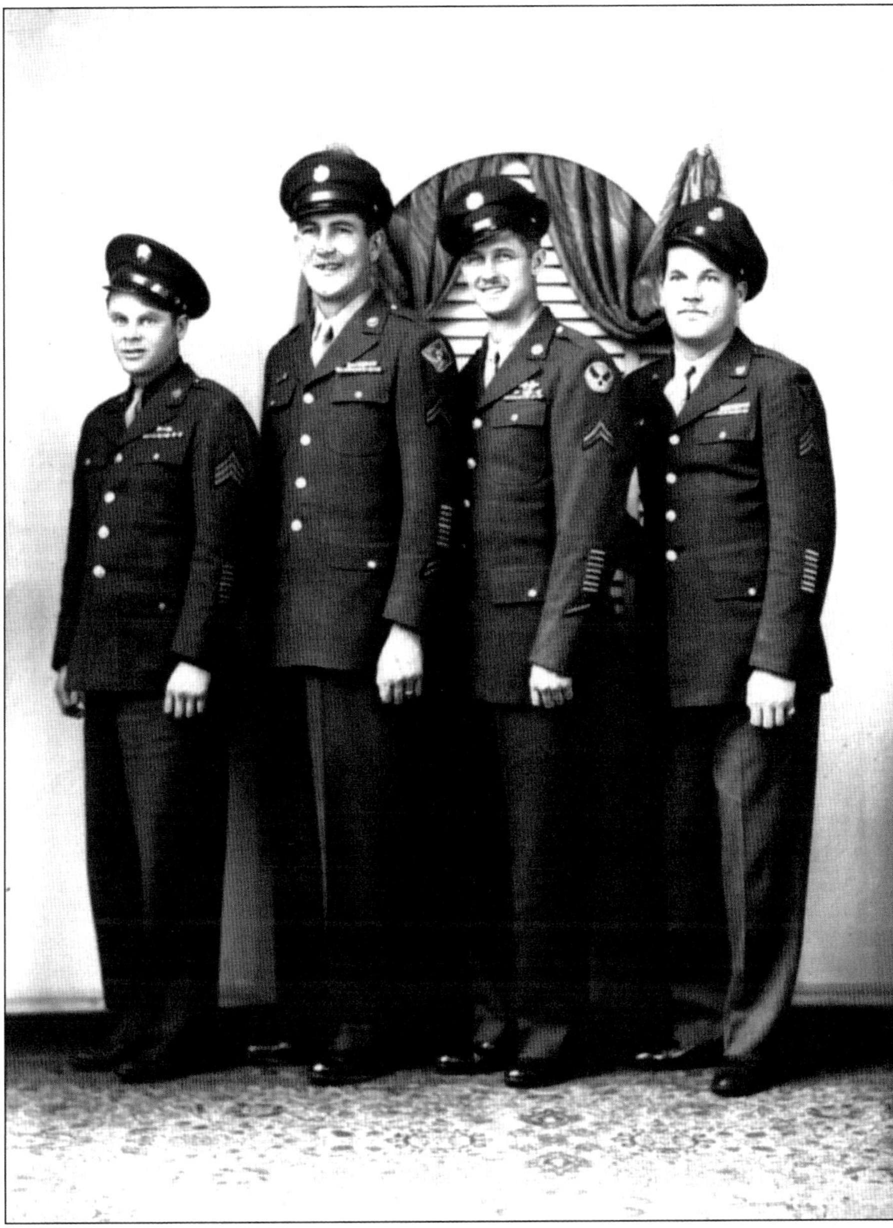

World War II inspired many young men from Norvelt to join the army. Homesteader Steve Cibulas said, "A special gathering was held as the first Norvelt draftees departed via Street Car from the Hurst High station to the Greensburg Depot. They were told this would be for a two year military obligation. But, of these initial recruits, one was stationed at the Schofield Barracks in Hawaii when the Japanese attacked on December 7th, 1941. And five were stationed in the Philippines when it was over run and occupied by the Japanese. The war then became very personal to us." Five of those boys, John "Swede" Emerick, Vinson (Vince) Hatcher, Everett Horrell, Joseph (Joe) Sherbuck, and Corbett (Corby) Marks, left Norvelt and found themselves together in the Bataan Death March. Pictured from left to right are homesteaders George Smollock, John Emerick, Vince Hatcher, and Choppy Bednar posing after enlistment. (Courtesy of Sophie Pipak.)

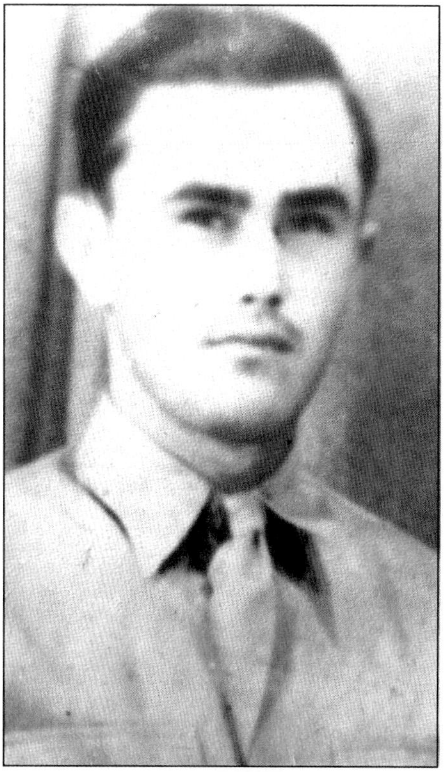

Joe Sherbuck begged his parents until they gave in to sign for him so he could join the army and be with his buddies. He and Corby Marks died during their imprisonment. Sherbuck, pictured at left, was imprisoned in the Philippines, working in the kitchen. He would steal food to give to others at risk to himself. In 1942, he was being transported to a prison in Japan when the ship sank after being torpedoed by an American sub. (Courtesy of Catherine Sherbuck Bosich.)

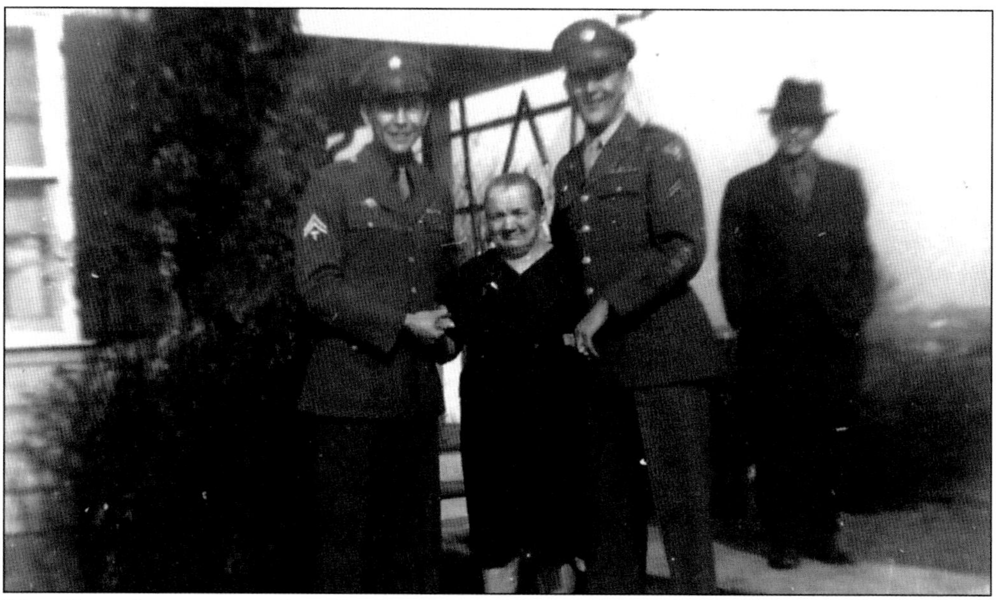

John Emerick was assigned to the Army Air Corps and became a noncommissioned officer training new recruits. During the siege in Corregidor in the Philippines in 1944, he served in the infantry and, after four months of fighting, was captured. He was shipped to Japan on the prison ship *Noto Maru* and served the rest of the war in Hanawa Prison Camp. In this photograph, taken before heading off to war, from left to right are brother Joe Emerick, mother Mary Emerick, John Emerick, and father Valentine Emerick. (Courtesy of Sophie Emerick Pipak.)

Everett Horrell, left, was also captured in Corregidor and marched 75 miles. Weighing only 85 pounds when liberated, his return home was delayed for a few months. He returned home early in November 1945 after hitchhiking on the turnpike. He left the turnpike at Carpentertown and walked five miles home. He married Norvelt girl Annabelle Porterfield and remained in the army until retirement. (Courtesy of Marie Horrell.)

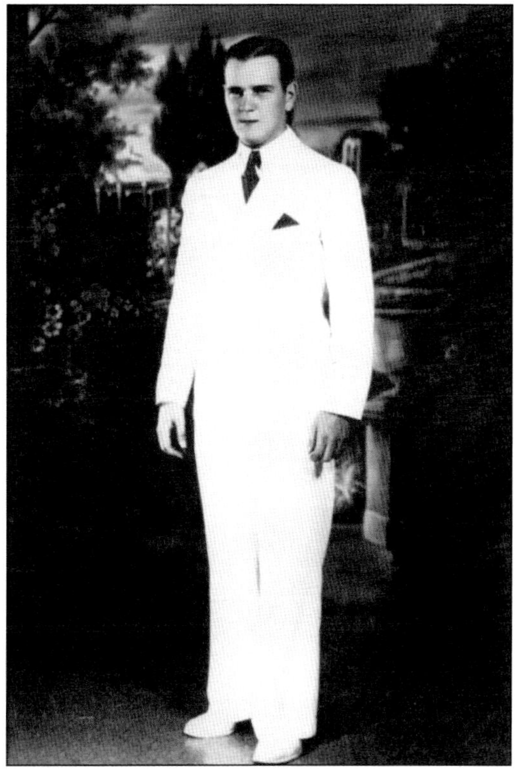

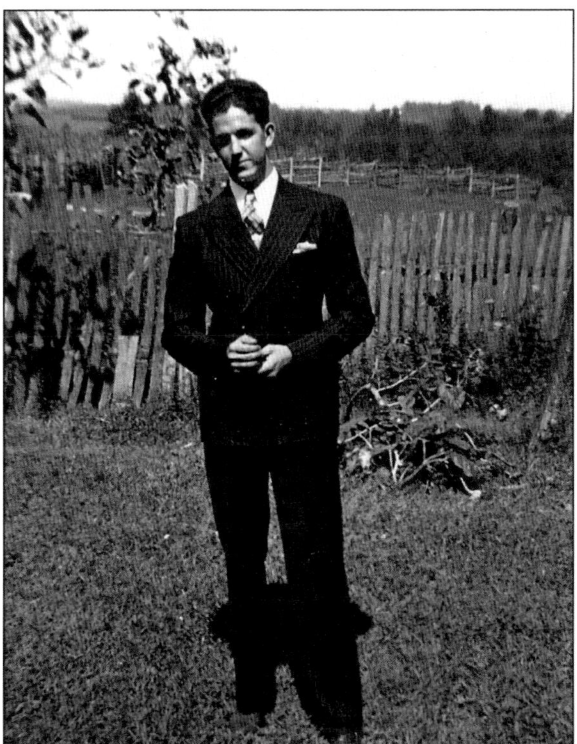

Corby Marks, six feet four inches tall, was a star athlete at Hurst High School and worked as a cutter at the garment factory before joining the army to be with his friends. He died of malnutrition and disease in a Japanese prison camp. (Courtesy of Doris Weaver.)

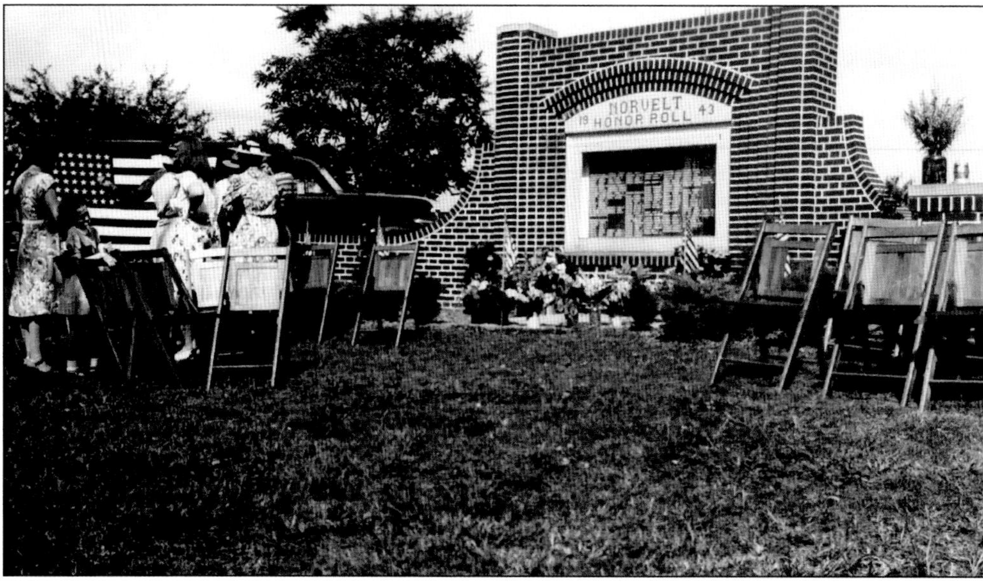

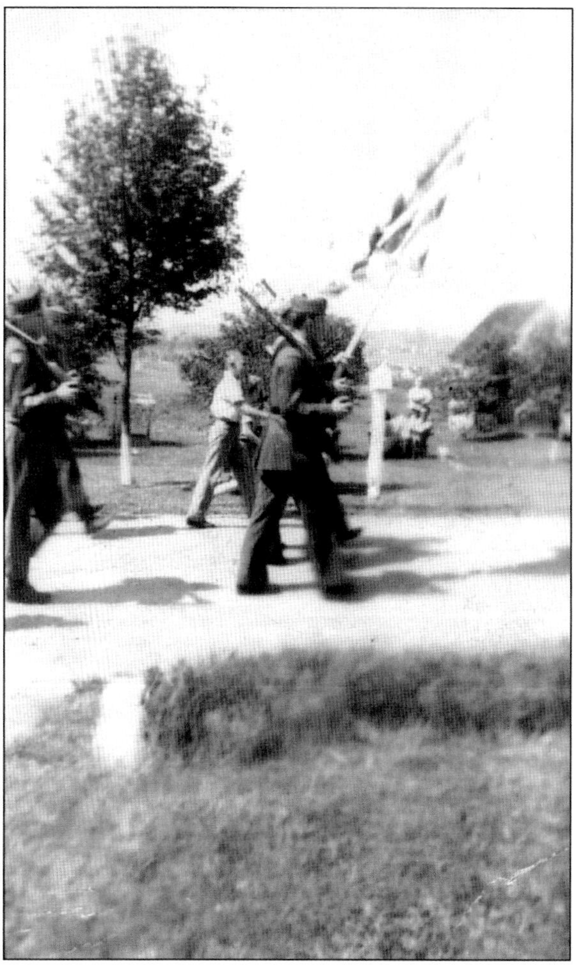

Two other boys from Norvelt, James Kurtz and Harry Dull, lost their lives in the war. Norvelt's Everett Percy Horrell returned after being a prisoner of Japan. The photograph at left was taken in 1946 at Westmoreland Homesteads first Memorial Day parade. It was a grand affair as the community celebrated the return of their sons and daughters from World War II. The day also honored those who died in service. The biggest-ever homecoming parade that day featured the returning veterans marching down the main street, dressed in their uniforms, to the honor roll (above) for a special ceremony followed by a full day of games and socializing, ending with a dance at the firemen's hall. (Above, courtesy of Patty Pavick Kelly; left, courtesy of John Sofranko.)

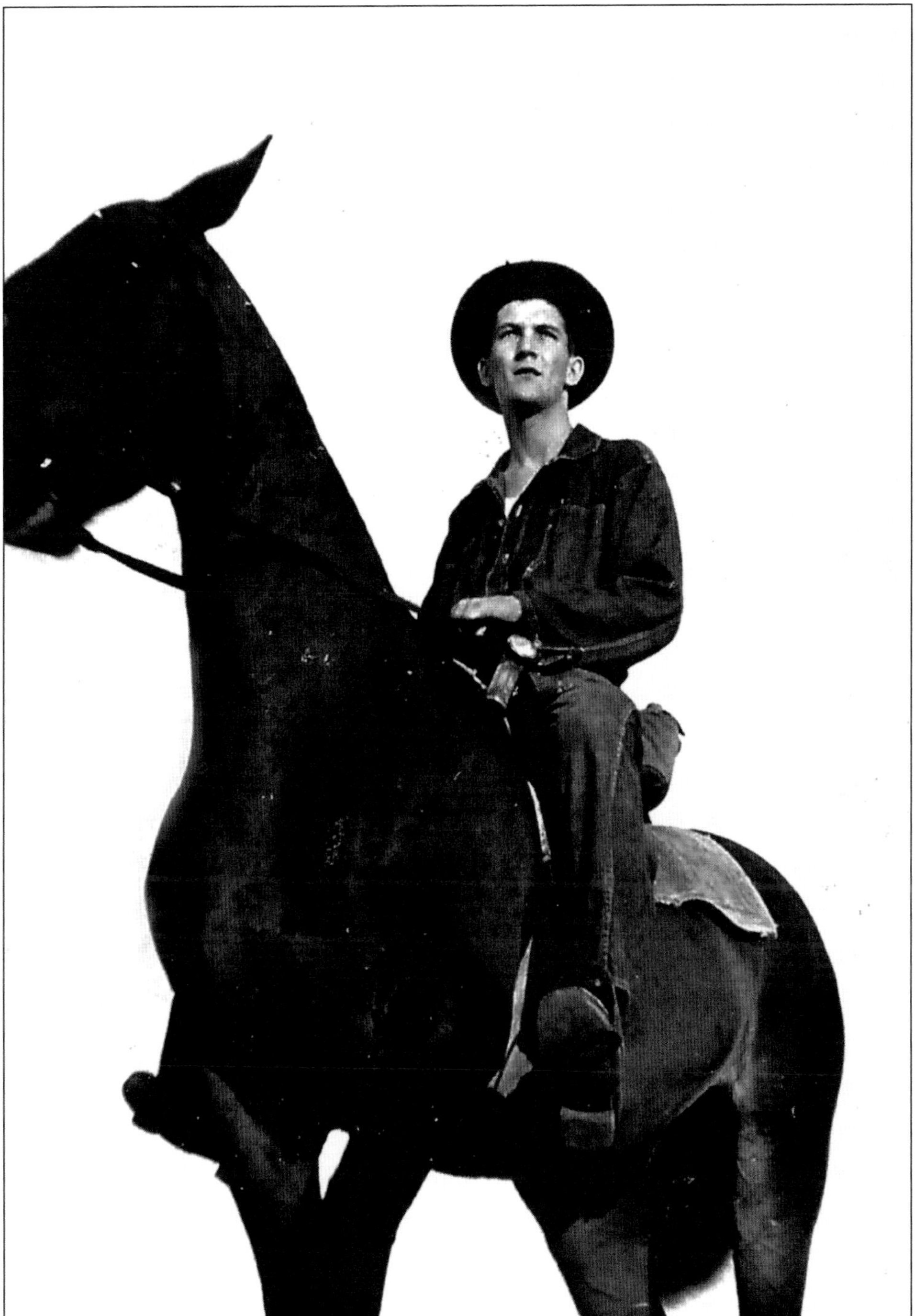

John Emerick returned to Norvelt and married Theresa Urban, also of Norvelt. The above photograph of John Emerick was taken during his military service. Having served as a national commander, Emerick and a group of former POWs established the American Defenders of Bataan and Corregidor (ABAC), now a recognized veteran service organization devoted to getting services for POWs. (Courtesy of Sophie Emerick Pipak.)

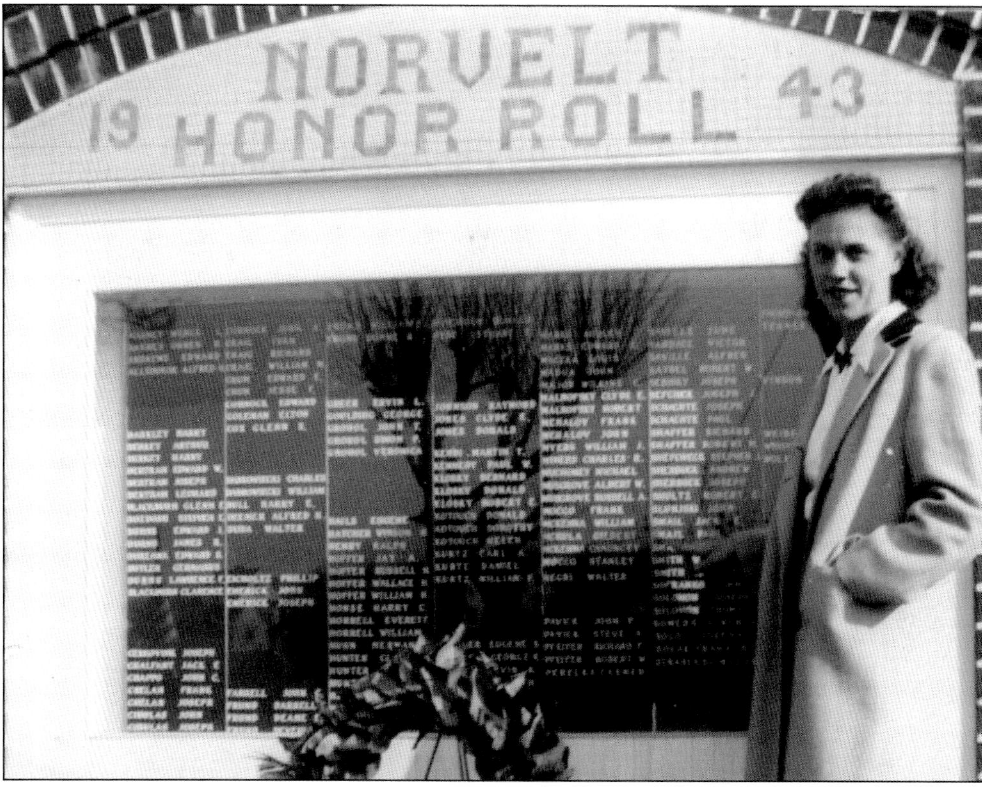

Helen Pavick stands beside the honor roll in front of the fire department dedicated in 1943. (Courtesy of Patty Pavick Kelly.)

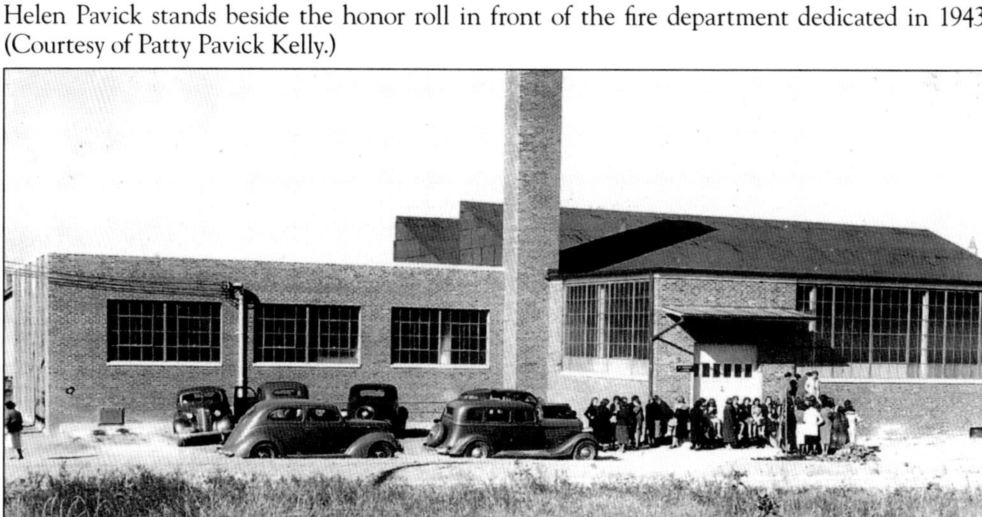

The town stood behind its boys in the military during World War II. This photograph shows the garment factory workers honoring veterans. Many garment workers had family members serving in the military. Catherine Sherbuck was working at the pants factory when she was called out and handed a telegram from the Department of War informing her family that their son had died in action. They had another son, Andy, serving, and the telegram did not say which son had died. She had to go home and tell her parents. Caty wrote to the Department of War and soon it was confirmed that Joe had died. (Courtesy of Valeria Sofranko Wolk.)

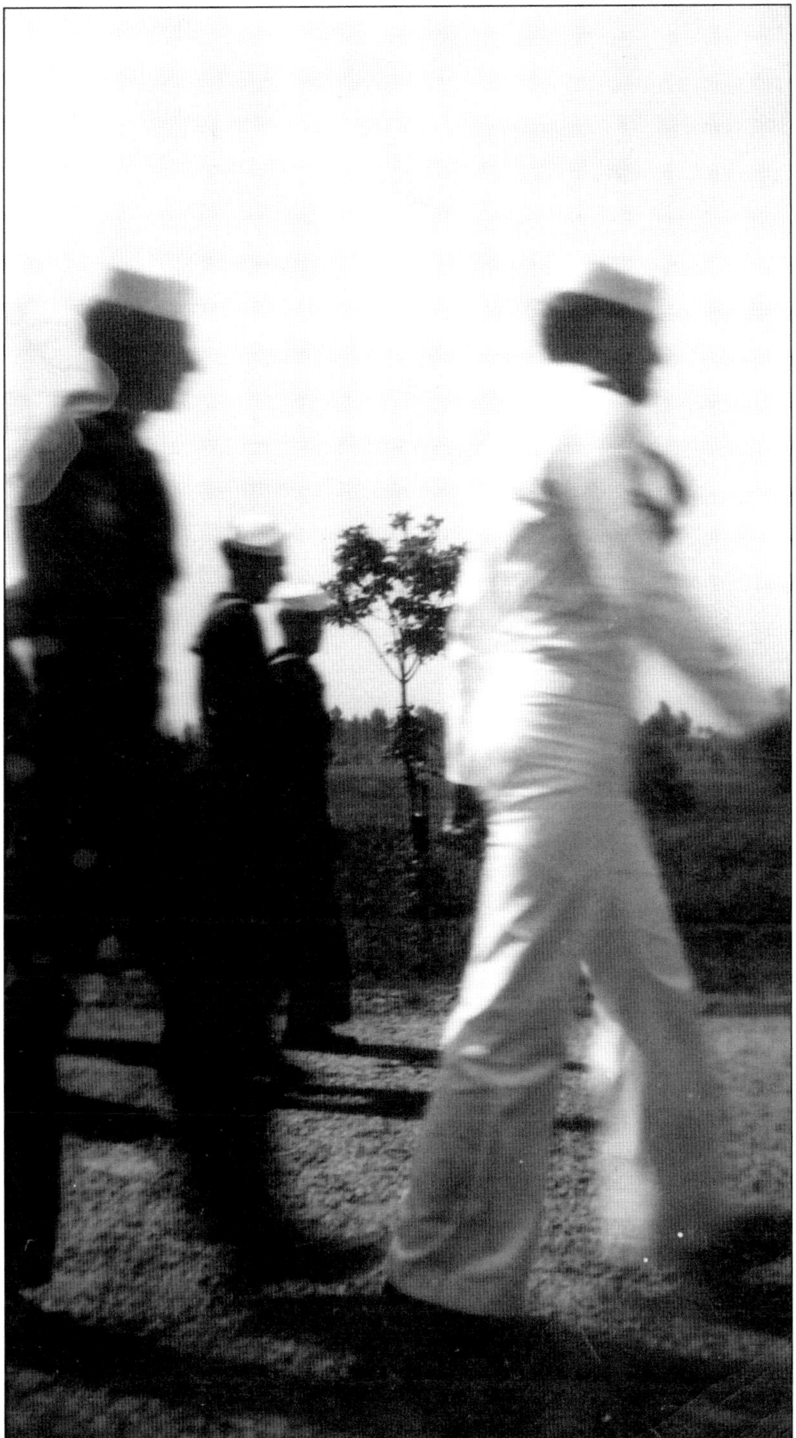

Soldiers and sailors marched side by side on that 1946 Memorial Day celebration. In this photograph is John Solomon, wearing the white sailor uniform, marching down Main Street in Norvelt in the biggest-ever homecoming parade. (Courtesy of Valeria Sofranko Wolk.)

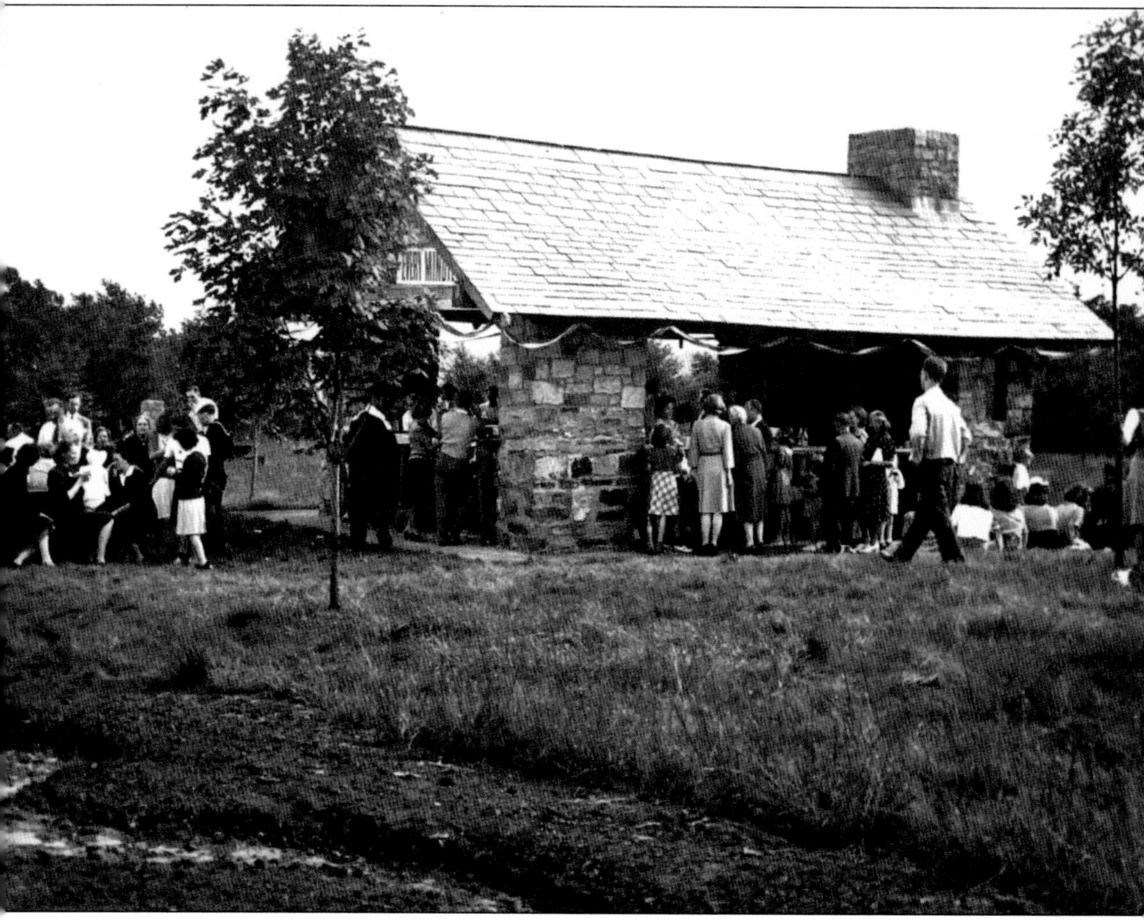

Eleanor Roosevelt visited Norvelt on May 21, 1937, accompanied by Elinor Morgenthau, wife of the secretary of the treasury, and 10 other friends. After driving to the homes of the Kelleys, Riddles, Millers, and Terneys, she drove her own car from E section, through United to D section and from there to Calumet and C section, stopping for a gathering on Reservoir Hill where they could look out over the town. Their tour ended with a visit to the nursery school and grade school. (Courtesy of Gail Hoffer.)

Six

THE HOMESTEADERS

By 1940, all homes were occupied. In 1940, Dairyman's house C-39 on Kecksburg Road was occupied by William Wilson. The farm foreman, residing at the Knopsick House on Hecla Road, was Elmer Linden. The Steele Farmhouse on Brinkerton Road was occupied by Clifford Andrews. The Kuhn Farmhouse on Brinkerton Road was occupied by Anthony Castorino. The LaBuda Farmhouse south of Kecksburg Road was occupied by John Gradish. The town was proudly known as Norvelt.

Norvelt was ready to come to life. The community building was the center for square dances, canning classes, picnics, and activities to get acquainted and socialize. Community dances were held in the Dillon Farm barn located at the site of the present fire station in Norvelt. George Marks, Bill Wilson, and two Musgrove boys would provide the music with their stringed instruments. Deacon Jones and his seven-piece band played for fund-raisers for the fire company. Frank Dudgeon, radio singer and "West Virginia Mountain Boy," was a featured entertainer. Music was an important part of community life in Norvelt. Spurred perhaps by Eleanor Roosevelt's early experience with the Chautauqua movement, she insisted that the arts be introduced into the homesteads. The WPA's Federal Art Project provided employment for unemployed artists and musicians. W. J. Simmons, a talented piano player and music teacher, touched many lives. Early on, the community raised money to purchase a Victrola, with several Gold Seal records, and a complete set of rhythm instruments. Simmons produced children's operettas as well as programs for adults.

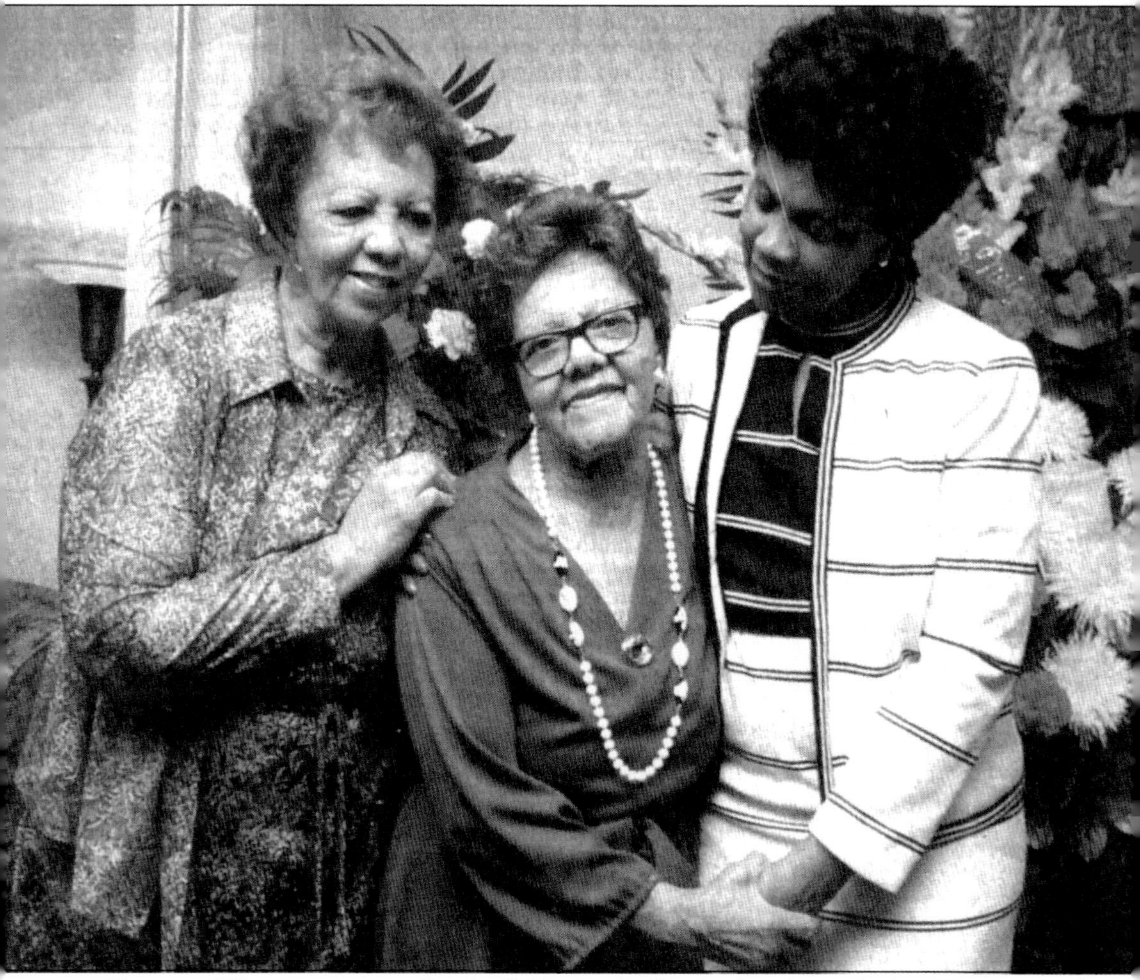

Chauncey White was repeatedly rebuffed by local officials when he applied to Westmoreland Homesteads. Just wanting the same chance as everyone else, White wrote a letter to the president about what was going on. Franklin D. Roosevelt wrote back that there would be no discrimination in the homestead. Shortly after, the Whites became the first and only black family in Westmoreland Homesteads. The August 8, 1935, issue of the *Homestead Informer* announced a contest to name the town. Addah, Chauncey's wife, wrote a letter to the editor suggesting the name Eleanorville after Eleanor Roosevelt or O'Dayville after Olive Day, David Day's wife. The contest would be won for her last suggestion: to combine the last letters of Eleanor and Roosevelt as the new name for Westmoreland Homesteads. The above photograph shows Addah White with her daughters Norma Williams and Sara White-Brown. (Courtesy of Earl Saville.)

Homesteaders remember Chauncey and Addah White's son, Doyle, for his gifted musical abilities. At an early age, Doyle played locally for schools and events. As an adult, he played piano with the New Philharmonic Orchestra. (Courtesy of Earl Saville.)

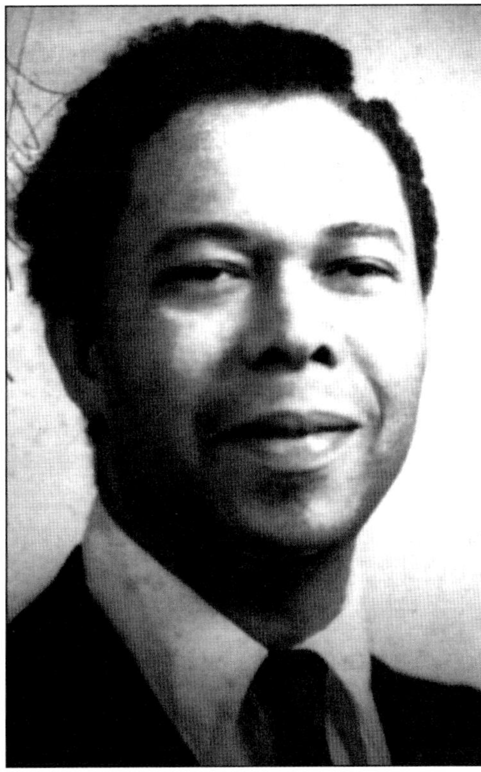

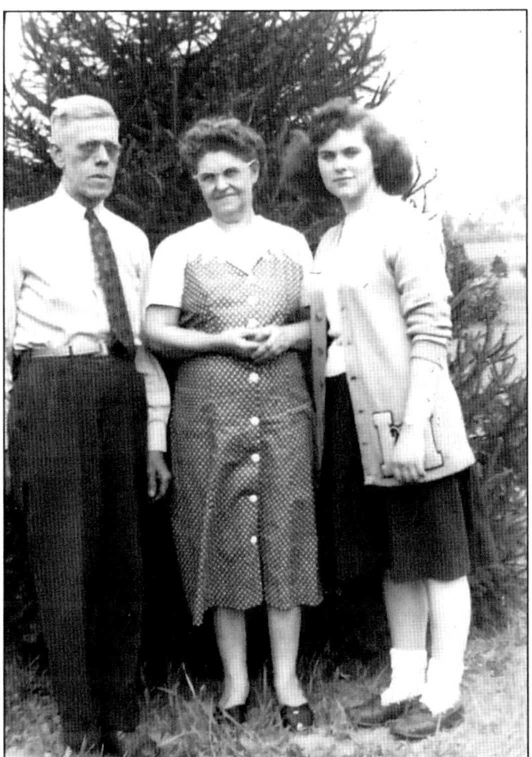

This photograph of Joe Saville, his wife Ella, and daughter Patty was taken on their front lawn in D section (D-16). Saville was a member of the volunteer firemen and lived on D section. (Courtesy of Earl Saville.)

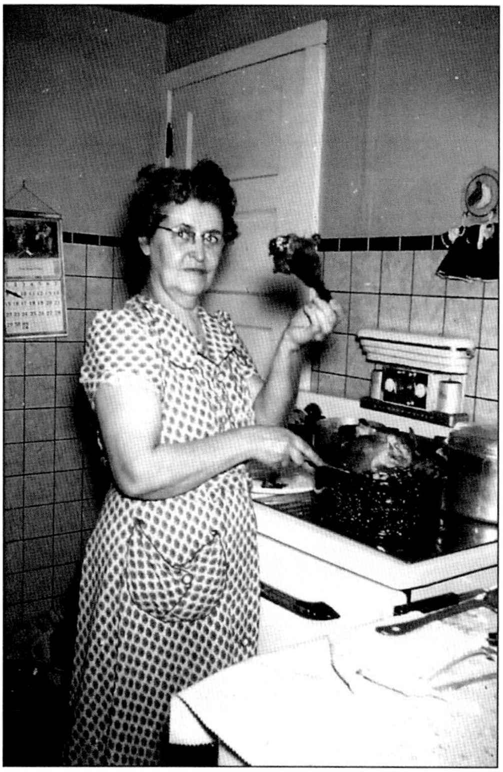

Ella Saville stands in her kitchen preparing Thanksgiving dinner. (Courtesy of Earl Saville.)

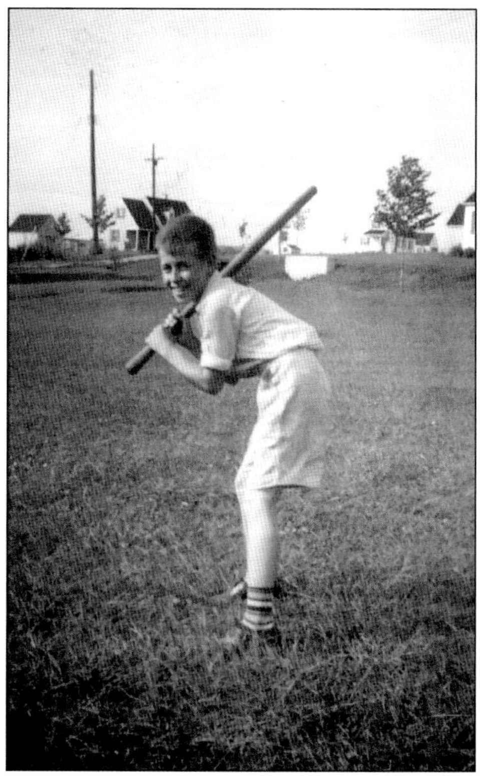

Earl Saville, at age 13, is ready to bat with a bat made by his uncle. Saville continues to reside in Norvelt and has been one of Norvelt's biggest advocates and most noted historian. He is a member of the Lion's Club. (Courtesy of Earl Saville.)

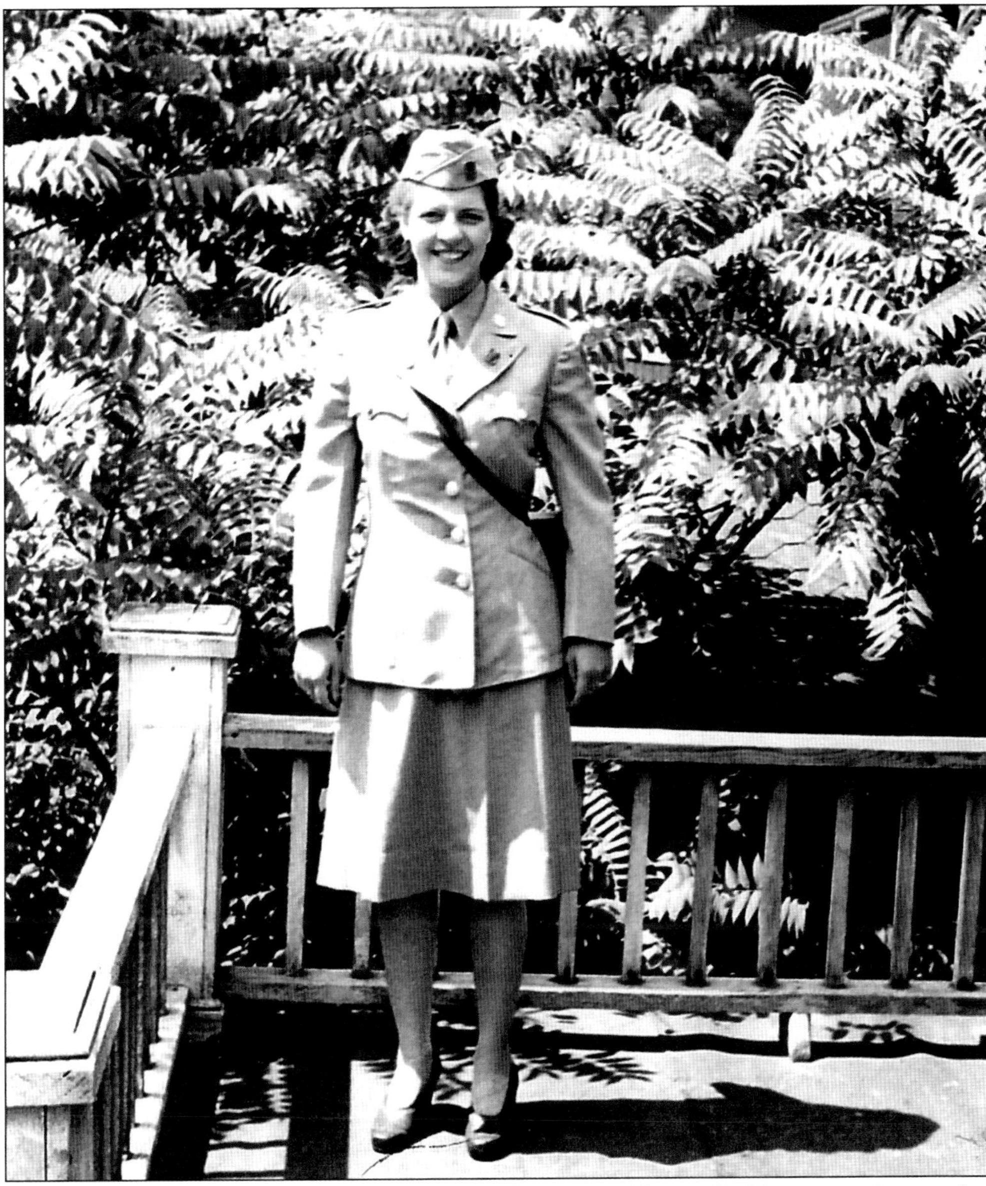

June Saville was in the Women's Army Corp during World War II. She is seen here in her uniform. (Courtesy of Earl Seville.)

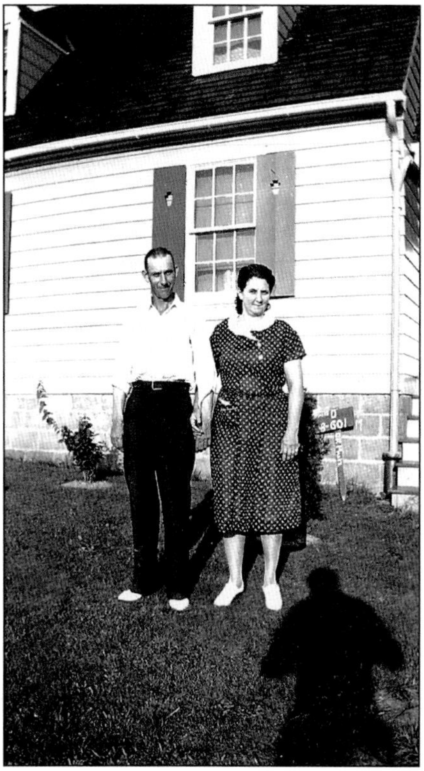

George and Blanche Marks of D section pose for a photograph in front of their home. The couple lost their son, Corbett, in the Bataan Death March. They had two other boys serving in the military during World War II. (Courtesy of Doris Weaver.)

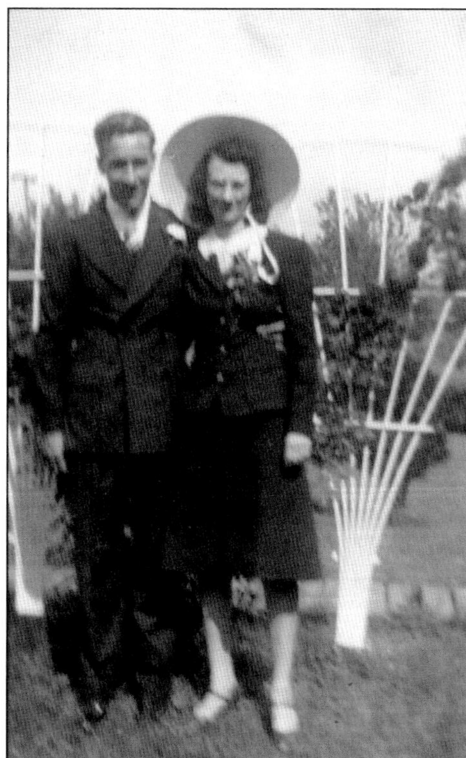

This photograph was taken on the wedding day of Louise Marks of D-38 to Herman Huhn of A section on June 14, 1941, at the home of Herman Huhn's parents. (Courtesy of Doris Weaver.)

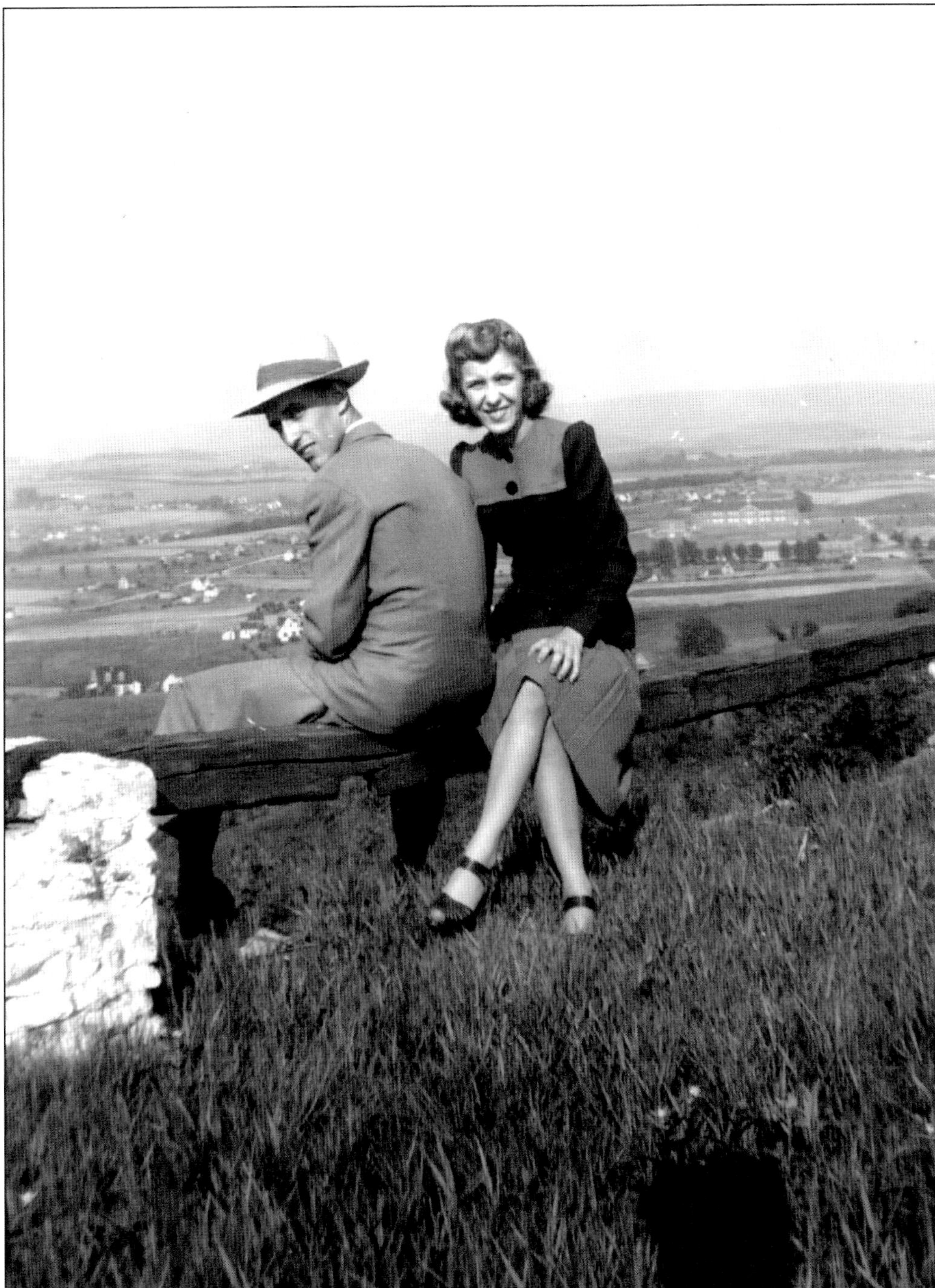

This photograph was taken in 1942 when Homer Huhn Jr.—known as JR—proposed to Josephine Hajduk Huhn, his wife, on Reservoir Hill overlooking Norvelt. After leading a very active life in Norvelt, Huhn worked at the Westmoreland County Courthouse as clerk of courts. In 1970, he was accepted by the Benevolent and Protective Order of Elks in Chicago to be grand secretary. He was voted unanimously to be grand exalted ruler from 1977 to 1978. He then retired to Latrobe with Josephine. (Courtesy of Doris Weaver.)

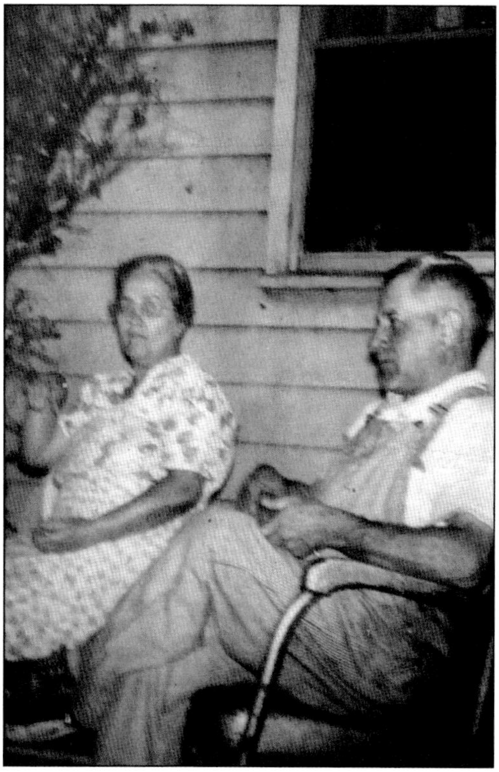

Homer Huhn Sr. walked from Calumet to the homestead every day to help build his home until it was completed. He was store manager and superintendent of poultry supplies at the poultry barn. He worked there until he started his own chicken business on his property in A section (A-2). (Courtesy of Doris Weaver.)

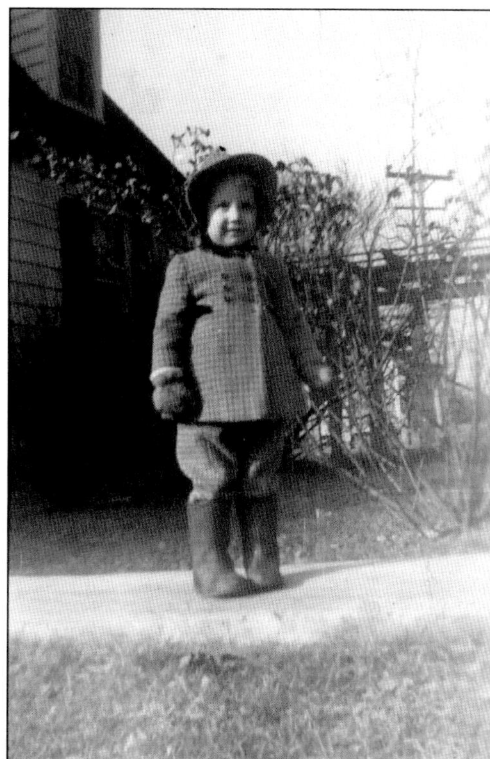

Roberta Huhn is the daughter of Nellie and Homer Huhn Sr. of A section (A-2). A young girl could be kept very busy growing up as a homesteader participating in Girl Scouts, tap-dancing lessons, art classes, and watching plays and movies at the school auditorium. (Courtesy of Doris Weaver.)

Joann "Josey" Whisdosh Walton stands in the front yard of her home in D section (D-9). Many young girls participated in the Little Mothers Sewing Club, which published a sample sewing book to get children interested in sewing. (Courtesy of Josey Whisdosh Walton.)

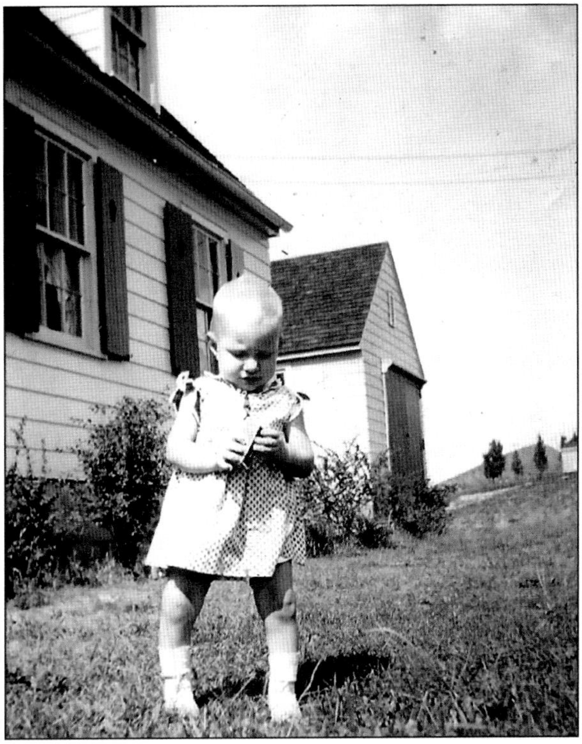

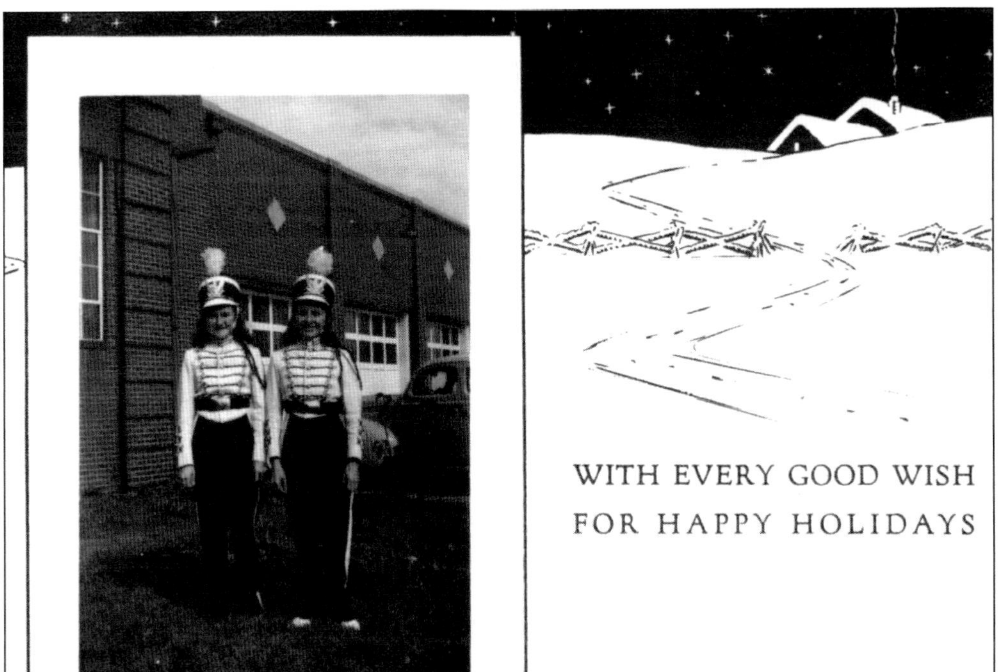

Agnes Whisdosh Shultz and Helen Whisdosh Kissell pose in their Hurst High School band uniforms in 1942. Hurst High School had a proud history of good marching bands. With scarlet-red pants and white jacket, they helped root the Scarlet Hurricanes to many victories. (Courtesy of Josey Whisdosh Walton.)

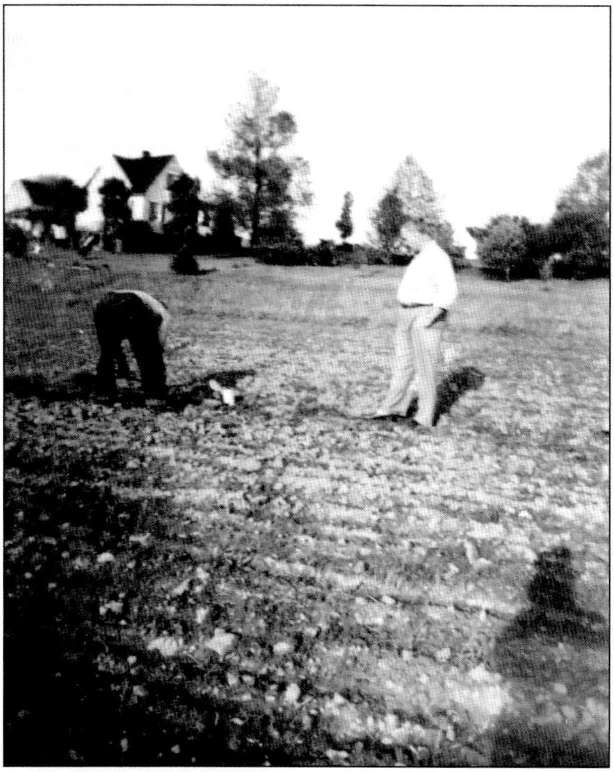

John Whisdosh of D-9 is planting his garden while a friend is watching with the Whisdosh home in the background. The co-op offered plowing and harrowing of gardens to homesteaders who were interested. (Courtesy of Josey Whisdosh Walton.)

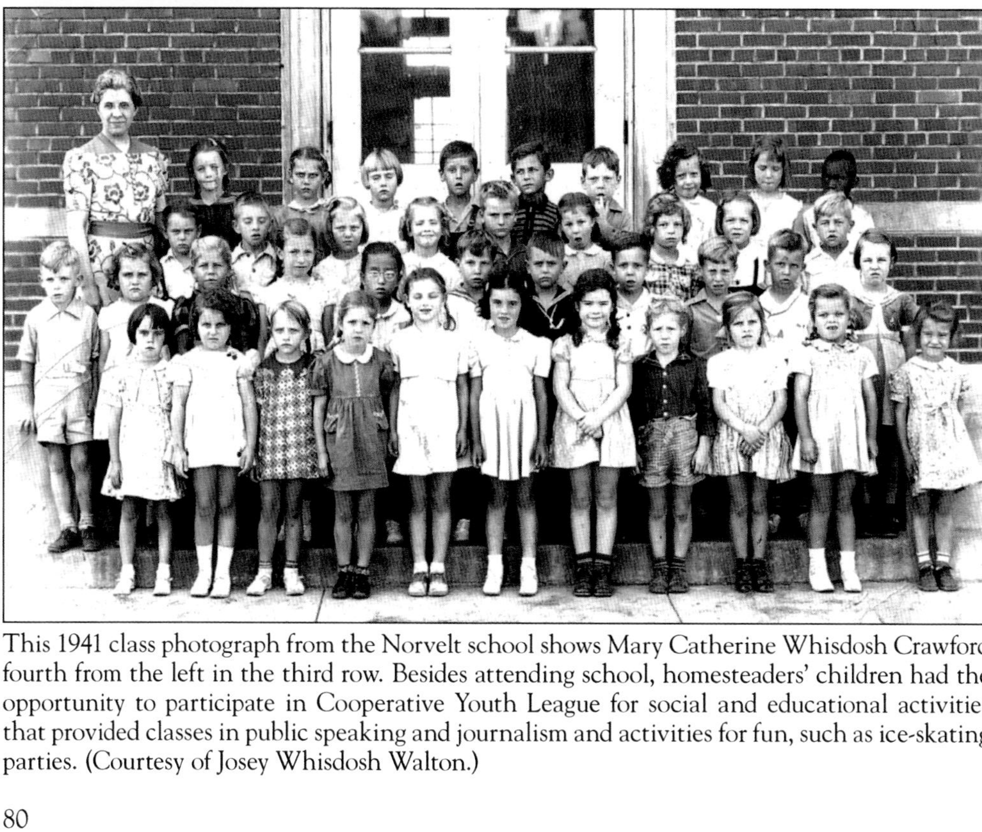

This 1941 class photograph from the Norvelt school shows Mary Catherine Whisdosh Crawford fourth from the left in the third row. Besides attending school, homesteaders' children had the opportunity to participate in Cooperative Youth League for social and educational activities that provided classes in public speaking and journalism and activities for fun, such as ice-skating parties. (Courtesy of Josey Whisdosh Walton.)

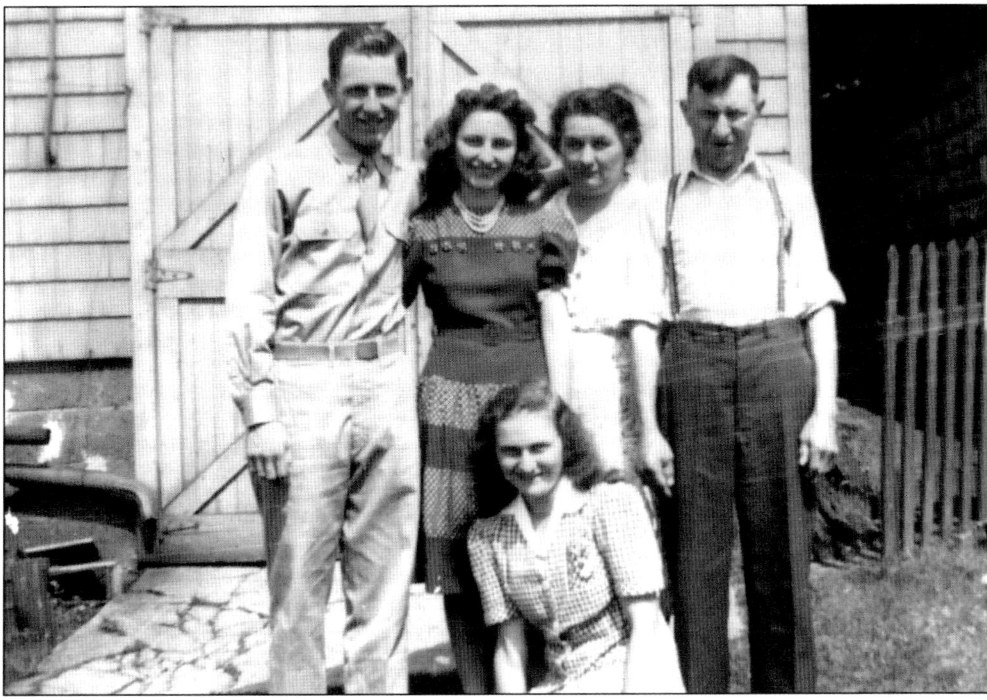

The Whisdosh family poses on July 19, 1943. The family includes, from left to right, Steve, Agnes Catherine Shultz, Agnes Kendi Whisdosh, Steve Sr., and (front row) Helen Whisdosh Kissell. The co-op provided guidance to homesteaders relative to any phase of gardening, landscaping, lawn making, and so on. (Courtesy of Stephen Whisdosh.)

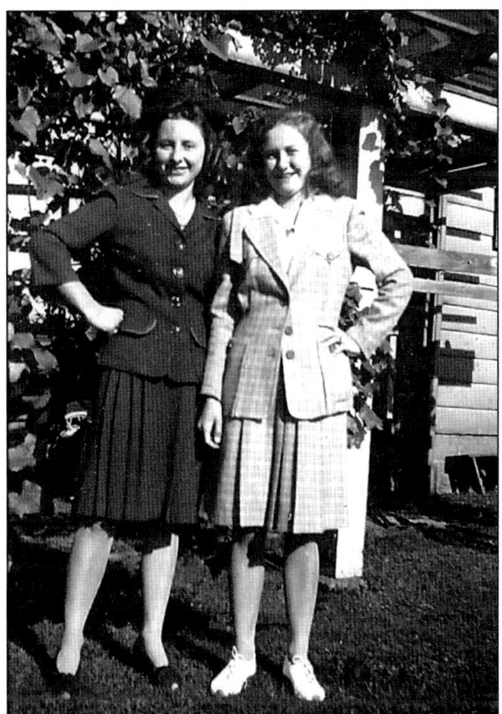

Agnes and Helen Whisdosh pose by the grape arbor on September 27, 1943. (Courtesy of Stephen Whisdosh.)

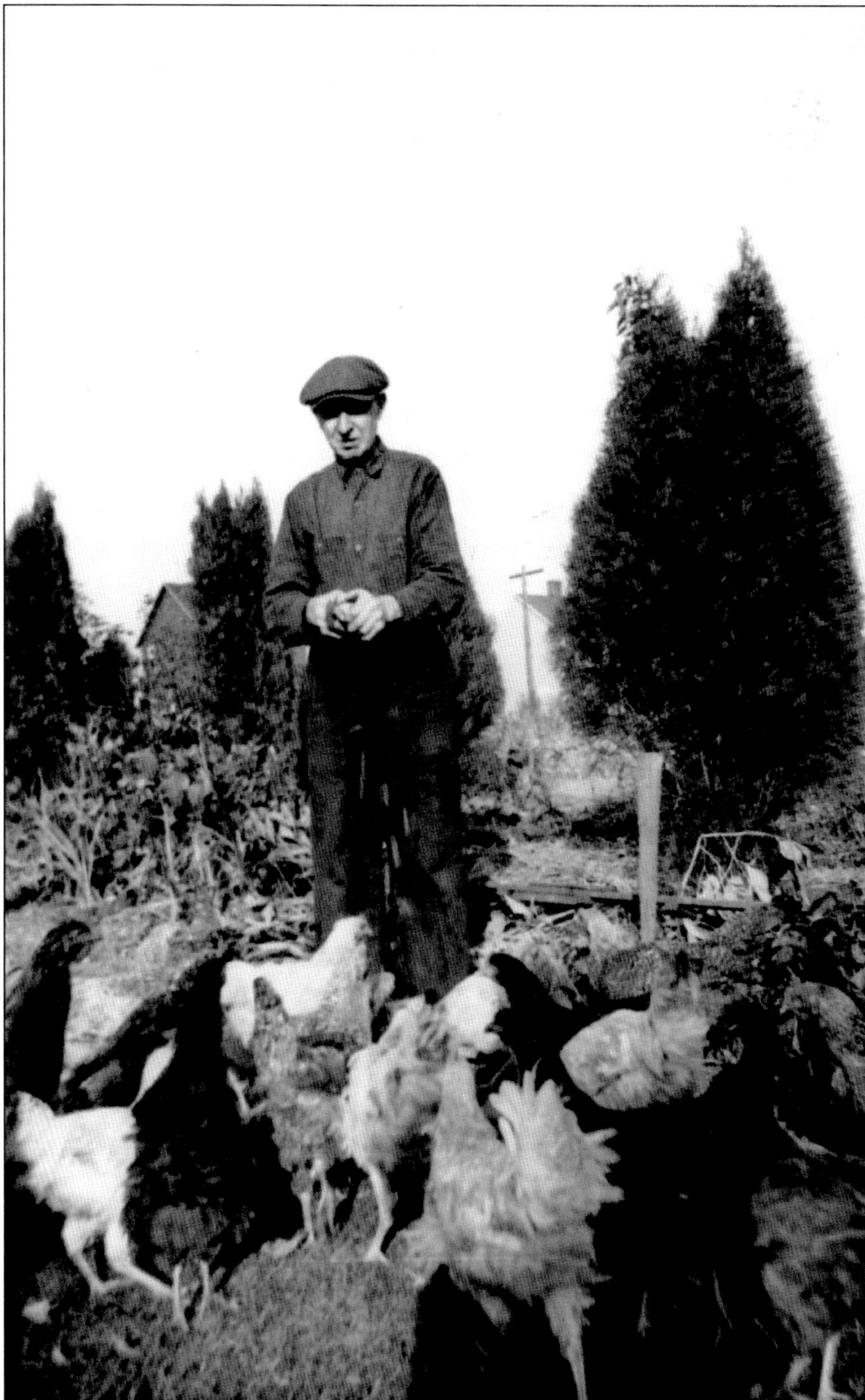

Steven Whisdosh Sr. feeds his chickens in his backyard. Study groups were arranged by the co-op and homesteaders were divided into groups to study various topics of interest and necessity for the homesteaders, such as the basic principles of all cooperatives and the care of baby chicks. (Courtesy of Stephen Whisdosh.)

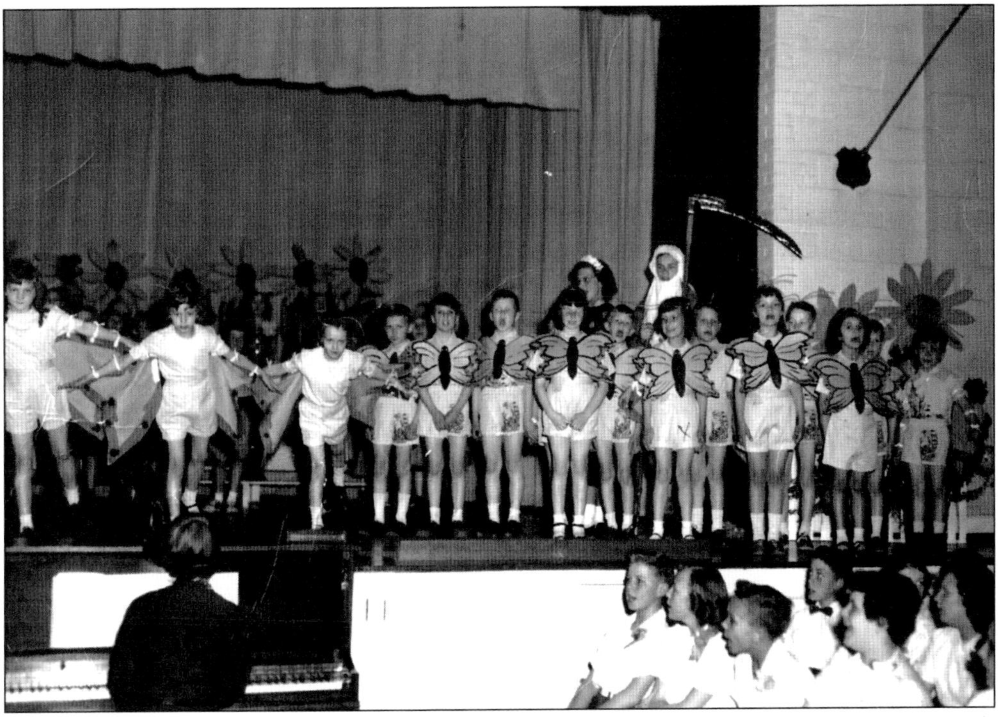

Homesteaders, young and old alike, could participate in drama clubs. The above photograph shows children at the Norvelt school putting on a special performance. (Courtesy of Shirley Jones Rusinko.)

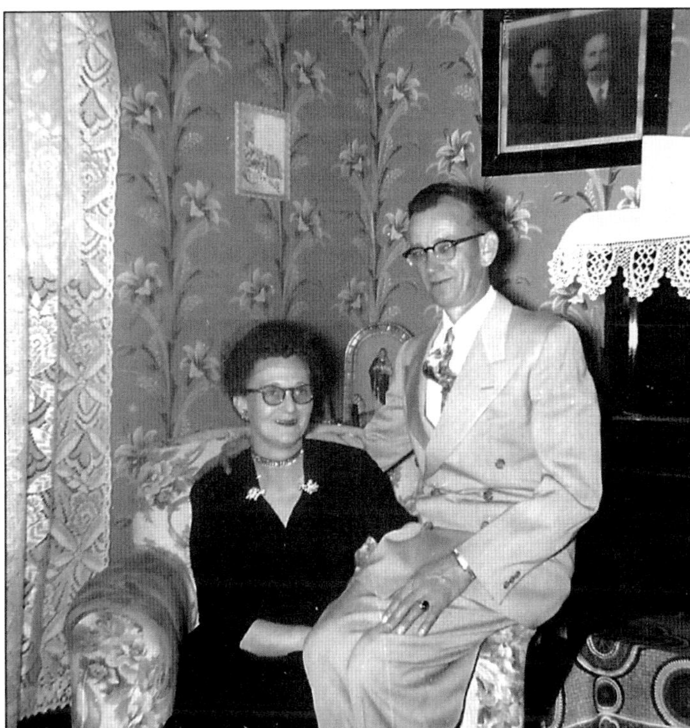

George and Mary Dzambo are seated in their living room. The Mother's Club hosted a meeting in 1936 at the Andrews family's Hurst House. Members dressed in costumes of many years ago to reflect the Colonial manor of the Hurst home. Mrs. Hatcher dressed as Martha Washington and won first place. Mrs. Fillmore won second place for a maroon velvet-trimmed dress with high neck, slim waist, and long full skirt. Runners up were Mrs. Dzambo, Mrs. Delynko, and Mrs. Kelly. (Courtesy of Geraldine Dzambo Mizikar.)

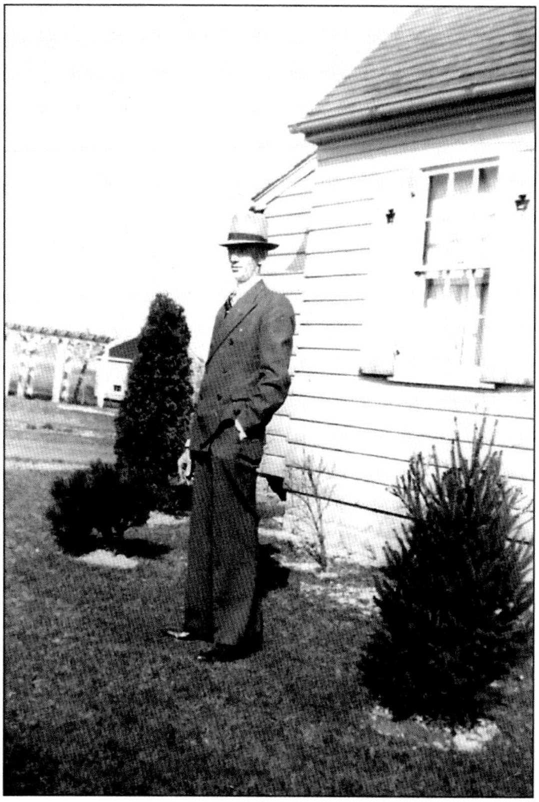

George Dzambo poses outside his home in E section (E-14). Dzambo was a fire chief and firemen's club bartender. The firemen sponsored many fund-raising barn dances at the community center with Deacon Jones and his seven-piece orchestra. Admission was 25¢ for adults and 10¢ for children. (Courtesy of Geraldine Dzambo Mizikar.)

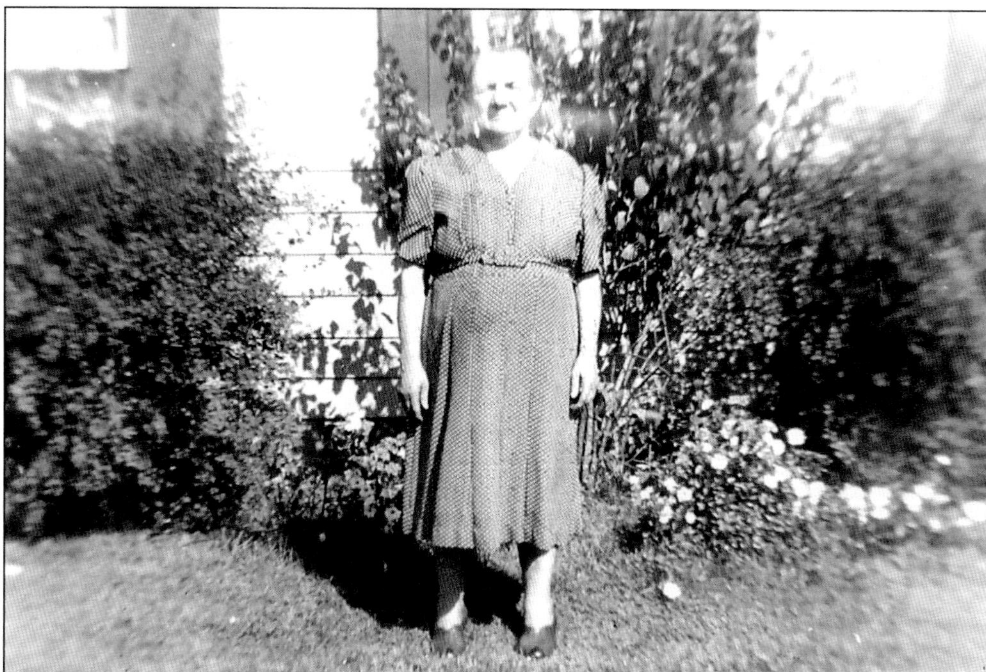

Mary Emerick, wife of Valentine Emerick, stands in front of her home. (Courtesy of Geraldine Dzambo Mizikar.)

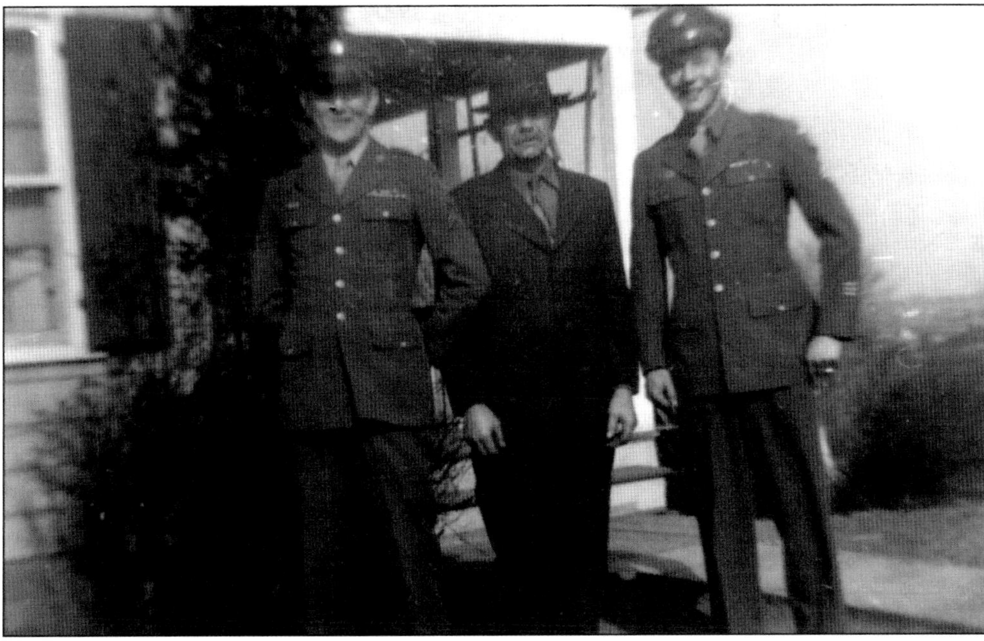

Valentine Emerick stands proudly between his two sons, John and Joe, as they were headed off to World War II. Both boys returned. (Courtesy of Sophie Emerick Pipak.)

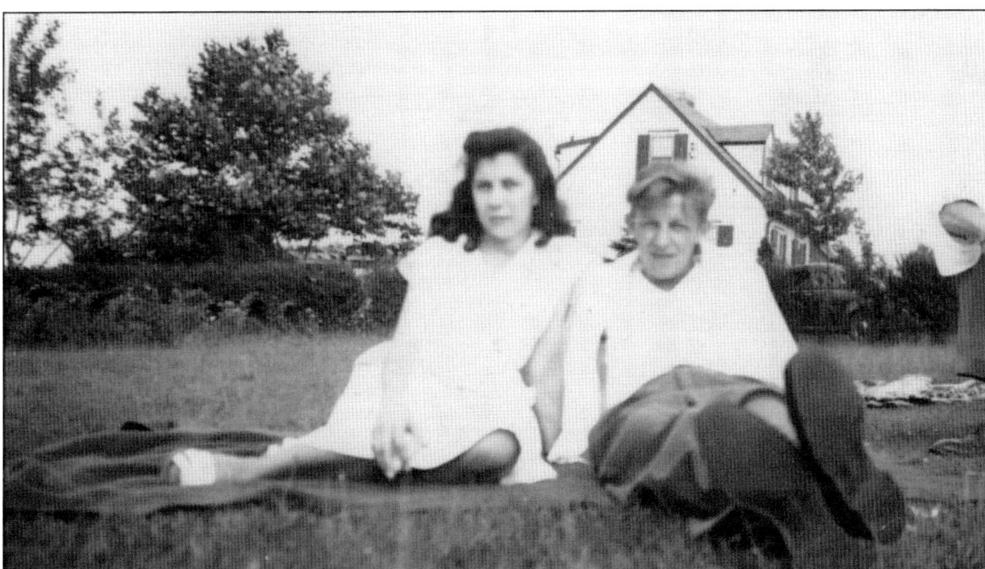

Frank Pipak sits on the grass with his wife, Sophie Emerick Pipak. (Courtesy of Sophie Emerick Pipak.)

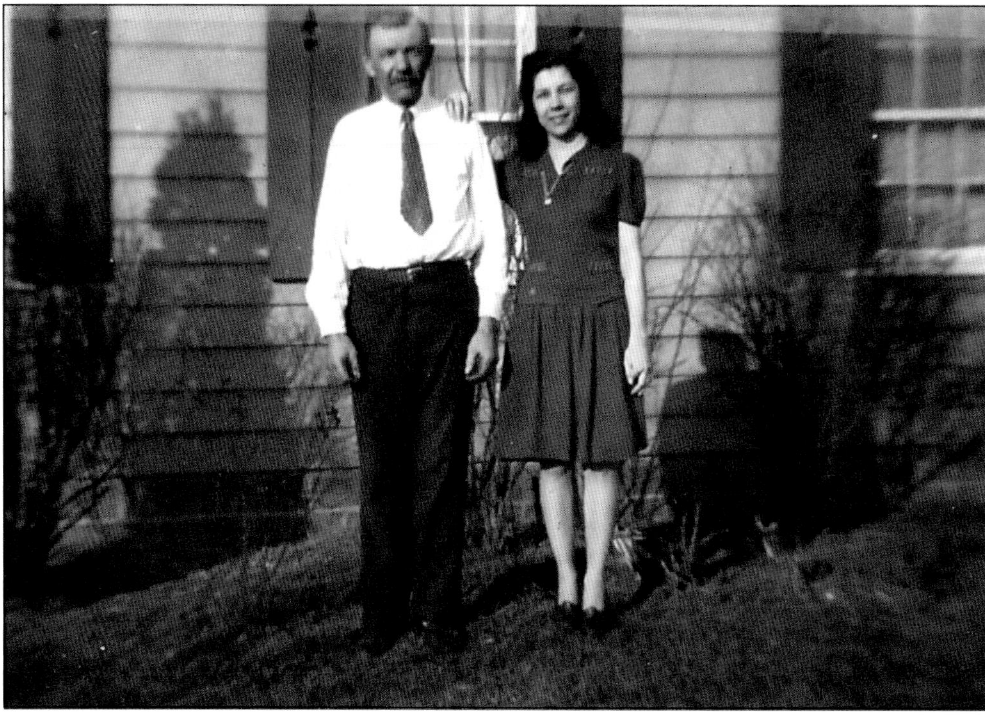

Valentine Emerick stands in front of the Emerick home with his daughter Sophie Emerick Pipak. (Courtesy of Sophie Emerick Pipak.)

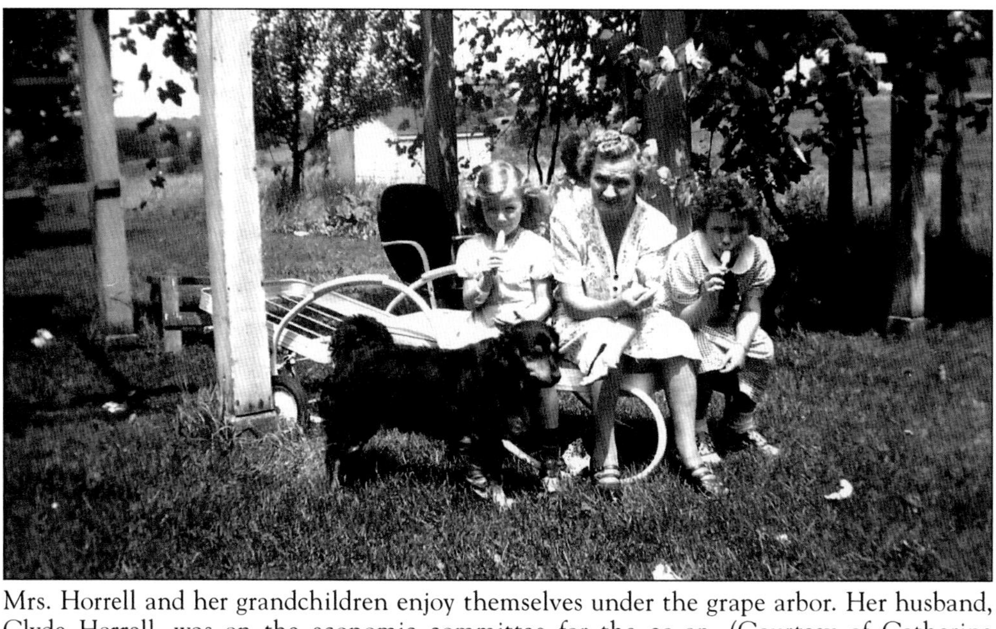

Mrs. Horrell and her grandchildren enjoy themselves under the grape arbor. Her husband, Clyde Horrell, was on the economic committee for the co-op. (Courtesy of Catherine Sherbuck Bosich.)

Everett Horrell, with wife and son, stands in his living room for this photograph. The *Homestead Informer* reviewed a social meeting with a short debate question, "Should both husband or wife be boss in the house. Mrs. Huhn and Mrs. Kelley plead the case for the wives. Mr. McFouse and Mr. Horrell for the husbands. The women bested the men so effectively that Mr. Candaez had to be called in; but he immediately cinched matters for the wives by saying that the women should be boss in the home. The debate was conceded to the women amid a lot of clapping, booing, and hissing." (Courtesy of Catherine Sherbuck Bosich.)

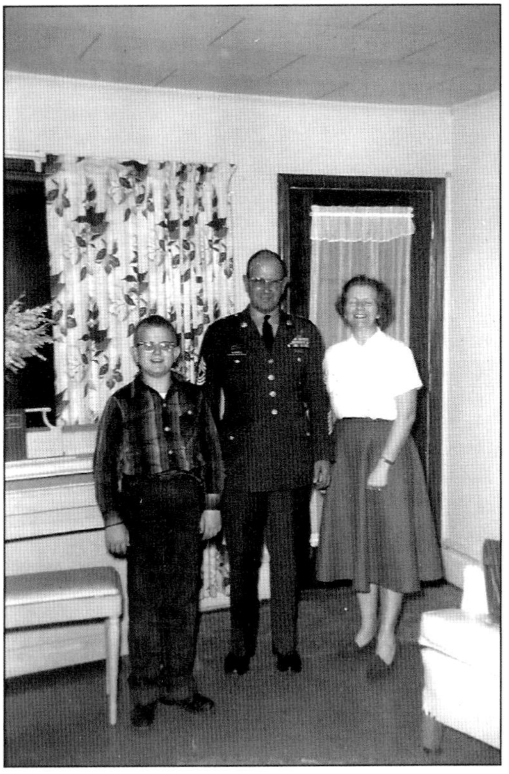

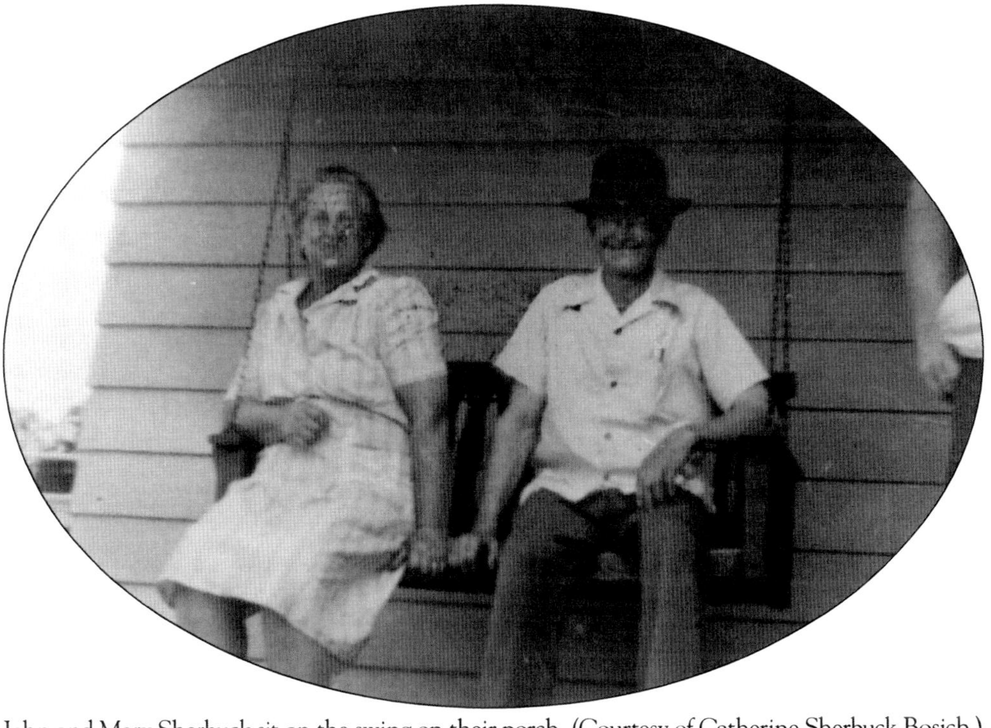

John and Mary Sherbuck sit on the swing on their porch. (Courtesy of Catherine Sherbuck Bosich.)

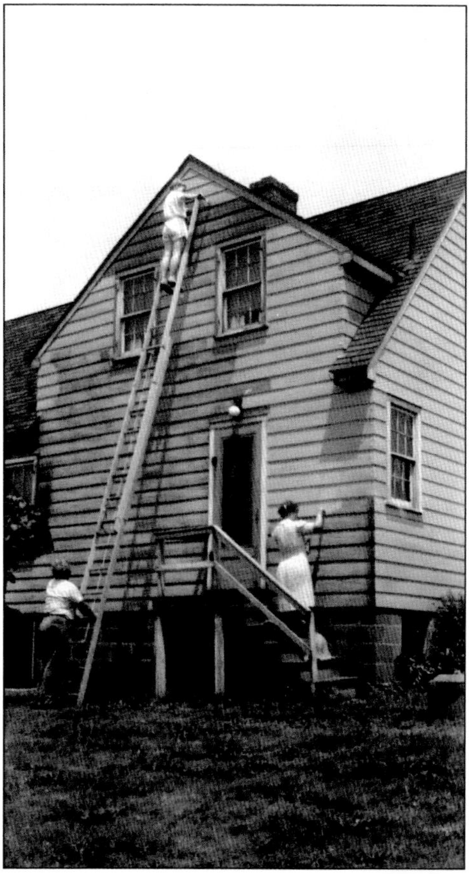

The Porterfield family paints the family home in B section in 1944. At the top of the ladder is Annabelle Porterfield. Below her are Evelyn and Clyde. Annabelle waited for Japanese POW Everett Horrell to return from World War II and married him. (Courtesy of Sharon Smith.)

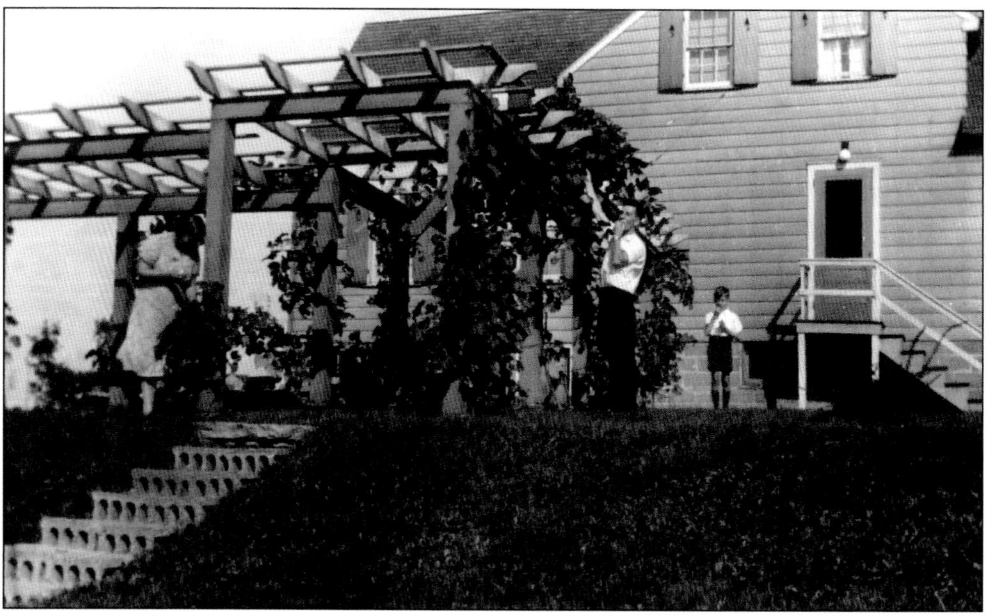

Tad Porterfield, Clyde Jones, and Evelyn Jones stand under a beautiful example of the Norvelt grape arbors in B section (B-39). (Courtesy of Connie Yasher Urban.)

Eva Porterfield sits and reads in the kitchen of her home. Her husband, Clyde Porterfield, was active as a business manager and actor in the Co-op Players. Annabelle was secretary of the sewing club. (Courtesy of Connie Yasher Urban.)

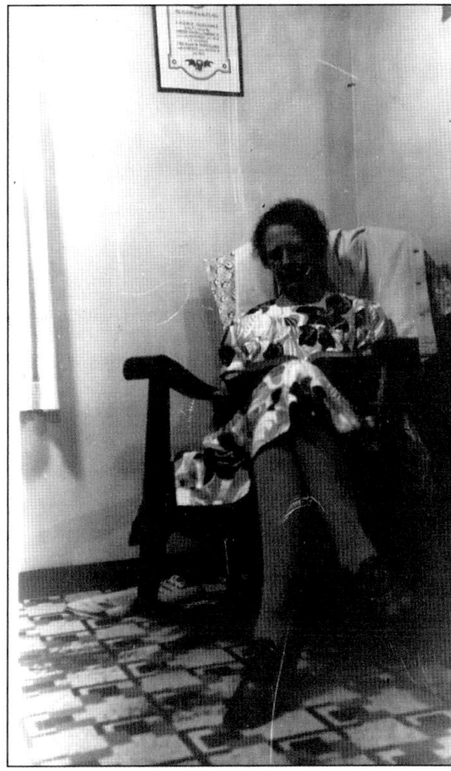

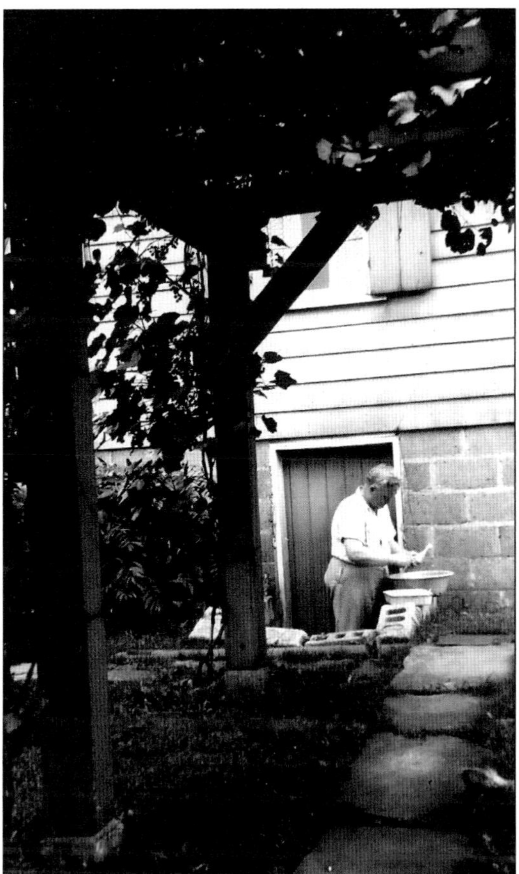

Clyde Porterfield cleans his vegetables outside on a clear day. He was a treasurer of the co-op and was foreman of the WPA. (Courtesy of Connie Yasher Urban.)

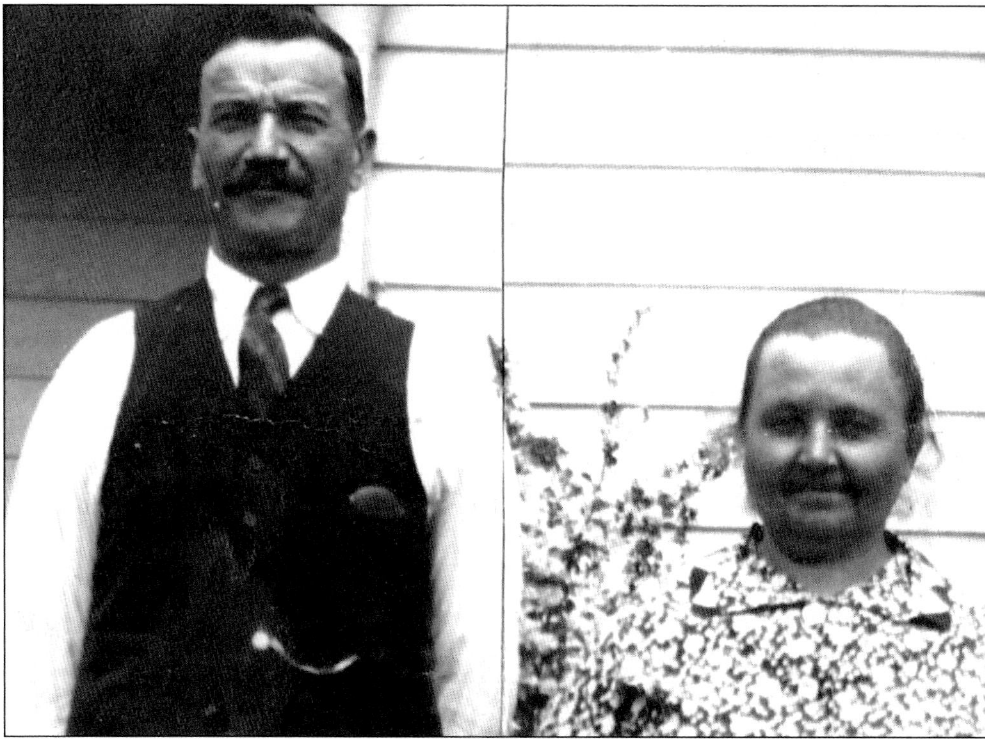

Homesteaders John and Helen Klosky of B section (B-18) enjoy some time to relax. (Courtesy of Connie Yasher Urban.)

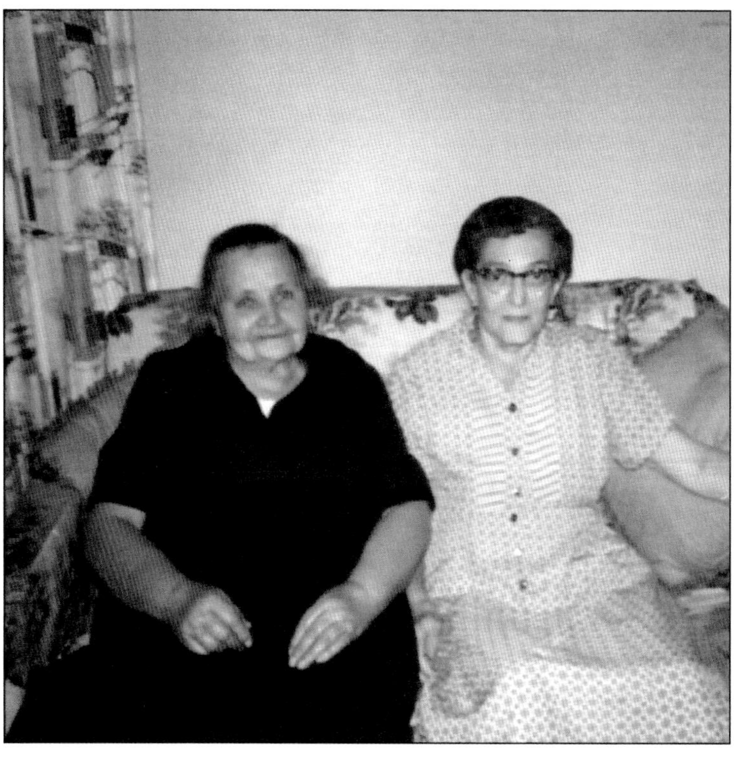

Kathleen Urban, wife of George Urban, and Helen Klosky, wife of Joseph Klosky, enjoy a visit. Mothers had a good outlet if desired to better their community. Members of Norvelt's Mother's Club were concerned about safe places for the children to play. Through their fund-raising, the club purchased $20 worth of play equipment for the community for the three playgrounds in August 1936. (Courtesy of Connie Yasher Urban.)

One-year-old Kathleen Urban and two-year-old Joanne Evans visit their grandparents, Helen and Joseph Klosky. Homestead mothers were interested in learning as much as they could and took their job as mother quite seriously. Homesteader Mrs. Straslicka hosted a class on "What is the Place of the Three R's in our School?" Other meetings reviewed articles in *Parents* magazine in Mrs. McKula's home on "If not Punishment, What?" (Courtesy of Connie Yasher Urban.)

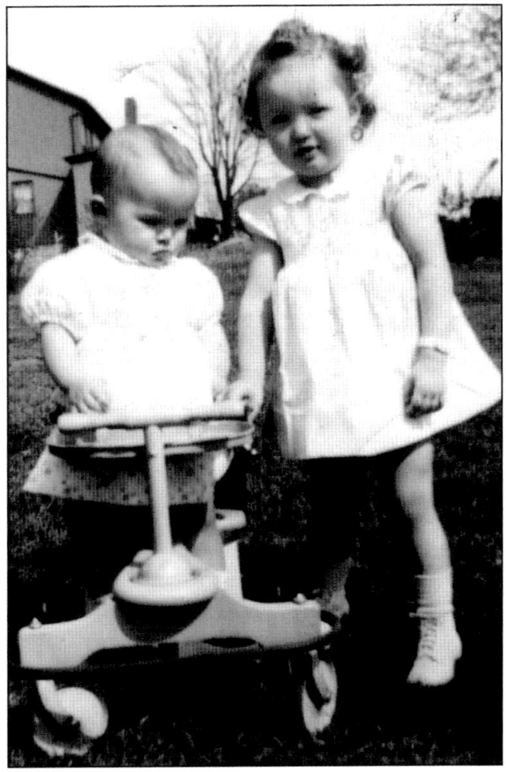

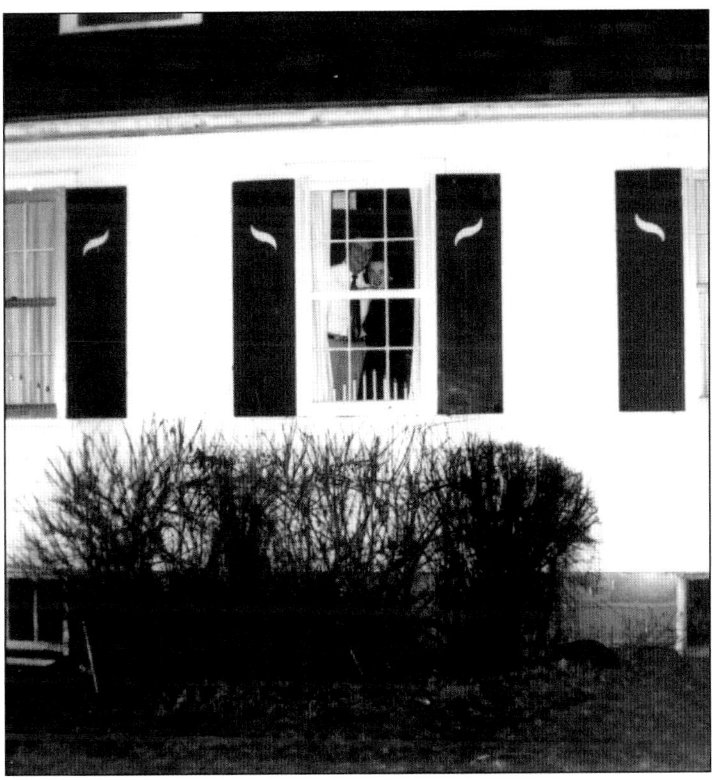

Roy Ewing and his wife look out the window of their home in D section (D-12) with the leaf motif on their shutters. Craft shops were open for the homesteaders to make finishing touches to their homes, like shutters, screen doors, and window screens. A weaving room was provided for residents to make blankets and rugs. All residents could participate and build their own home's special touches. (Courtesy of Patty Ewing Hawse.)

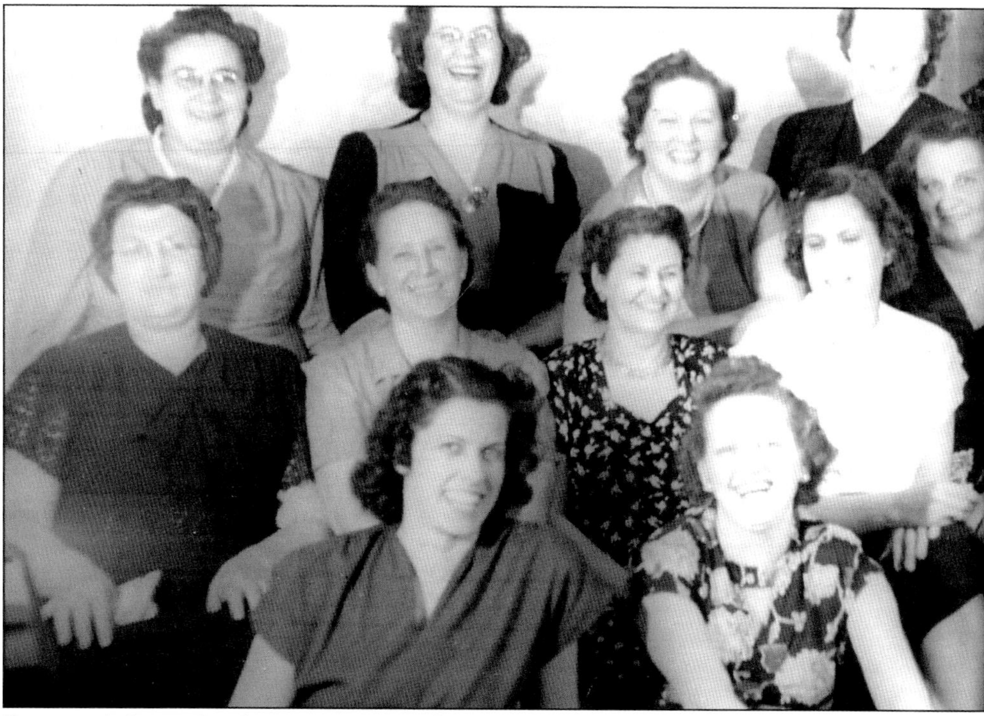

D section ladies gather for a party. Pictured from left to right are (first row) Kate Ewing and Betty Koenig; (second row) Peg Kotouch, Tina Bonkovich, Ella Saville, and Dot Caldwell; (third row) Elizabeth Bann, Marge Kirchner, Bunny King, Sara Malnofsky, and Stella Frederick. (Courtesy of Patty Ewing Hawse.)

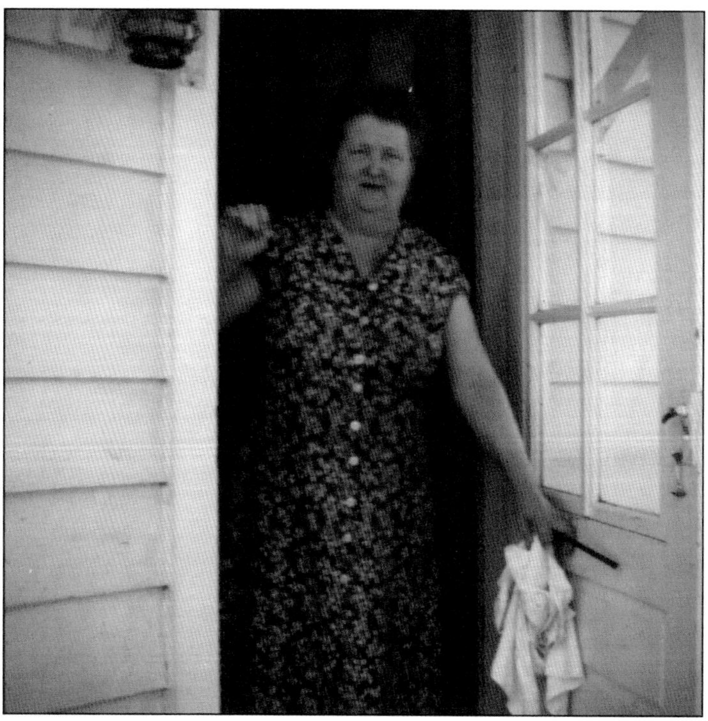

Suzanne Bosdosh looks out her back door. All adults could participate in an adult school that was introduced to the community in October 1936. David Day announced the first line of courses to include art, economics, weaving, home nursing, soils, wood craft, and philosophy. (Courtesy of Marsha Bosdosh.)

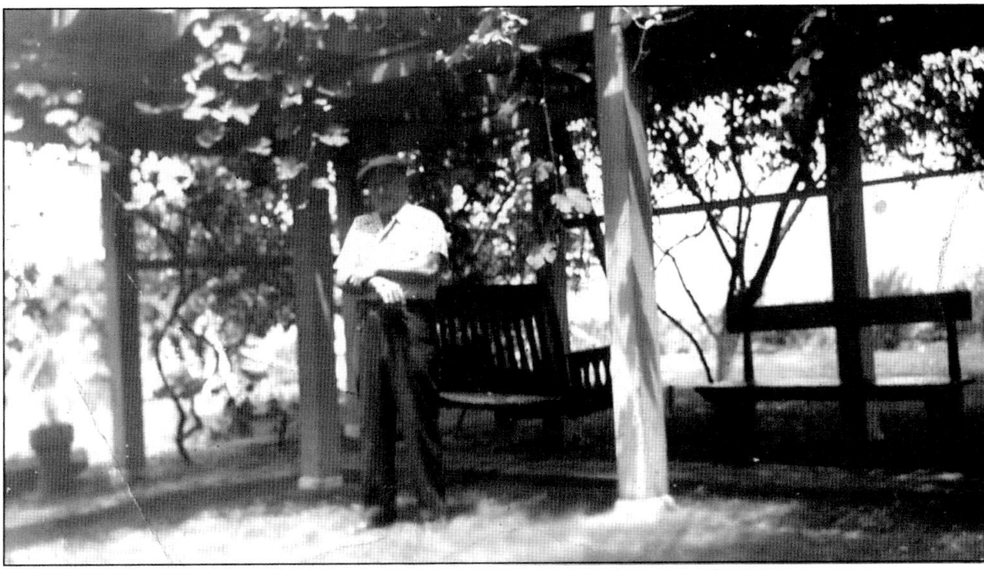

Steve Bosdosh is standing under his cozy grape arbor at his C section (C-18) home. Homesteaders could enjoy Saturday night at the movies. The Norvelt school auditorium provided the perfect house for moving pictures featuring Charlie Chan, Popeye the Sailor, and the Three Stooges. (Courtesy of Marsha Bosdosh.)

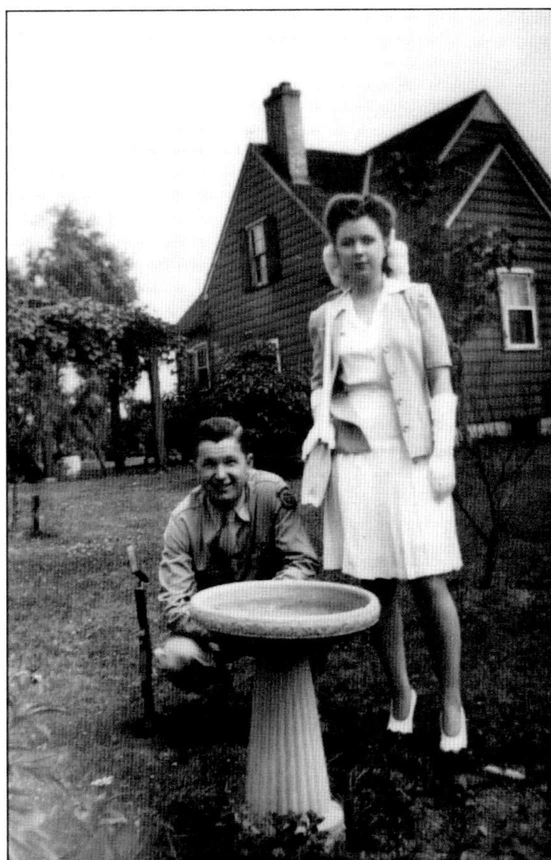

The children of Steve Bosdosh Sr. are Steve Jr., in his army uniform, and Suzanne. Young people could participate in the Cooperative Youth League, which arranged for the group to travel to Laughlintown, Pennsylvania, in a cooperative institute with other young people from resettlement communities of Arthurdale, Tygard Valley, and Red House. The Farm Bureau Cooperative of Pennsylvania assisted in plans, speakers, and finances. The focus of discussion was the history and principles of the cooperative movement and pubic speaking. (Courtesy of Marsha Bosdosh.)

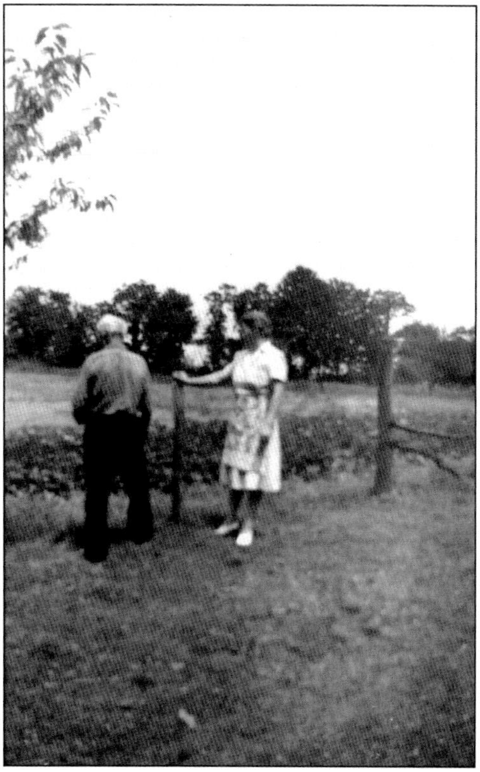

Mr. and Mrs. Steve Bosdosh stand over their garden while planning for the next planting. Resident artist Dick Kenah in an April 1, 1936, article in the *Homestead Informer* responded to "why would an artist want to live in Westmoreland? . . . Westmoreland is a fine place to draw and paint. There could hardly be a better one. Anywhere that people are living and working is a good place; and here in the Homesteads this condition is sharpened by excitement and hope for the success of the project." (Courtesy of Marsha Bosdosh.)

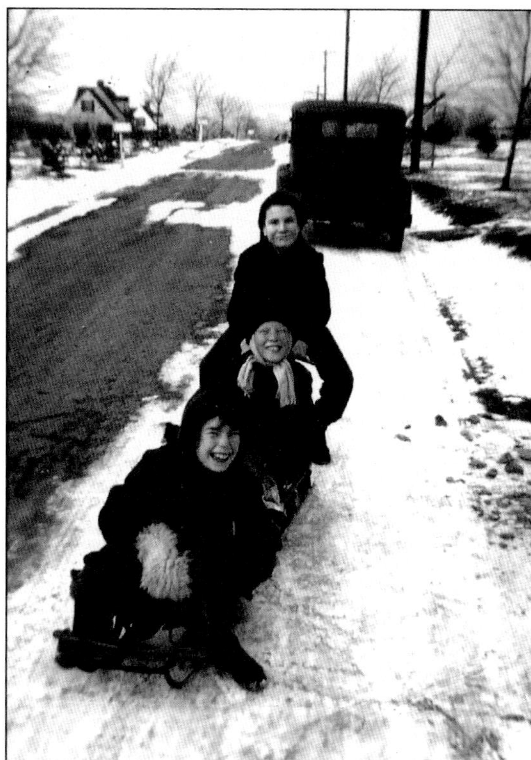

Children of B section homesteaders in this photograph, from left to right, Bob Burns, Jimmy Golding, and Carol Lowry, enjoy the winter snows. When not at play, the Cooperative Youth League held at the schoolhouse for social and educational activities provided classes in public speaking, journalism, and activities for fun. (Courtesy of John Kennedy.)

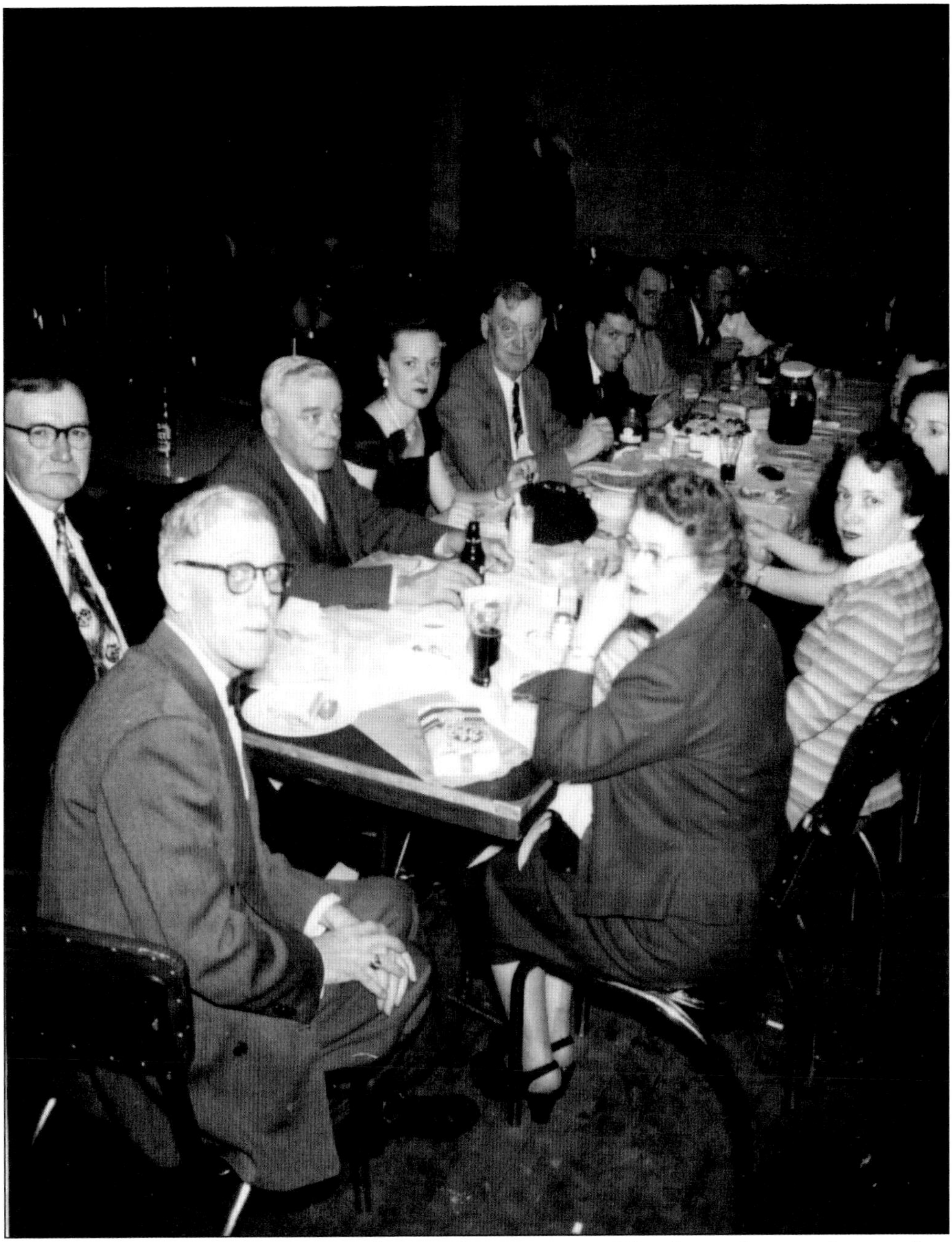

Joe and Ella Saville were active members in the community. The above photograph was taken at a fire department banquet. (Courtesy of Earl Saville.)

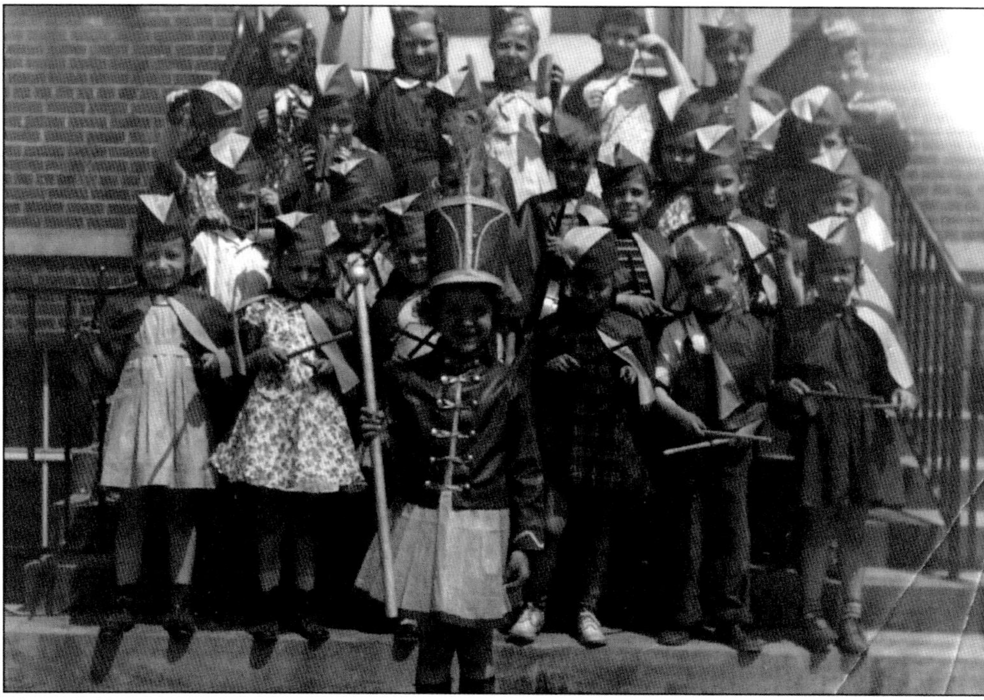

The Children's Rhythm Band, pictured above, was directed by W. J. Simmons, music director and talented piano player. Sponsored by the WPA, he taught music and produced dramas for adults and children. He produced a children's operetta at the close of the school year. He had his own radio show on WHJB in Greensburg stationed at the Penn Albert Hotel, behind the broadcasting window, where he would play the piano and talk between his songs. (Courtesy of Geraldine Dzambo Mizikar.)

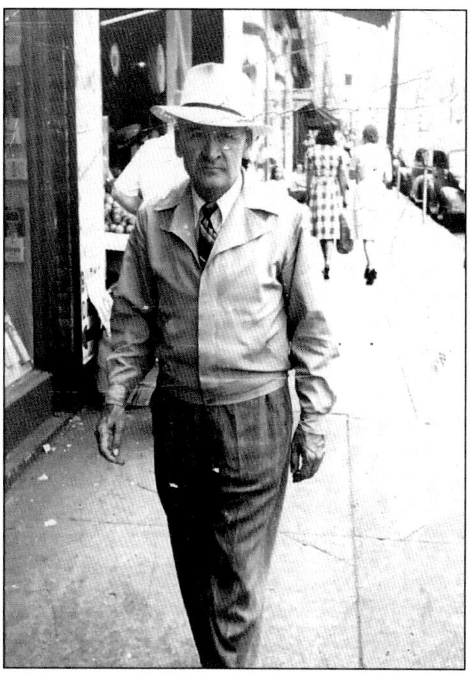

Alvy Jones of B section (B-19) was a foreman in the mines and moved to Norvelt from the mining town of Whitney. He and his wife, Emma, were happy to raise their children, Bessie, Donald, David, Jean, Clyde, and Frieda, in Norvelt. The Mother's Club members often donated health supplies to the community, and in 1936, Emma Jones donated a hot-water bottle and baby hot-water bottle. (Courtesy of Shirley Jones Rusinko.)

Pictured from left to right, Don and Dave Jones stand in front of their homestead. Dave was a cub reporter for the *Homestead Informer* in July 1936. Don became the first member to be in charge of and maintain responsibility over the Cooperative Youth League's portable confectionary stand. He also was a news reporter for the *Homestead Informer* and was in charge of lighting in the Co-Op Players dramatic group. (Courtesy of Shirley Jones Rusinko.)

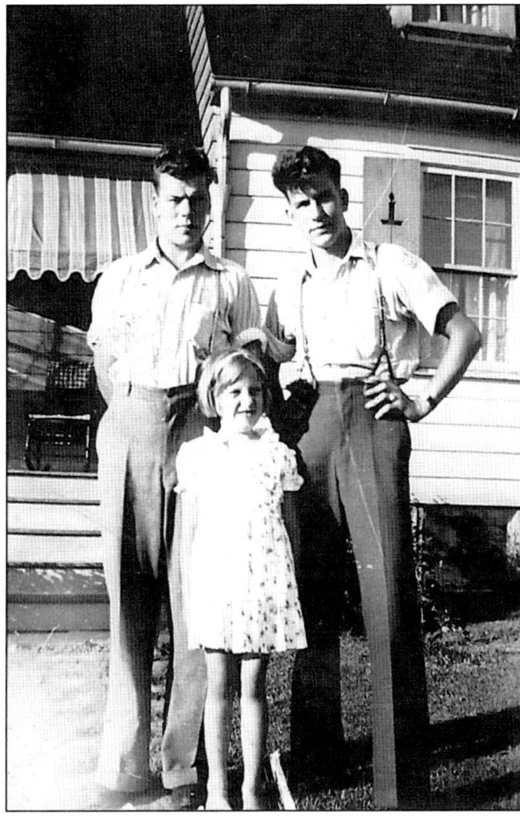

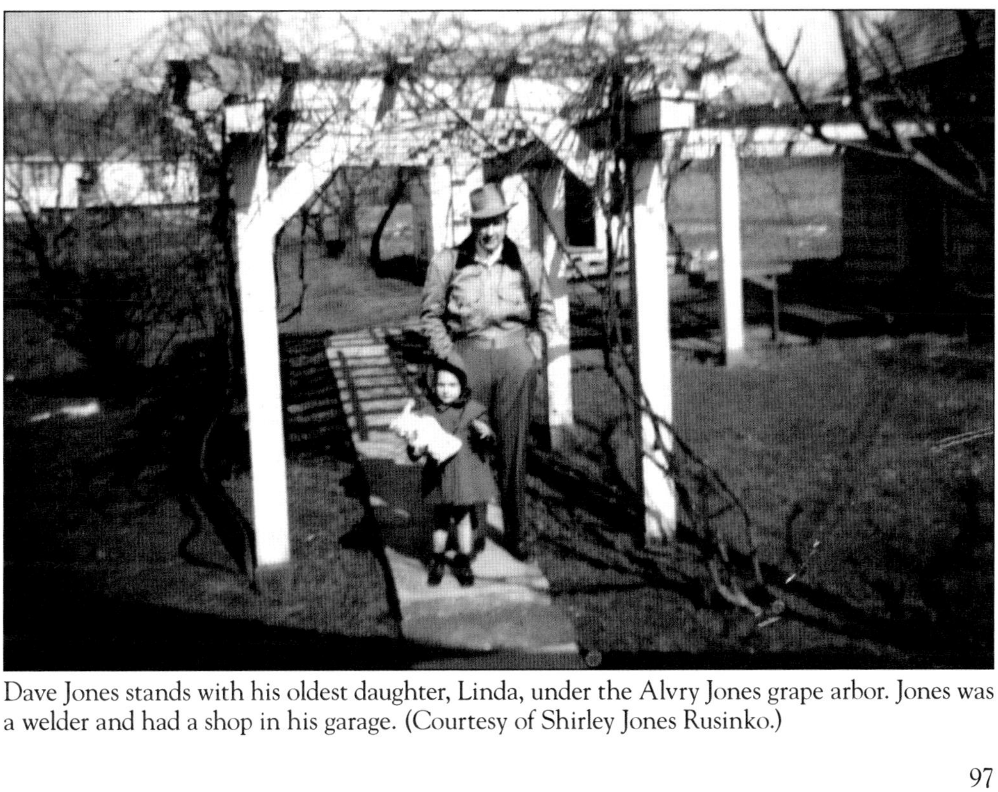

Dave Jones stands with his oldest daughter, Linda, under the Alvry Jones grape arbor. Jones was a welder and had a shop in his garage. (Courtesy of Shirley Jones Rusinko.)

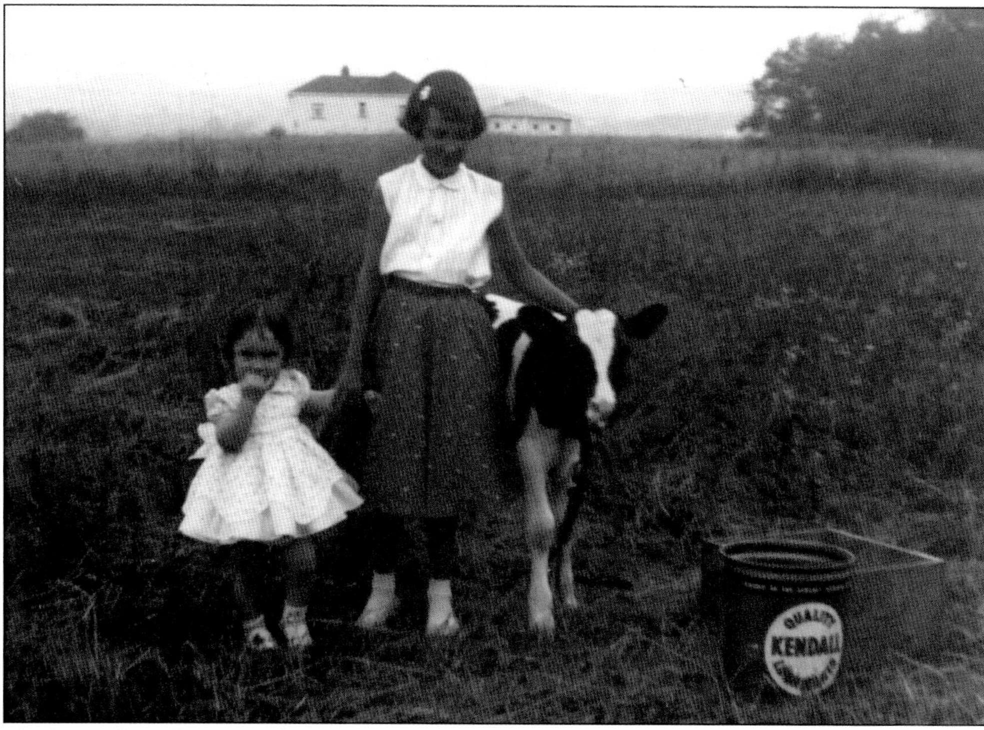

Shirley and Linda Jones, daughters of Dave and Iona, stand with their calf in the backyard. Each homestead was large enough that many homesteaders raised cows and horses. (Courtesy of Shirley Jones Rusinko.)

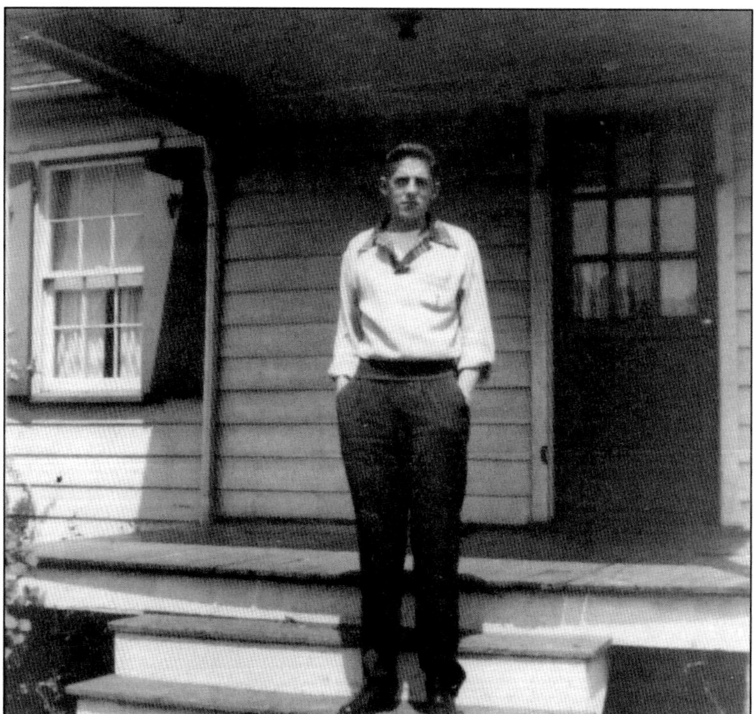

Elmer Linden was the farm foreman. He was a director on the co-op board and truck driver in the homestead construction. Here his son Bill stands on the porch of the family home. (Courtesy of Josephine Linden.)

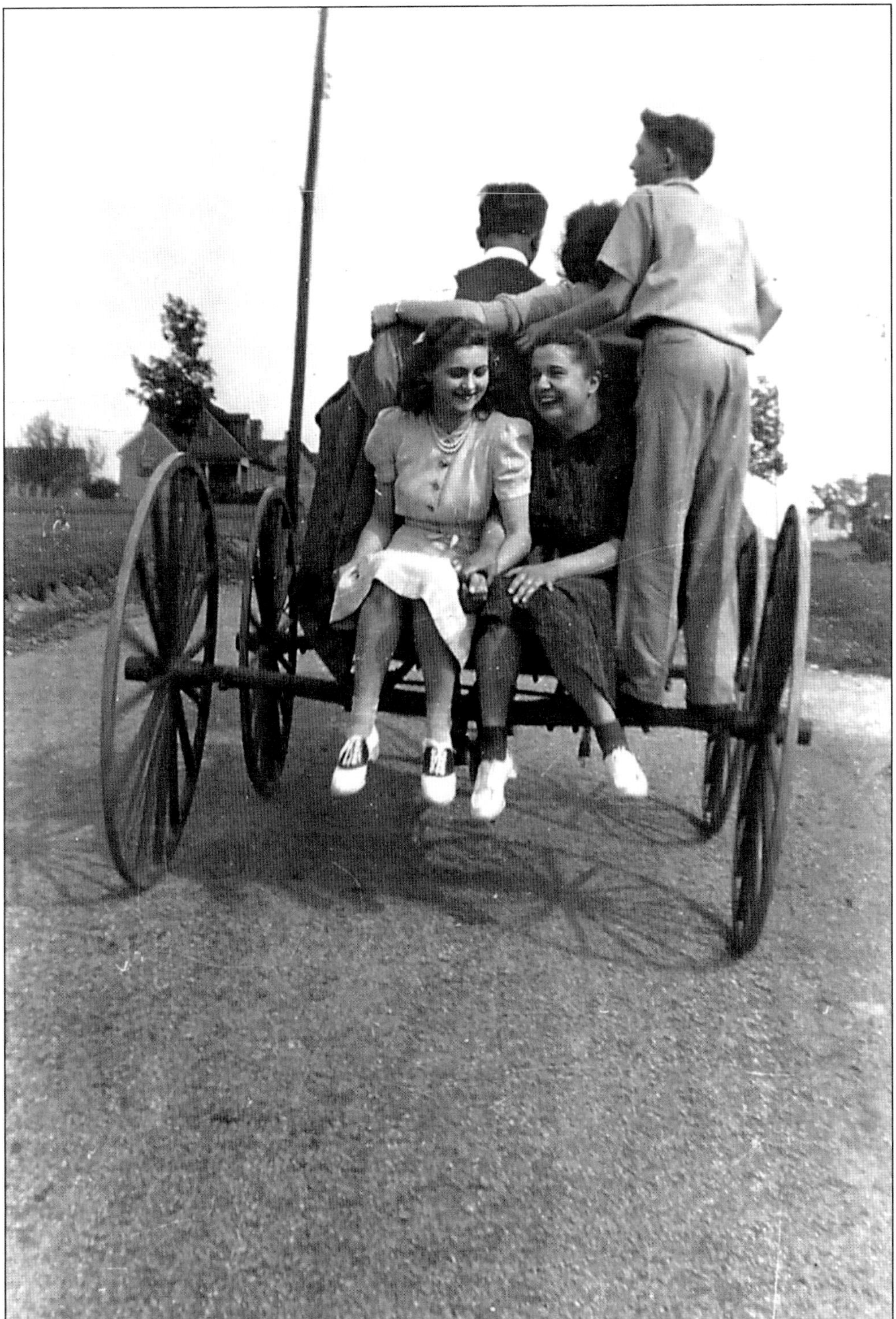

Andrew and Juliana Urban ride in the front of this horse and carriage with friends on the back. (Courtesy of Andrea Urban Dominick.)

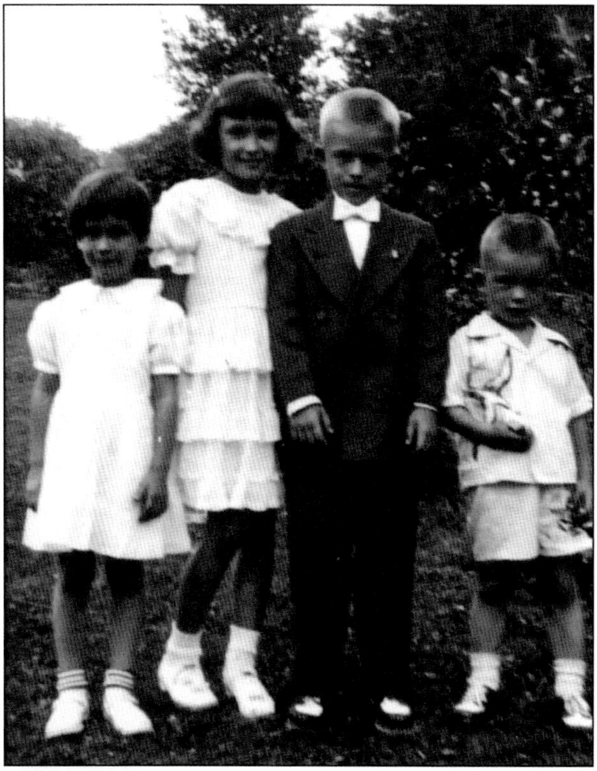

Morgan, Kathleen, Stephen, and John Urban stand in the homestead orchard. The homesteaders' gardens were judged annually on cleanliness, arrangement, number of essentials, vegetables grown, and surplus above family needs. W. S. Treager, company agent, chose the following winners in September 1936: Walter Kocinski, George Gradish, Louis Solak, Albert Kurtz, and George Urban. (Courtesy of Andrea Urban Dominick.)

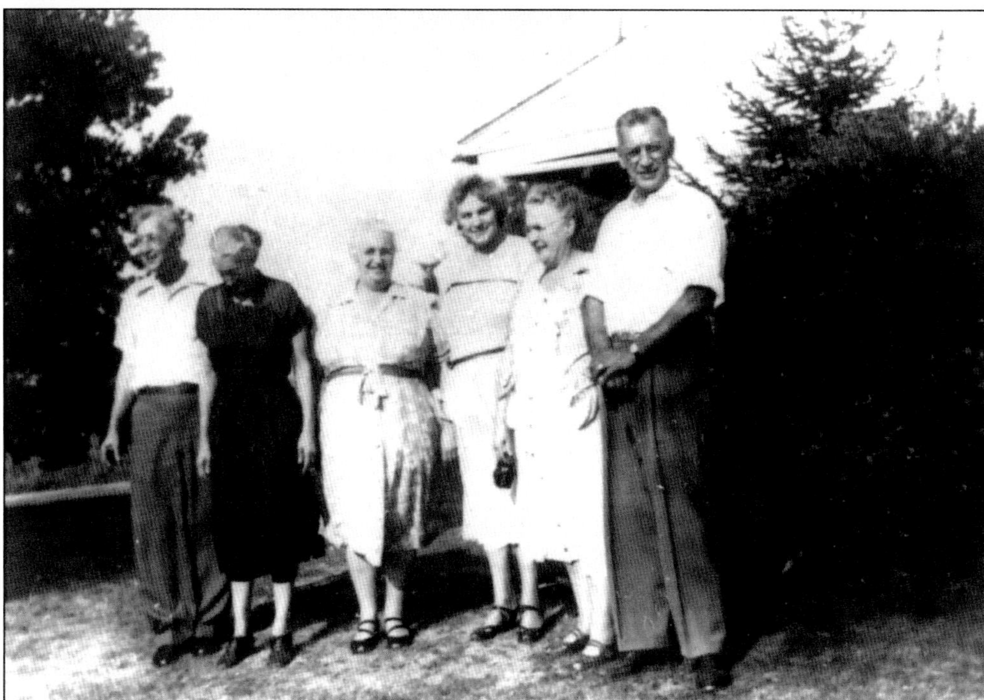

Homesteaders Tom Hyde, Kathryn Hoffer, Anne Smith, Margaret McKenna, Elizabeth Goodman, and George Hyde pose together at Herbert Hoffer's homestead. (Courtesy of Gail Hoffer.)

The Craig family is gathering on the front lawn of their homestead in B section. William was president of the credit union and co-op, Cooperative Quarterly Forum director, and the chairman of the committee of games and sports for Westmoreland Homesteads Fair the weekend of September 25, 1936. He coordinated dances at the community auditorium. Along with square dancing, he also aided in teaching dance. His wife served as the *Homestead Informer*'s newsperson for B section. (Courtesy of Kimberly Sulzer.)

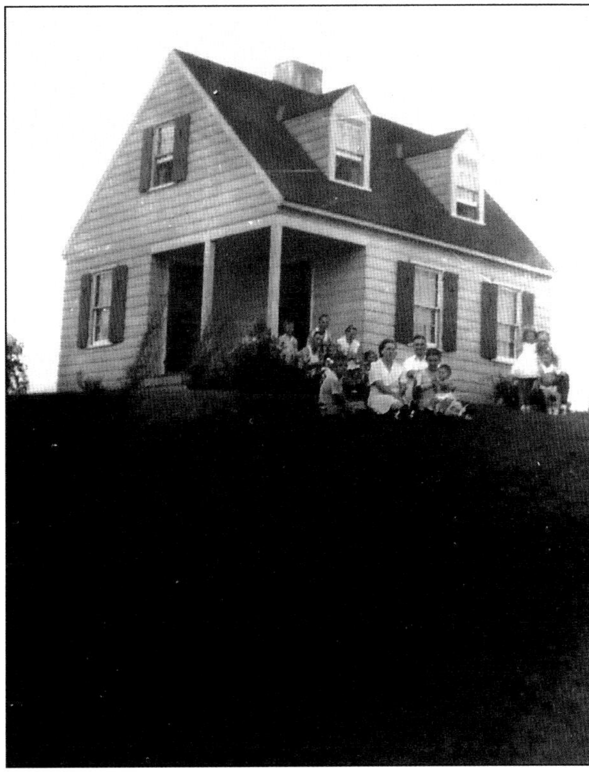

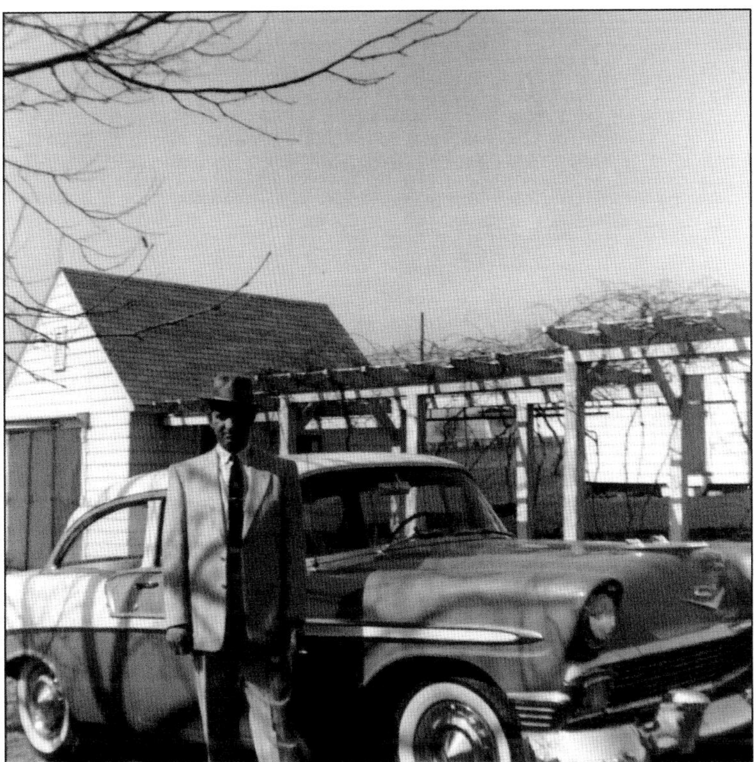

Harry Craig stands in front of his new car. His brother Dick Craig was president of the Cooperative Youth League and was the first homestead young man to be married. (Courtesy of Kimberly Sulzer.)

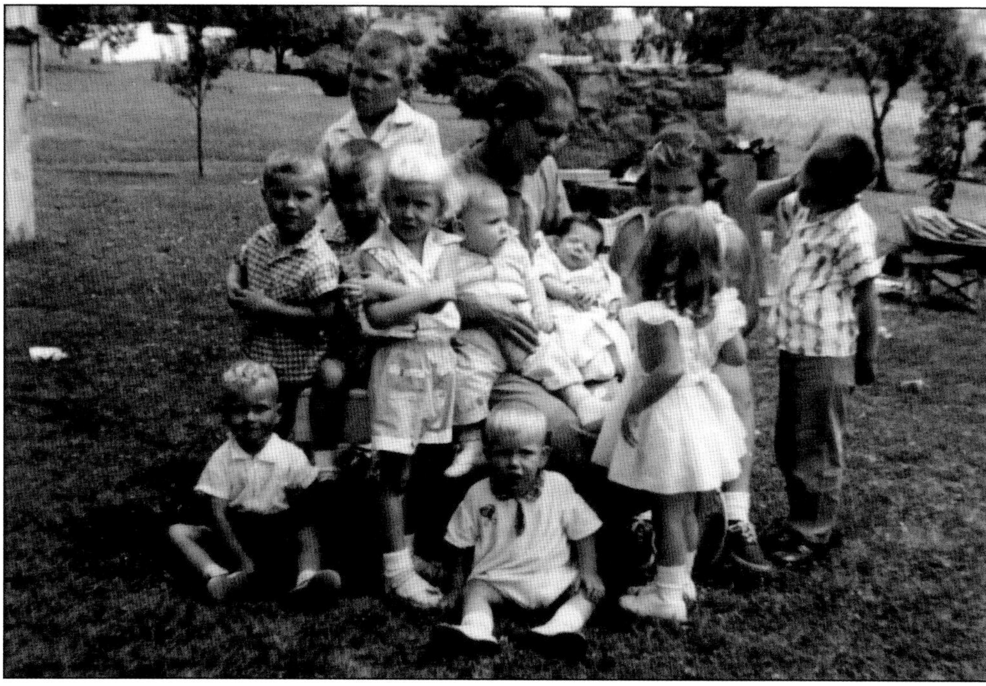

Anne Hajduk Cibulas is surrounded by her grandchildren in her backyard. She resided in B section with her husband, John, and their children. John and Anne took personal satisfaction in contributing to John's communal farm assignments. Son Steve Cibulas said of his parents, "Our parents had a 'can do' type of mindset with focus on rising above the challenges they faced. This was also apparent with most of our neighbors and friends. In retrospect, the communal environment was a means for energizing them and their families to set and meet high personal goals." (Courtesy of Catherine Cibulas.)

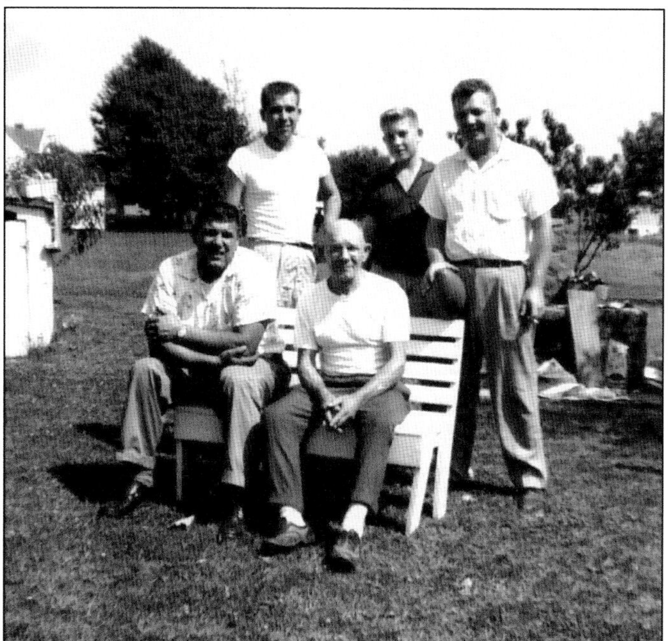

Steve Cibulas explained, "We took special pride in our community Honor Roll which listed the names of all the military personnel from Norvelt including our brothers. Our Father was one of the volunteers who constructed it which has given us very special pride." Pictured from left to right are (first row) Joe and their father John; (second row) Bill, Bob, and John Jr. (Courtesy of Catherine Cibulas.)

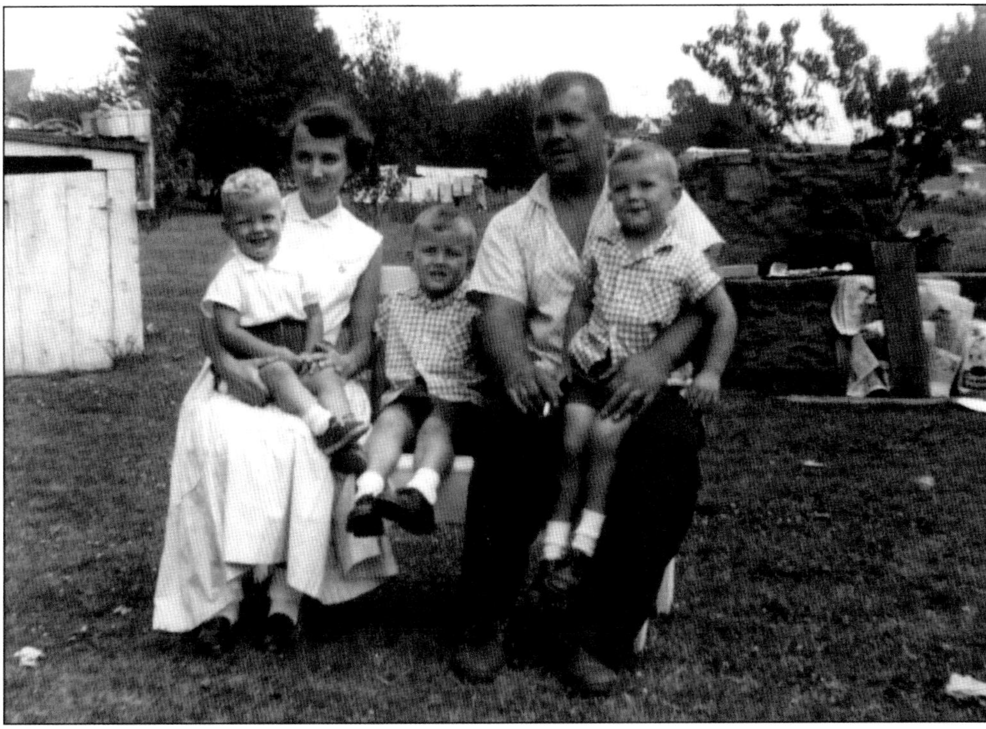

According to Steve Cibulas, "This educational infrastructure, combined with the experiences developed in the 'homesteading' environment helped us mature and grow well beyond that of our parents' expectations. They planted in us the desire and will to succeed in any venture we chose while preserving our family and these unique Norvelt roots . . . There are now close to 100 members in just our family." Ed Cibulas, Catherine Kissell Cibulas, and their three sons pose here. Ed and his wife have remained active, planning annual homesteader reunions. (Courtesy of Catherine Cibulas.)

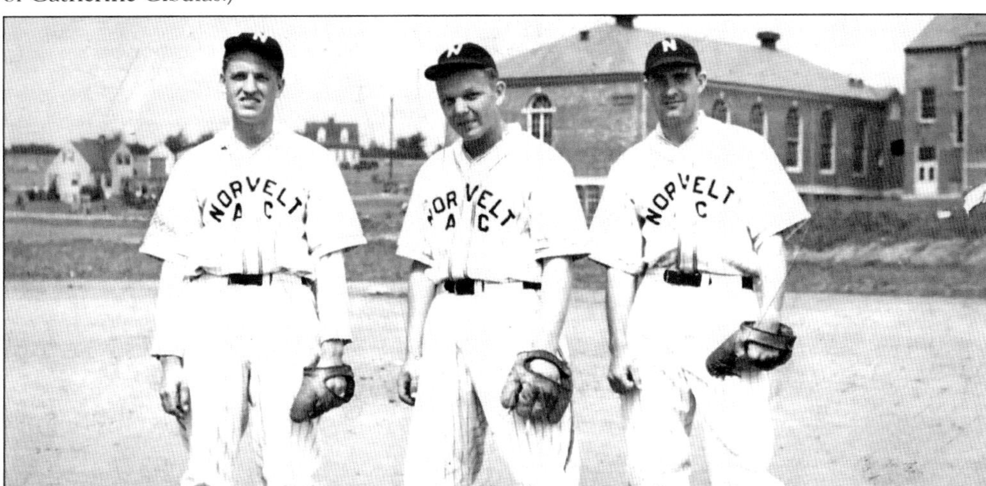

Many boys participated in Boy Scouts, the baseball team, and athletic club until adulthood, enjoying the community building with its pool table and Ping-Pong table. In the above photograph from left to right are Carl Kurtz, John Cibulas, and Dick Craig, star baseball players. (Courtesy of Kimberly Sulzer.)

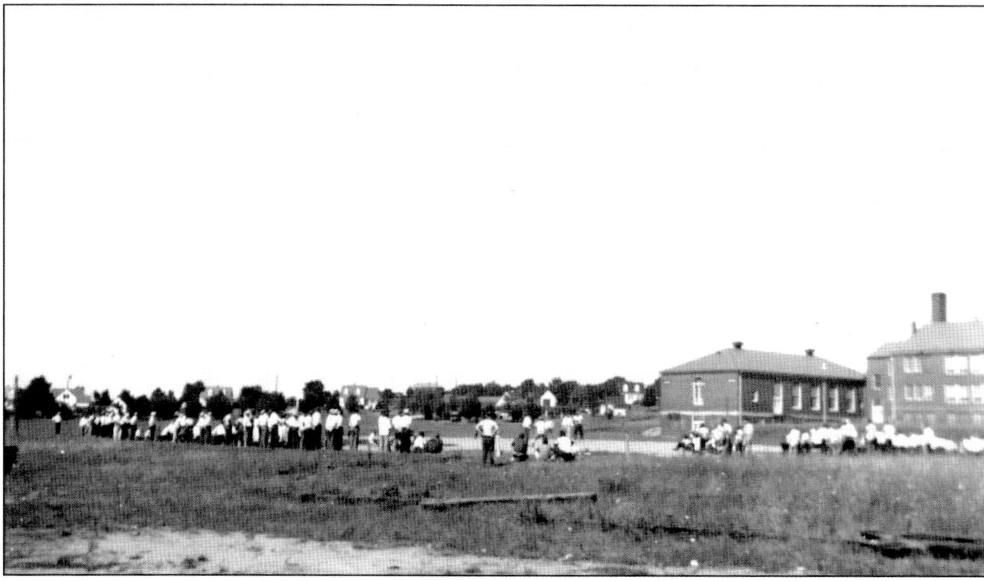

The athletic club's baseball team was a big draw for summer-evening games. Located between the Norvelt school and firemen's club, the ball field is still in use. (Courtesy of Sharon Smith.)

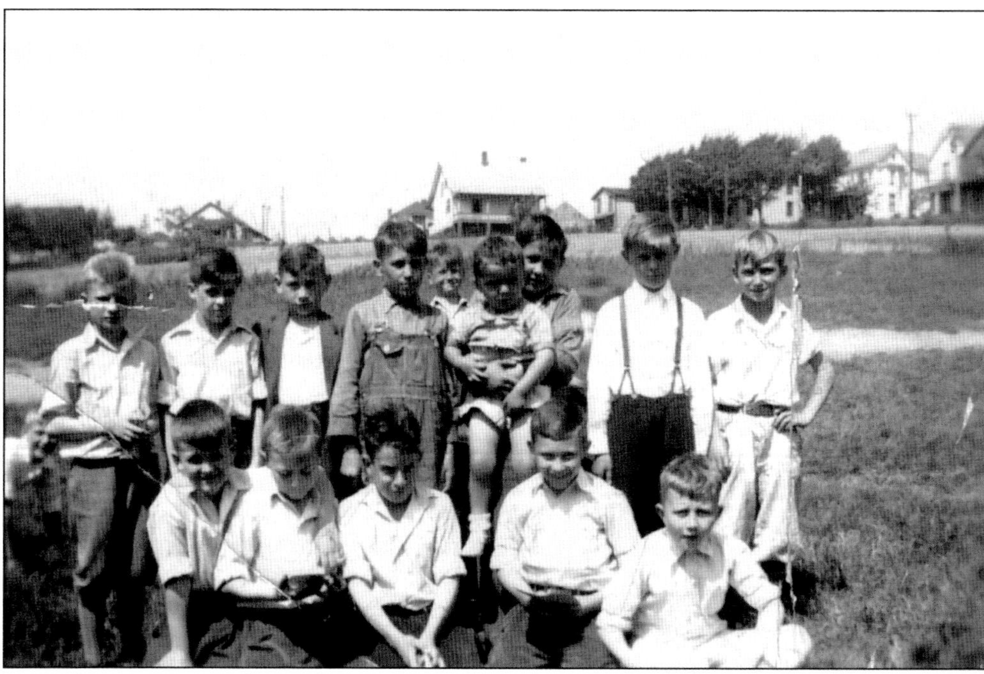

Young boys participated in pickup games. In this photograph, the boys pose before their game. (Courtesy of Earl Saville.)

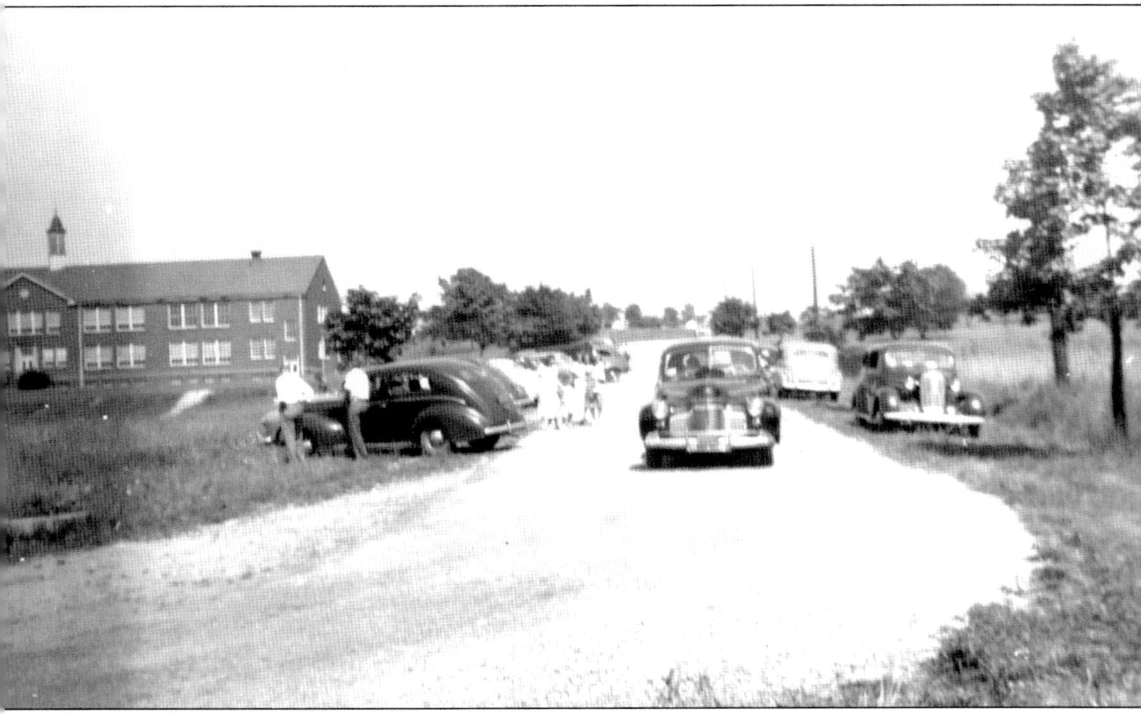

The Norvelt Athletic Club was the 1939 Westmoreland County champions and included team members Joe Wolk, Homer Huhn Jr., Oran Allen, Joe Schwab, Frank Obrocto, Clarence Gorinsky, Wallace Hoffer (coach) and Mr. Swanson (coach), Bill Baker, Joe Solomon, John Cibulas, Pud Pavick, Al Rollins, Jim Santymyer, Moe Koshusko, Tom Solomon, Don Jones, and Sam Grohal. This photograph shows cars and fans starting to arrive at the big game. (Courtesy of Joseph Wolk.)

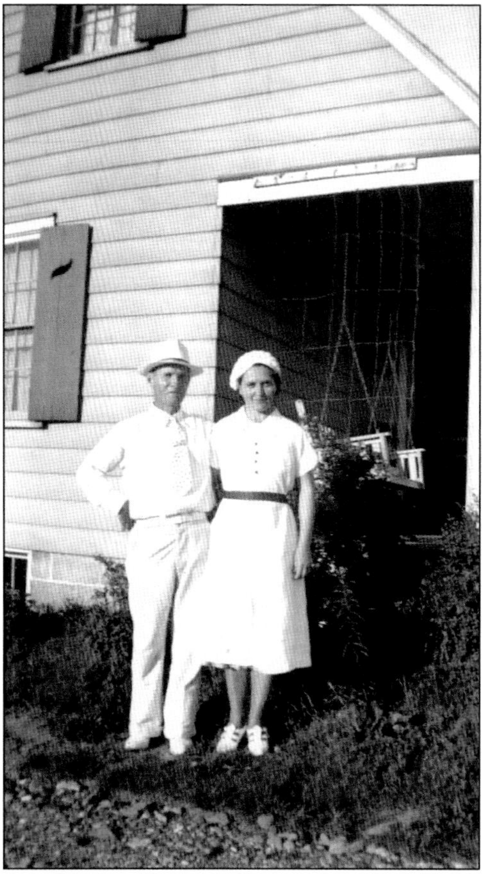

Stephen and Theresa Berdak Sofranko, at left, grew up in coal patches and moved to Norvelt from Standard in Mount Pleasant. Stephen was a miner since age 12. He was a survivor of the Carpenter Mine explosion of 1952, when six miners were killed from a methane gas explosion. They raised rabbits, and he is remembered for his flourishing rose gardens. (Courtesy of Dorothy Sofranko Vidakovich.)

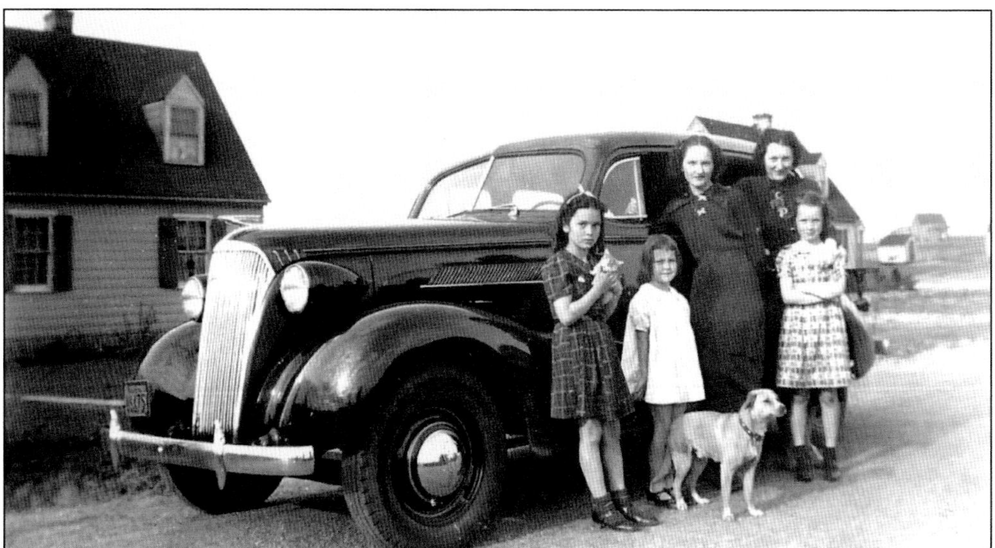

Four of the Sofranko children and a friend gather in front of the family car. All homes in Norvelt had garages. Pictured from left to right are neighbor Lindy McKenna, Dorothy, Helen, Margaret, and Valeria Sofranko. (Courtesy of Valeria Sofranko Wolk.)

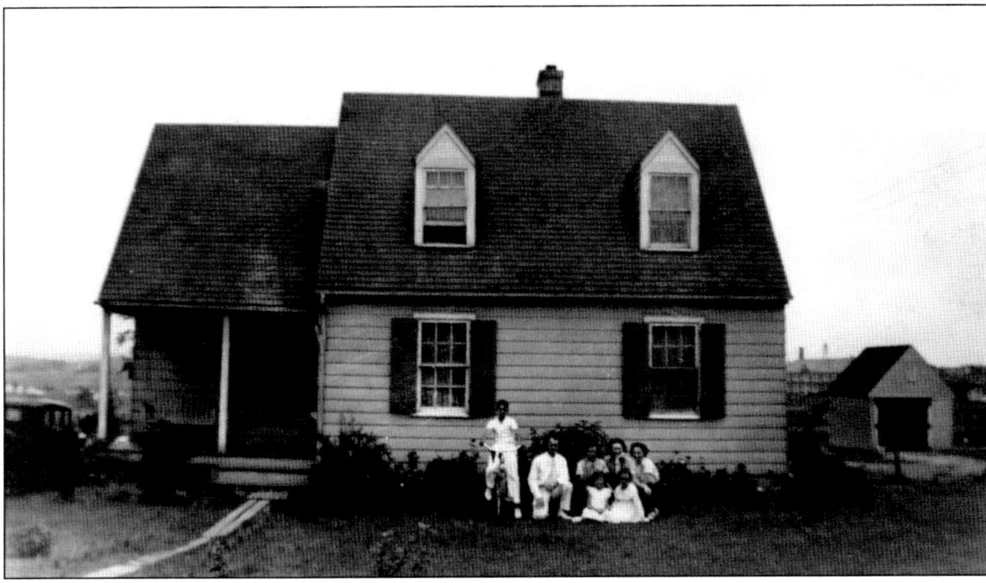

The Sofranko family enjoyed attending moving picture shows held at the Norvelt school auditorium. Pictured from left to right are (first row) Dorothy and Valeria; (second row) John, Betty, Margaret, and Helen. A whole family was able to participate in dances, dance lessons, stage shows, and musicals hosted and conducted by local citizens. Art classes were held for schoolchildren and adults. (Courtesy of Valeria Sofranko Wolk.)

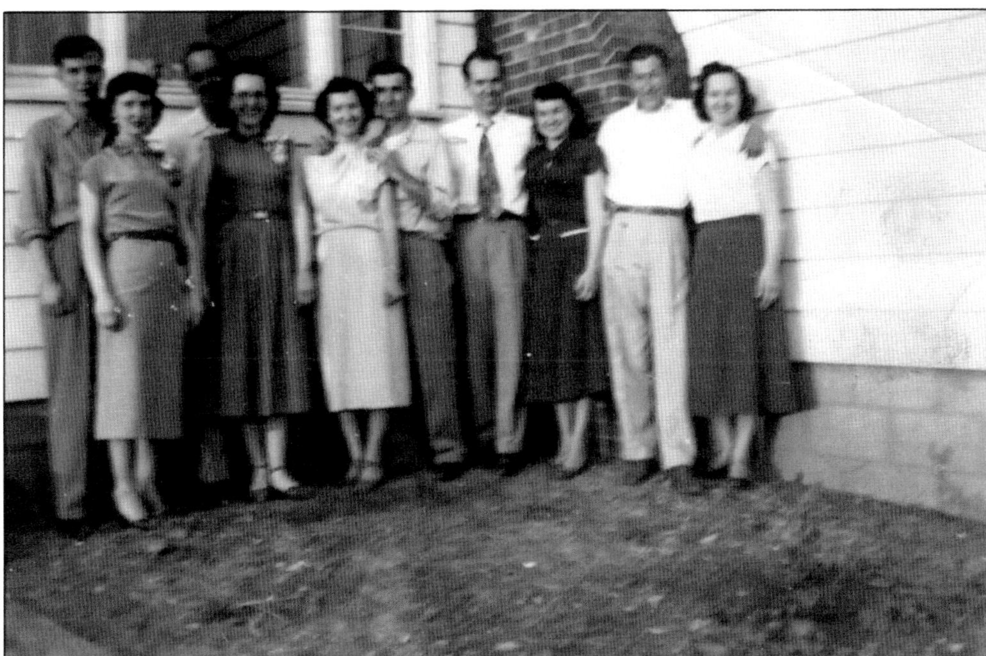

Like so many homesteading families, all of the Sofranko children ended up living in homes in Norvelt. Pictured from left to right are Joseph and Valeria Wolk, Mike and Peg Pavick, Helen and John Kapura, John and Betty Sofranko, and Joe and Betty Tirdil. (Courtesy of Valeria Sofranko Wolk.)

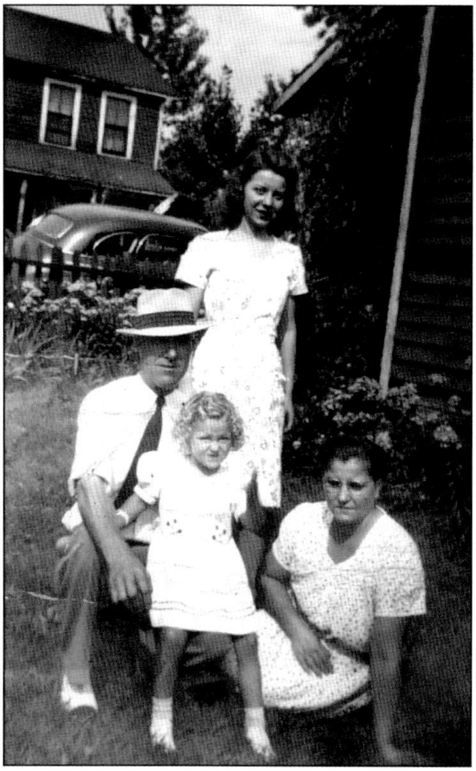

The Anthony Wolk family moved to the homesteads from the Whitney patch. Anthony was a miner and carpenter. Mary worked in the sewing factory until her retirement. Pictured here from left to right are Anthony, Marian, Florence (standing in back), and Mary. Mary Wolk participated in a quilting group, rug-making group, and canning group. She volunteered with the 4-H Club and taught Sunday school. (Courtesy of Joseph Wolk.)

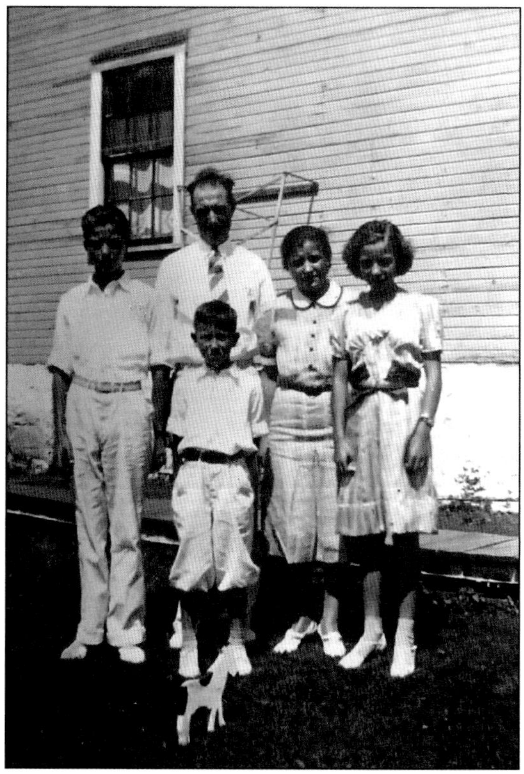

The Anthony Wolk family, from left to right, Joseph, Anthony Jr., Anthony Sr., Mary, and Florence, stands for this photograph. The *Homestead Informer* reported a story of the nursery school teacher thanking all who helped get the preschool ready and that Mary Wolk "took the trouble to hunt me up to tell me she wanted to help with nursery but couldn't leave her boy and growing chickens very well. She begged me to send all 14 blankets home with her and the very next day an express wagon drawn by a little girl and boy stopped at our home with 14 blankets washed and pressed. I've been most grateful to her ever since." (Courtesy of Joseph Wolk.)

Anthony Wolk was active in carpentry and building in the early community. He enjoyed woodworking and made furniture in his free time. The March 18, 1936, *Homestead Informer* contained a notice for homesteaders to use the craft shops to "make the finishing touches," such as shutters, screen doors, and window screens for their homes. Instructors had been brought into the community to teach residents how to operate woodworking machinery so that people could make their own furniture and other things for the home and to make household repairs. (Courtesy of Joseph Wolk.)

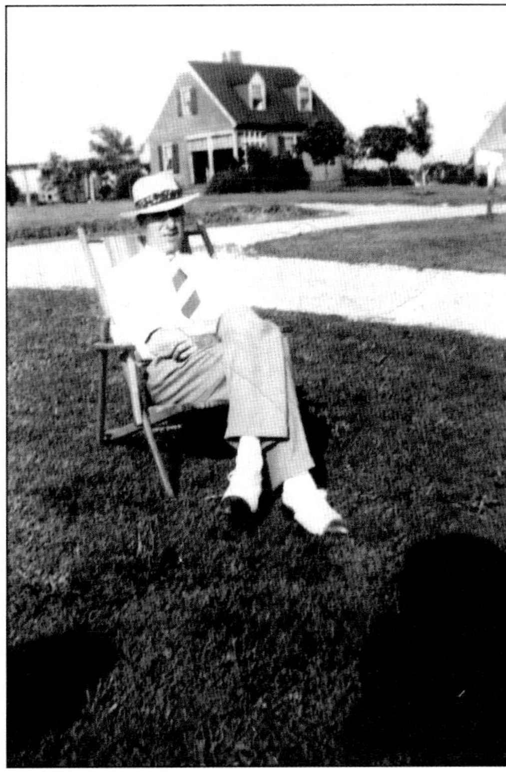

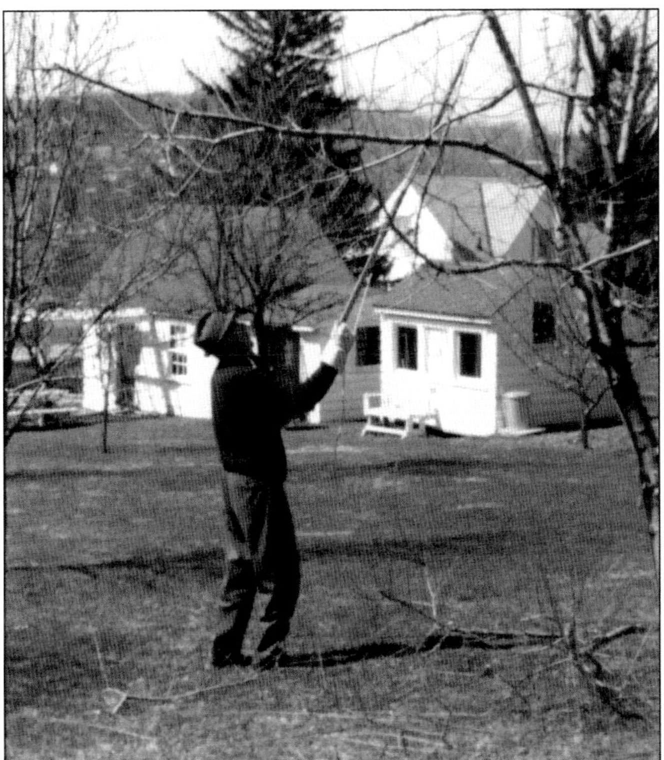

Anthony Wolk is trimming his fruit trees in the orchard behind his home. All homesteaders were provided fruit trees for their orchards. Cherry, apple, and pear trees made delicious pies, jams, butters, and juices. The federal government provided the community an agricultural advisor, W. C. Sterrett, who had his office in the community building. (Courtesy of Joseph Wolk.)

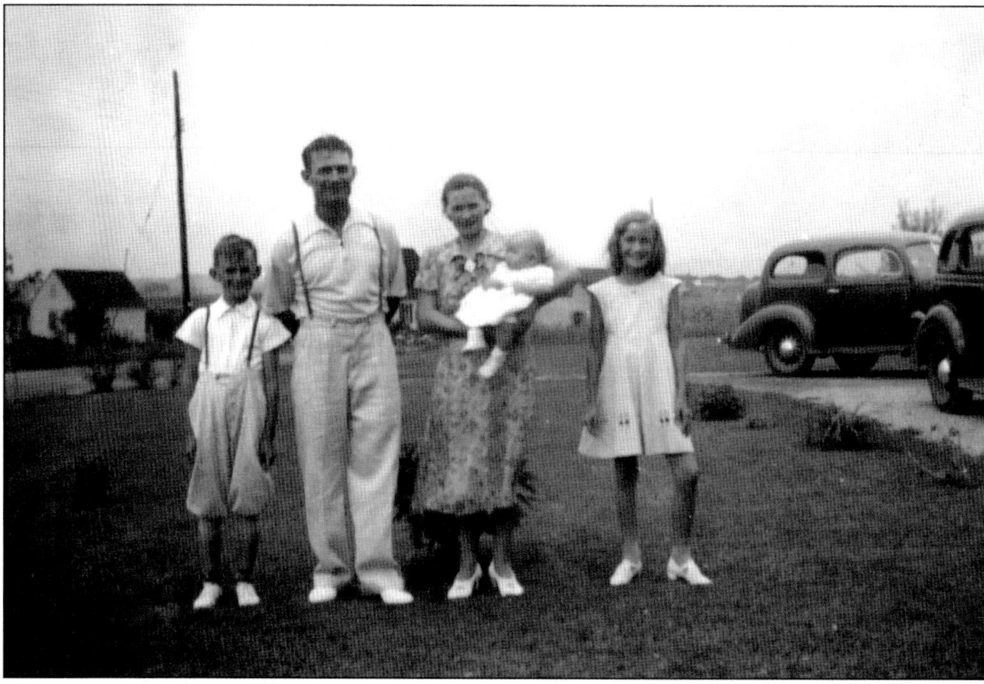

The Boytim family moved to the homesteads from United, where John Sr. worked in the coke yard. Pictured from left to right are John, John Sr., Susan holding Betty Sue, and Virginia. (Courtesy of Virginia Boytim Vahaly and Betty Sue Boytim Mondock.)

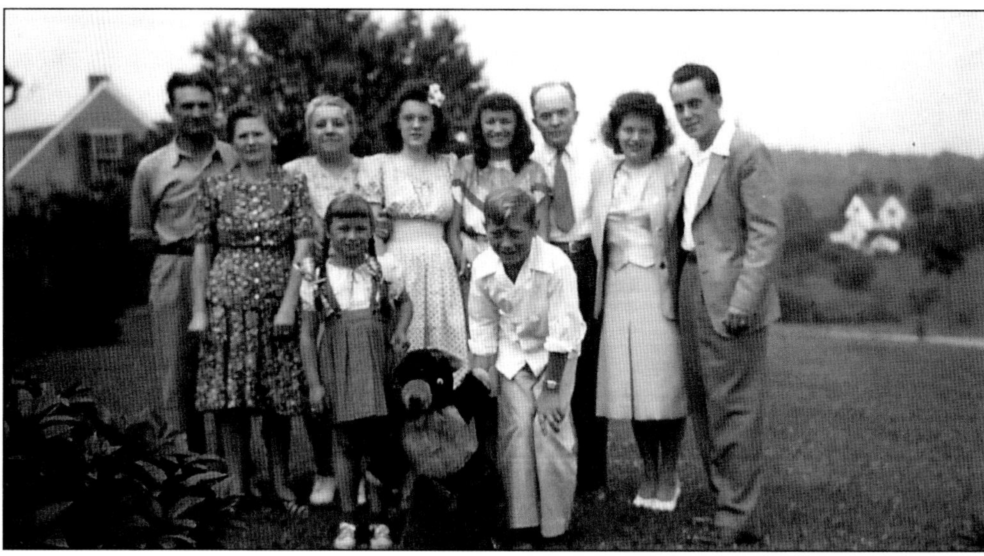

John Boytim, his wife, two daughters, and relatives from Ohio stood for this photograph in their yard. Homesteaders were able to enjoy community events for both children and adults. Community lawn festivals were common; homesteaders were invited to bring cakes, apple pies, and buns. Receipts from the sale of ice cream would go to the community Sunday school. Performers like Frank Dudgeon and the West Virginia Mountain Boy would perform. (Courtesy of Virginia Boytim Vahaly and Betty Sue Boytim Mondock.)

Betty Sue Boytim Mondock stands with her dad on the evening of a parade. Betty Sue was a majorette in the firemen's band, and her father was a fireman. Summers were busy as the local fire departments supported each other by marching in other's bands during carnival season. (Courtesy of Virginia Boytim Vahaly and Betty Sue Boytim Mondock.)

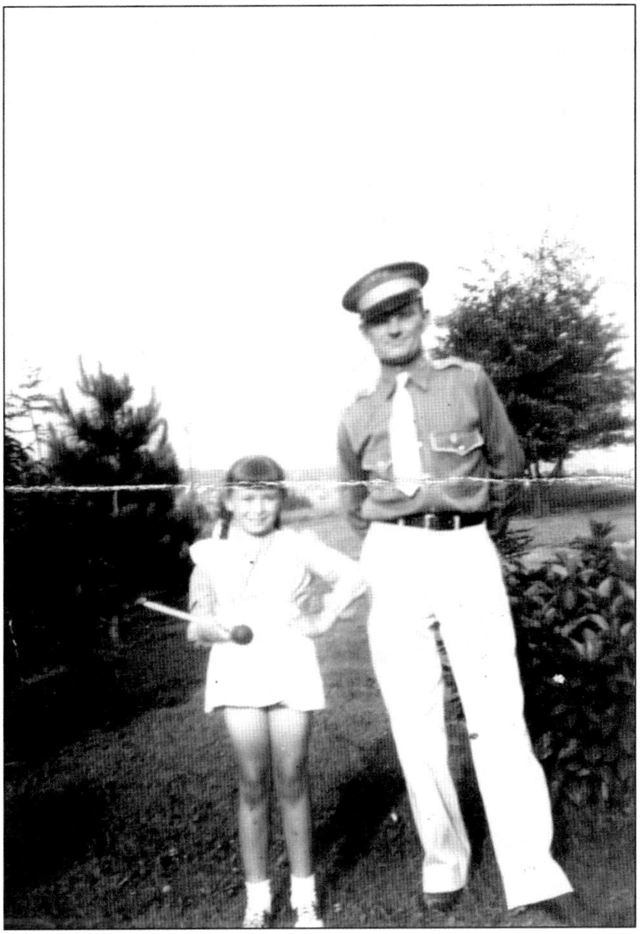

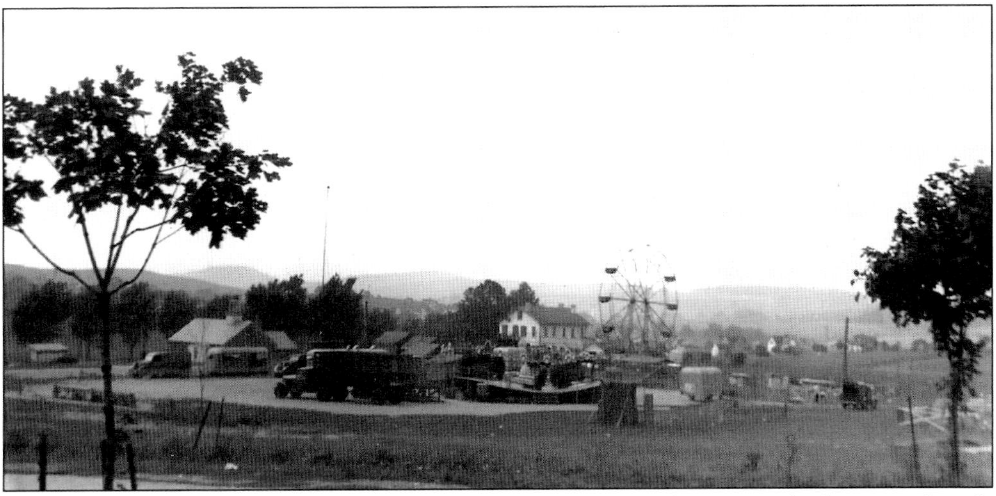

The Fireman's Fair, held every summer, was the highlight of the season for homesteaders. It was a good time to socialize, dance, play bingo, chuck-a-luck, and enjoy carnival rides. The above photograph shows the carnival rides being set up with the firemen's club and community building in the back. (Courtesy of Sharon Smith.)

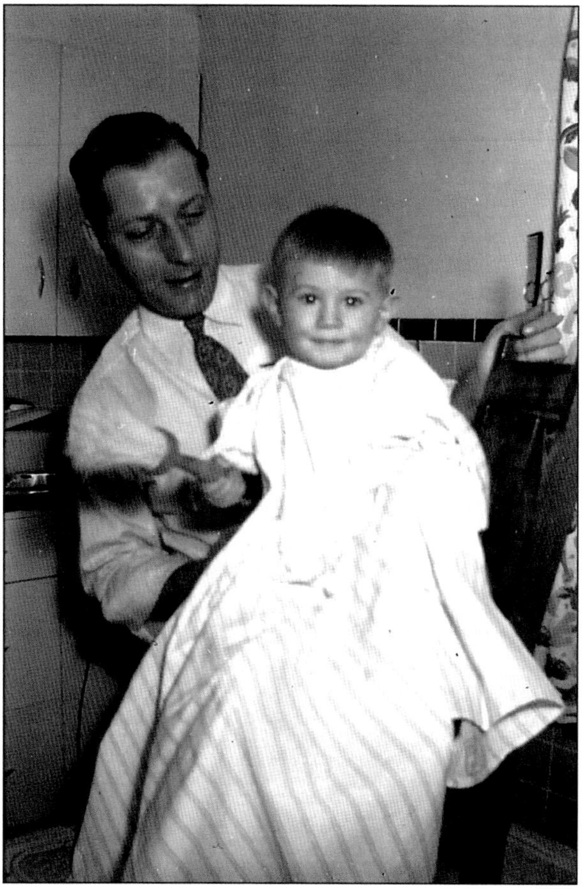

Herb Black was the local barber in Norvelt. This photograph of Richard Vahaly, son of Andrew and Virginia Boytim Vahaly, shows him getting his first haircut. (Courtesy of Virginia Boytim Vahaly and Betty Sue Boytim Mondock.)

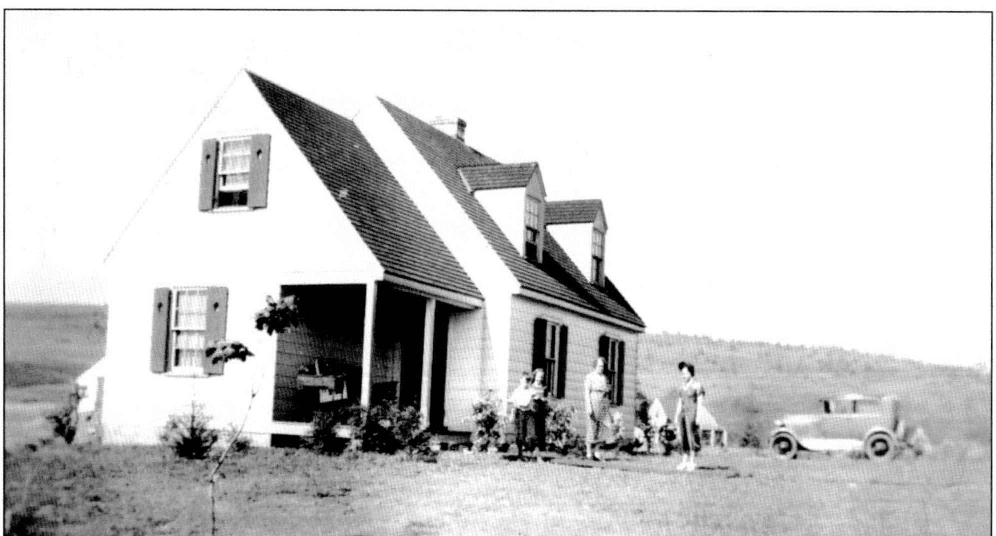

This is a photograph of the completed Shrader home in A section (A-72) with, from left to right, Mary Rose, Bob, Mrs. Shrader, and Mrs. Shrader's mother. Mrs. Shrader was a news reporter for the *Homestead Informer*. (Courtesy of Lois Weyandt.)

Paul K. Schlingman and his wife, Sara Florence Lewis Schlingman, stand outside their home. Paul was a very active fireman. Sara was a gifted piano player who entertained her family. (Courtesy of Lois Weyandt.)

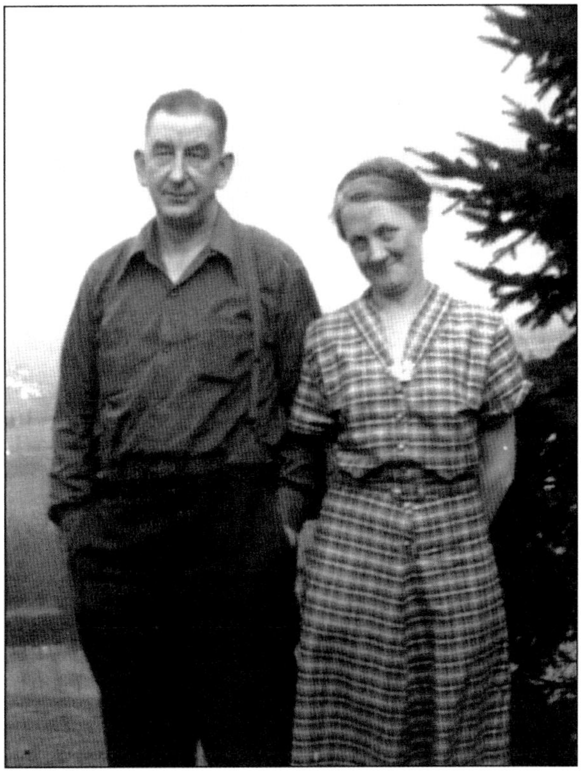

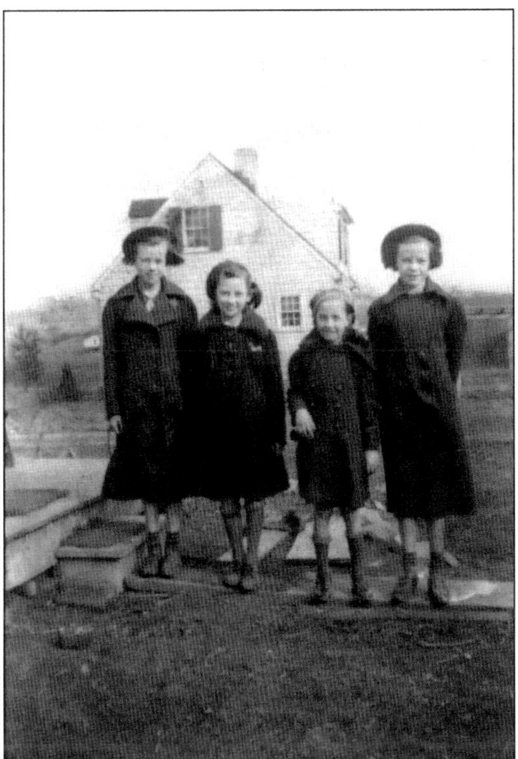

The four Weyant girls, from left to right, Jane, Lois, Patty, and Jean stand outside their home. Lois has remained very active in Norvelt and was instrumental in getting a historical marker for Norvelt. (Courtesy of Lois Weyandt.)

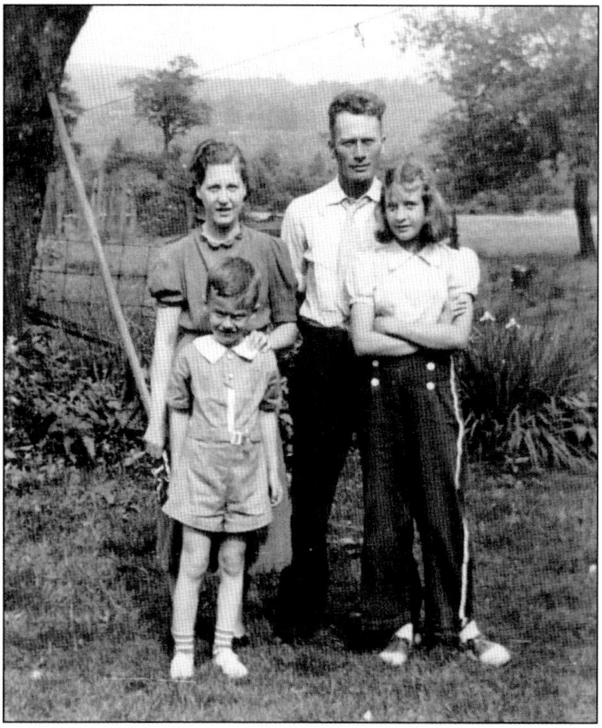

John and Emaline Kennedy of Section B stand with their children, Joe and Carrie Lou. Emaline was active in Mother's Club and was a member of the cast of the Dramatic Club's first production, "Weiners on Wednesday." Carrie Lou sang with a group of girls on opening night. John and his son crafted their own furniture and were known for their carpentry skills. (Courtesy of Joe Kennedy.)

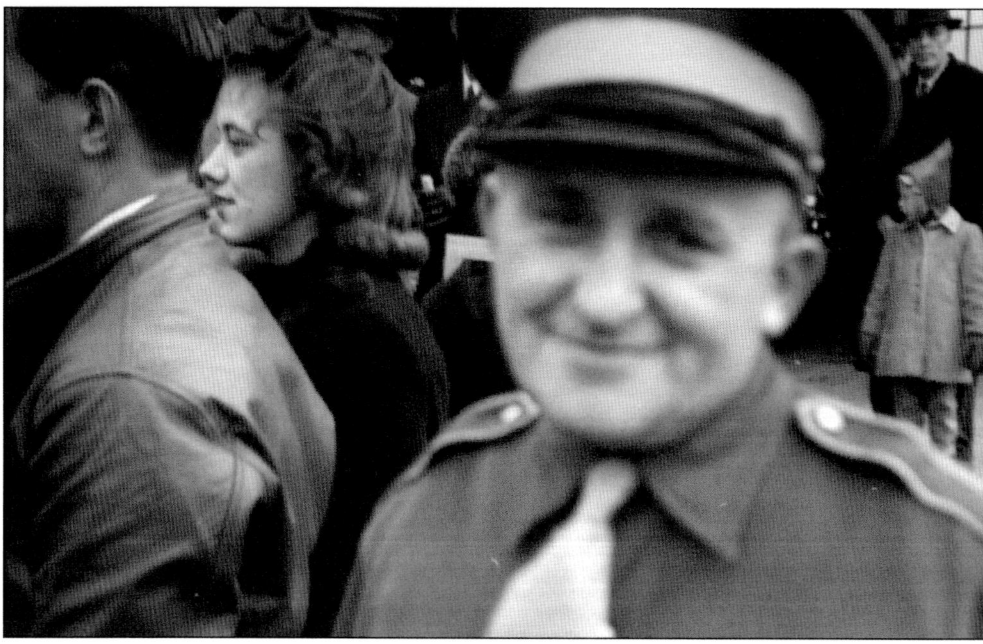

Steve Viazanko is pictured in his fireman's uniform on the day of a parade. Artist Richard Kenah commented, "People here are interesting because they are interested; and Westmoreland itself makes good picture material because of the activities of the people who live here. The idea that an artist should go to Palm Beach or to the West Coast in order to paint a good picture . . . is all wrong. The truth is that the picture is good if it tells a real story of real things. And Westmoreland is as good a spot as any in which to look for subjects." (Courtesy of Steve Viazanko.)

The Andrews family is shown on the entry to their home. Sitting is son Frank. Alice and Charles are in the background. Mrs. Andrews was in charge of costumes in the Co-Op Players dramatic group. The Andrews family resided in the 124-year-old Hurst House and Mrs. Charlie Andrews invited the Mother's Club for a meeting and to celebrate. The women dressed in period costumes, played old-fashioned games, and had a corn, wiener, and marshmallow roast. (Courtesy of Jean Crise Andrews.)

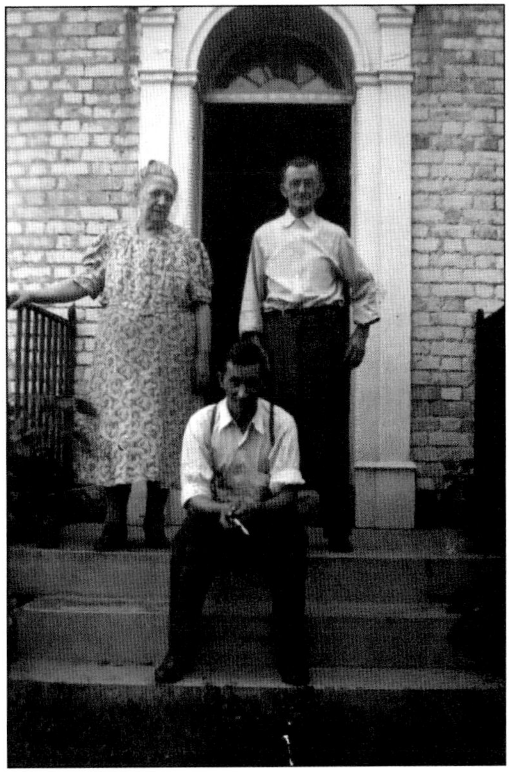

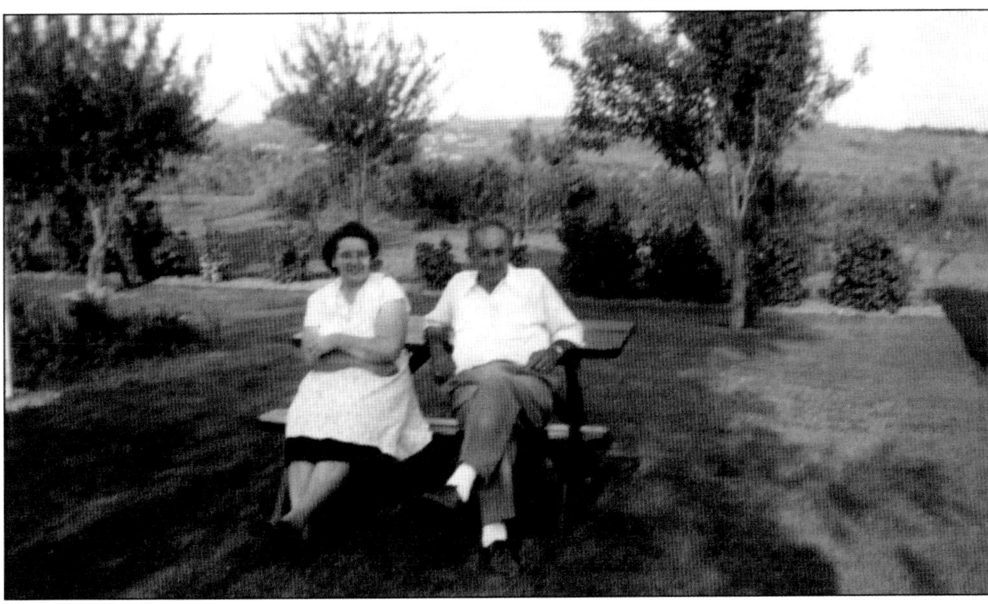

Joe Bann and his wife rest in their orchard. Homesteaders were encouraged to join in an agricultural and industrial research committee established to consider possible industrial activities for the co-op, such as dry ice, wood craft, metal craft, allied tradesman, weaving, co-op coal mining, agriculture lime, canning of tomato and meat, shoe factory, creamery, woolen mill, brewery, peat moss market, feed mill, mushrooms, summer resort, roadside stands, tobacco factory, coffee and peanut roasting, and popcorn raising. (Courtesy of Helen Bann Stefanek.)

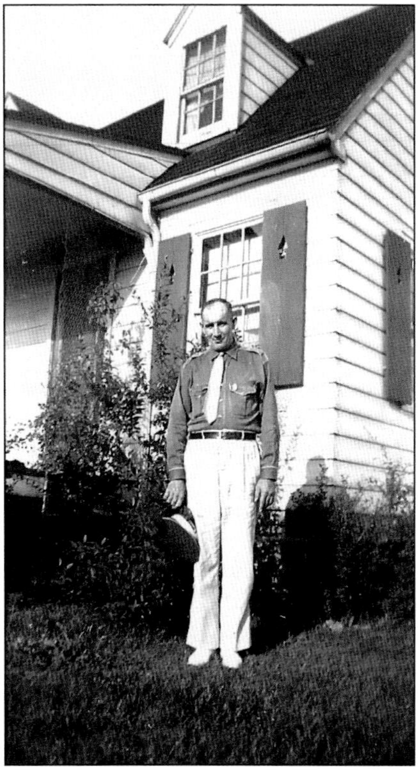

Joe Bann is pictured here in his fireman's uniform. (Courtesy of Helen Bann Stefanek.)

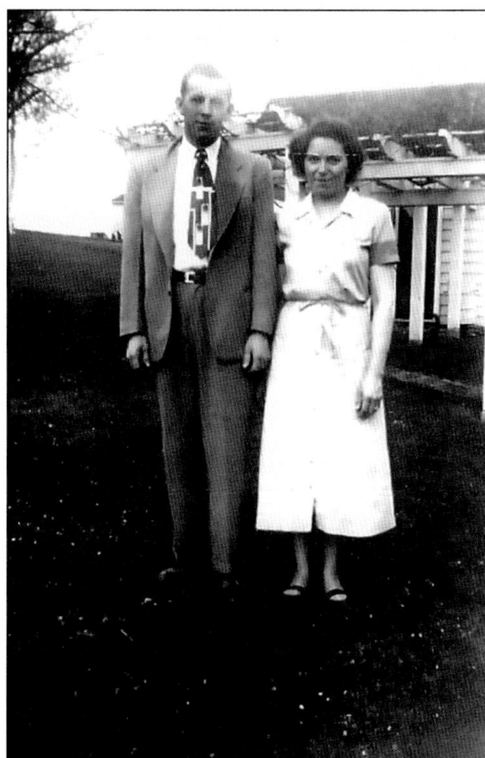

Sarah Kelly is standing with her son, Regis Kelly, who was Westmoreland County sheriff. Sarah Kelly was a president of the Mother's Club. Her husband John Kelly was active in the early days of the homestead. He was selected to attend the Mine Sealing Conference at the U.S. Bureau of Mines in Pittsburgh with speaker Dr. Edith MacBride, secretary of health for Pennsylvania. (Courtesy of Sally Fetter.)

Sarah and John Kelly pose with daughter Sally Kelly Fetter getting ready for the May Queen festivities at St. Florian Church. (Courtesy of Sally Fetter.)

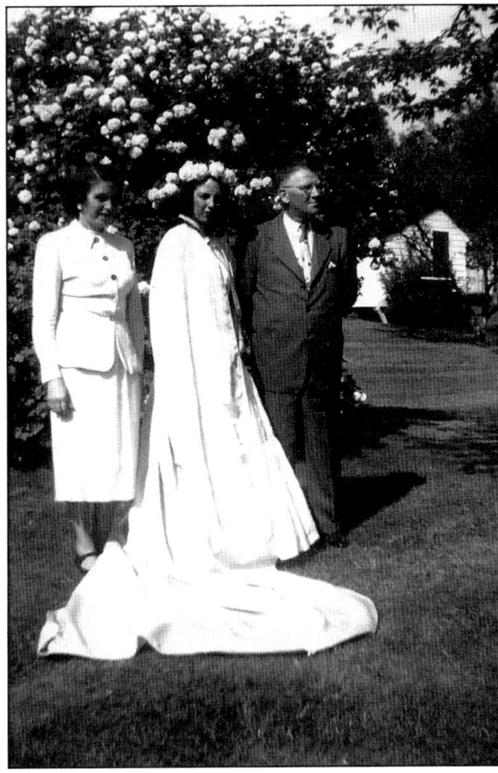

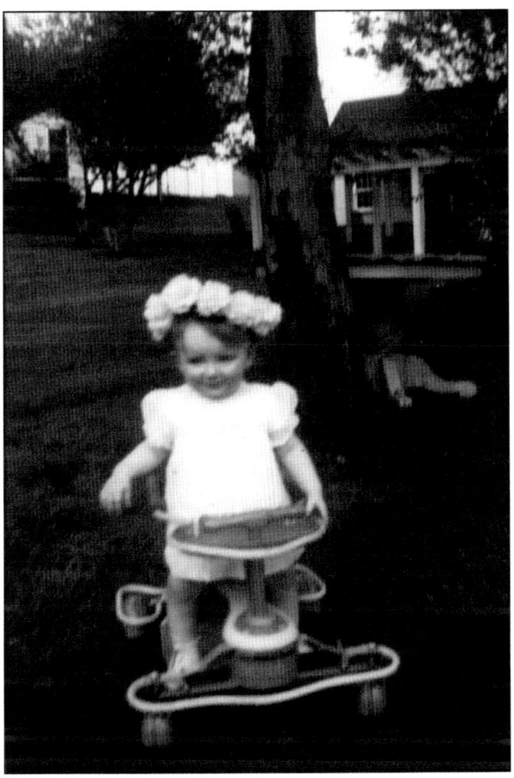

Kathleen Kelly posed in the May Queen crown. Early on, the homestead made sure children had ample places to play. Three playgrounds were established, one at the community center in A section, E section, and D section. (Courtesy of Sally Fetter.)

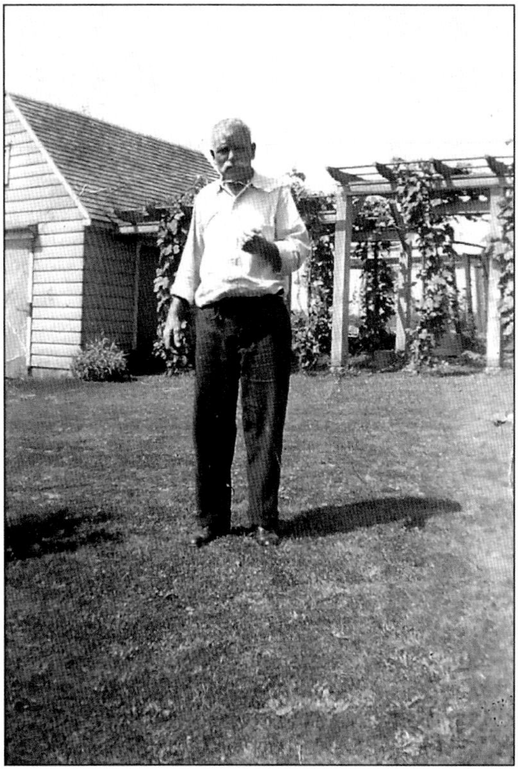

John Slunjski, pictured at left, lived in B section with his wife Elizabeth. (Courtesy of Barbara Kepick.)

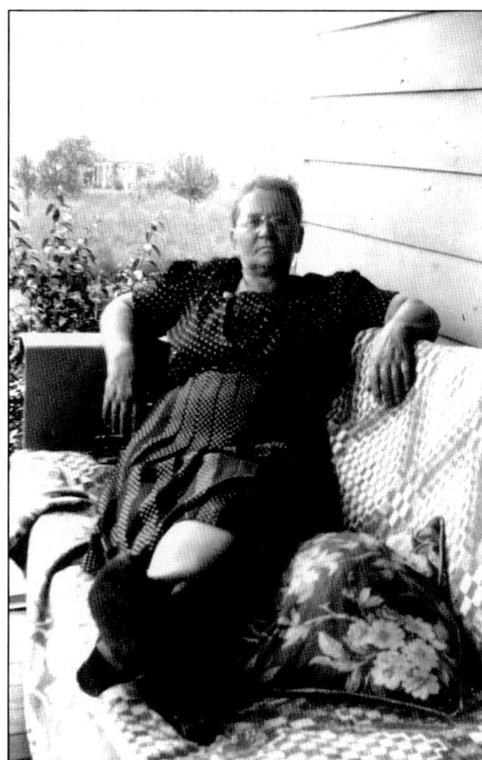

Elizabeth Slunjski sits on her front porch in this photograph. The homes were built with front porches and this permitted residents to socialize with neighbors and feel more a part of the community. When interested, a weaving room was provided for residents to make blankets and rugs so residents could participate and make their own home's special touches. (Courtesy of Barbara Kepick.)

Ann Slunjski and friend Joe Chelan from Norvelt stand in the backyard. Many young members of the community joined the 4-H Club. Sixty-seven girls attended the first meeting held in 1937. The 4-H Club is part of extension teaching by the Extension Division of Penn State University and the U.S. Department of Agriculture, cooperating for rural boys and girls, 10–20 years of age. (Courtesy of Barbara Kepick.)

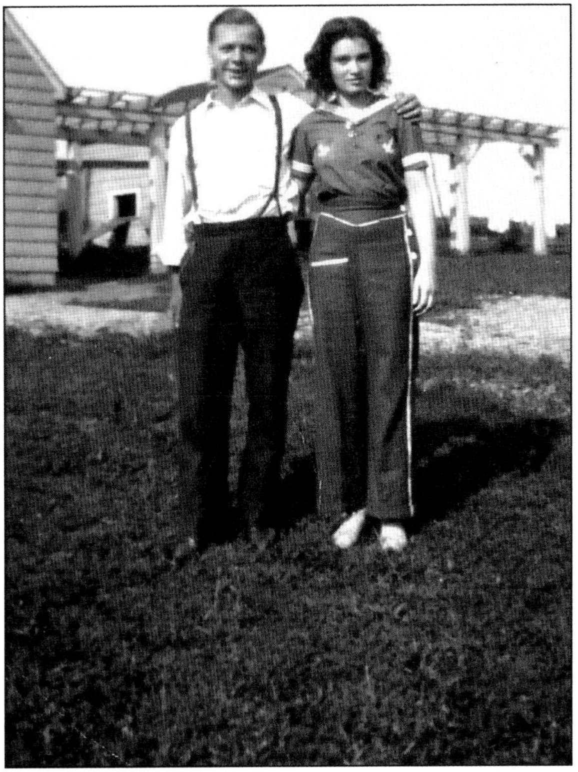

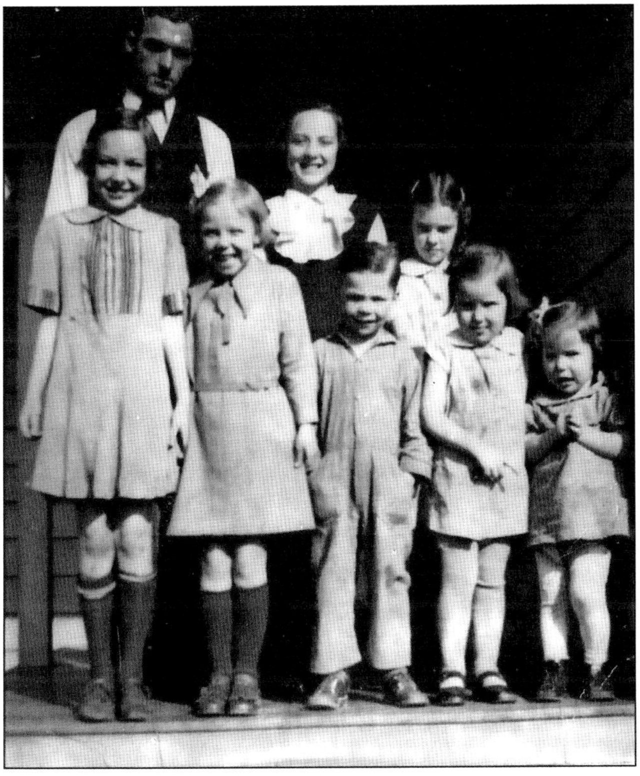

The Cunningham family moved to the homesteads in 1937. This 1938 photograph shows William Cunningham with his seven children, from left to right, Eleanor, Dot, Glennie, Shirley, David, Nancy, and Polly (Mary). The *Homestead Informer* expressed the sadness of the homesteaders and friends when William's wife passed away from pneumonia leaving the children, all under the age of 10, without a mother. (Courtesy of Glynnis Cunningham Waters.)

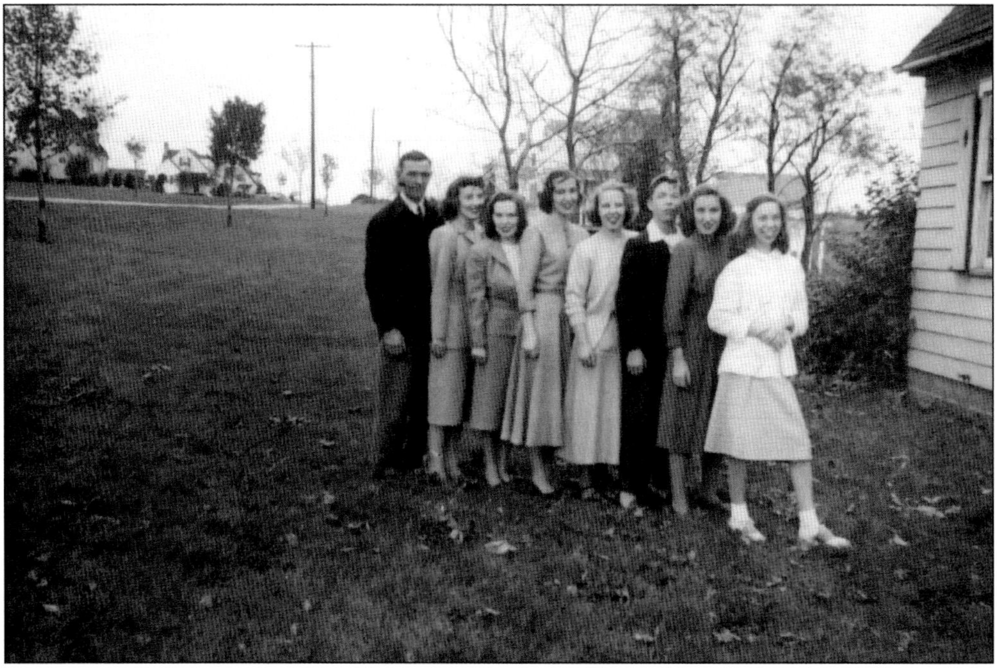

William Cunningham was well respected for raising his seven children. They are pictured here in 1948. (Courtesy of Glynnis Cunningham Waters.)

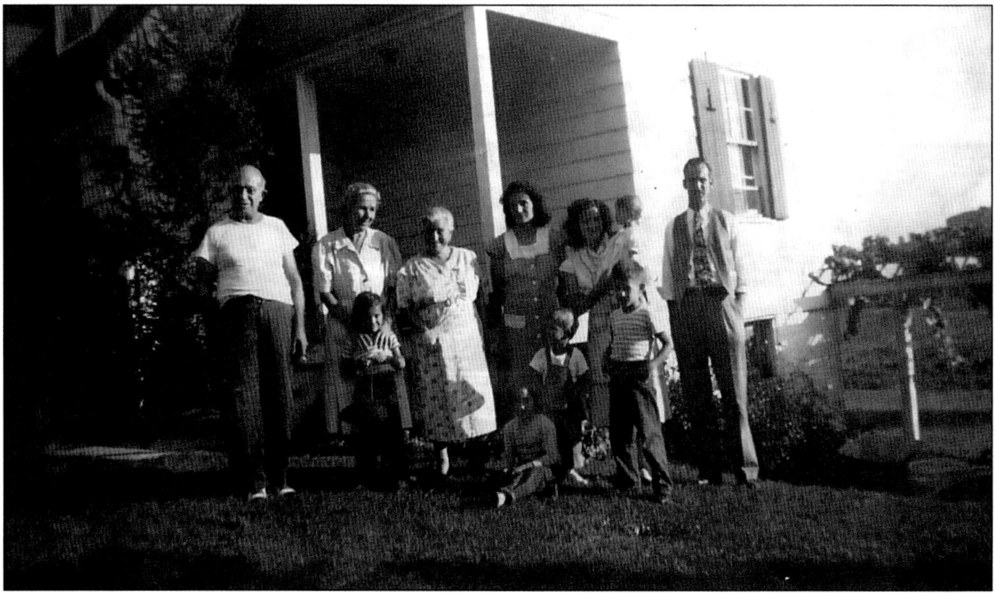

Louis Pastore was married to Nancy Cunningham and was known throughout Norvelt as the shoemaker. His office was in the bottom of the community store. (Courtesy of Ann Riggen.)

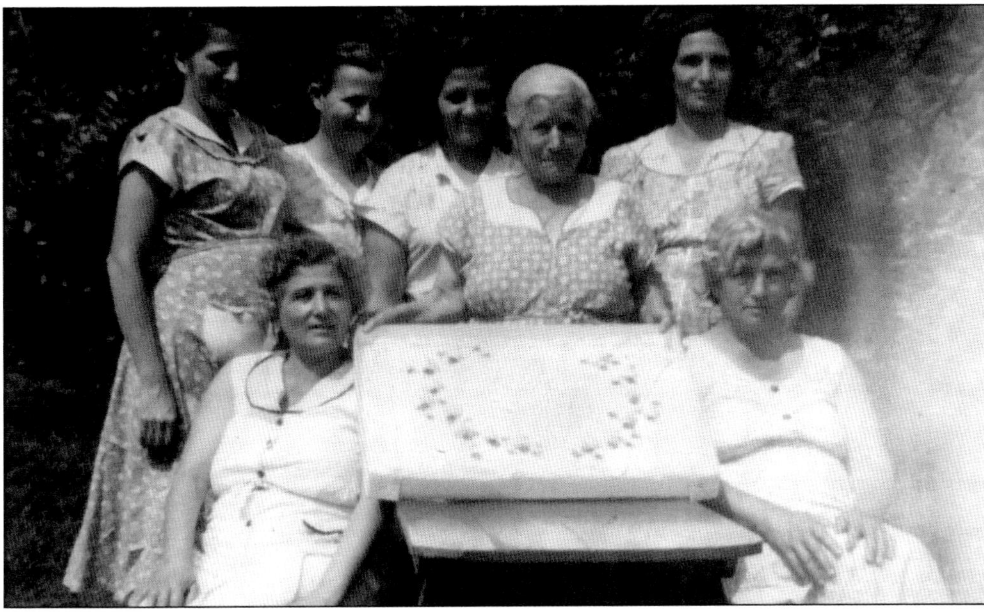

The Pastore family's six daughters are gathered in this photograph around their mother. Many homesteaders had large families, and caring for the health of families was important. The homestead developed a health club with the Medical Association of Westmoreland County. The 1937 issue of the *Homestead Informer* reported that the club would bring dentists to the community and hospitalization at special rates, and the surplus funds would be mounting to be ready for winter. Annual membership in this medical insurance program was $1.60. (Courtesy of Ann Riggen.)

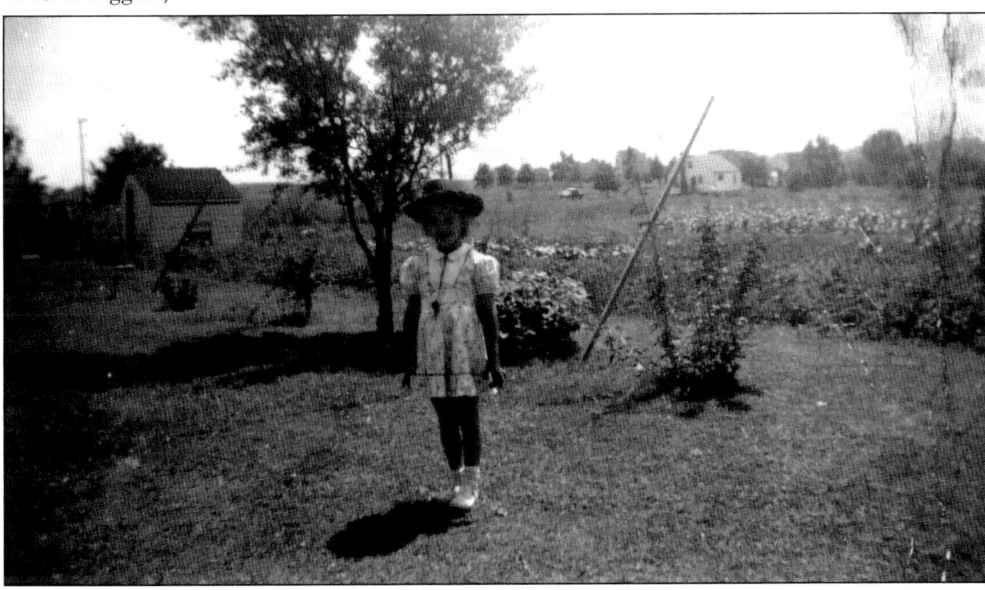

Louis and Nancy Pastore's granddaughter Anna Marie Solo poses in front of her grandparents' vegetable garden. Teachers were brought to provide education for the children, many of whom had never attended school before. A service, far ahead of its time, was the day care center started and staffed by AFSC volunteers. The day care center provided a much-needed service for parents who had to work during the day. (Courtesy of Ann Riggen.)

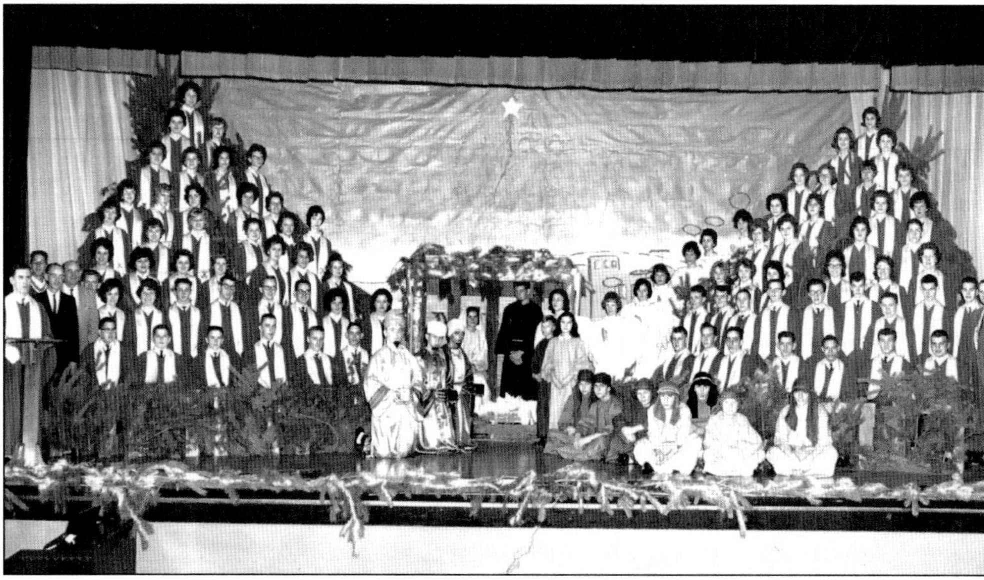

Concerts at Hurst High School were popular. In this photograph, the high school chorus is staging its annual Christmas program. (Courtesy of Shirley Jones Rusinko.)

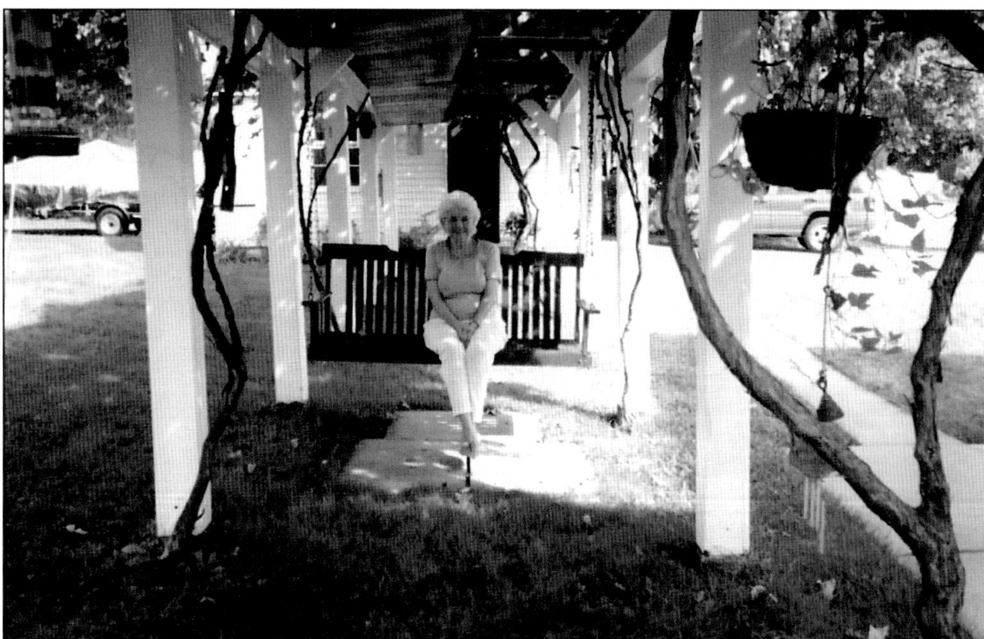

Evelyn Stairs is seated on the swing under her grape arbor. Care of home and yard was strictly enforced. Homesteaders were expected to keep their homes clean and neat. Homesteaders routinely entertained visitors with their plantings of vegetable gardens, flowers, and trees. (Courtesy of Mrs. V. Prue.)

Catherine Pavick, wife of John, stands with her son Michael, granddaughter Bonnie, and daughter-in-law Margaret Sofranko Pavick. By 1940, all of the homesteaders bought their homes. The subsistence program lost its federal funding in 1944. By 1950, the cooperatives were gone, including the poultry and dairy barns. In a *Homestead Informer* article one homesteader said, "Our Homestead has meant: better housing and living conditions, new friends, new outlook on life, co-op spirit (which has had ups and downs)." (Courtesy of Keith Pavick.)

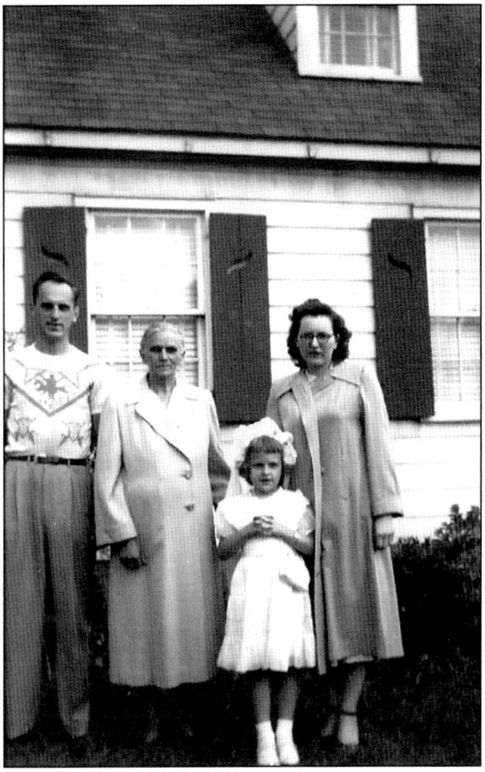

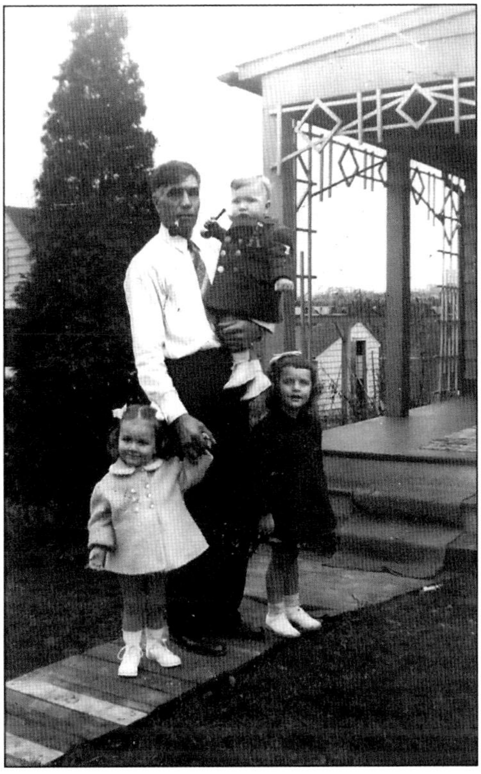

John Pavick stands with, from left to right, grandchildren Dolores Pavick, Bobby Pavick, and Patty Pavick Kelly. John ran the pig farm. The homesteaders chose to work in the private sector for higher-paying jobs and left the community farming jobs. Although the homesteaders of Norvelt did not embrace the socialist ideas of communal farming and becoming self-sufficient as was hoped, it was considered a success as a means to free people from poverty. (Courtesy of Keith Pavick.)

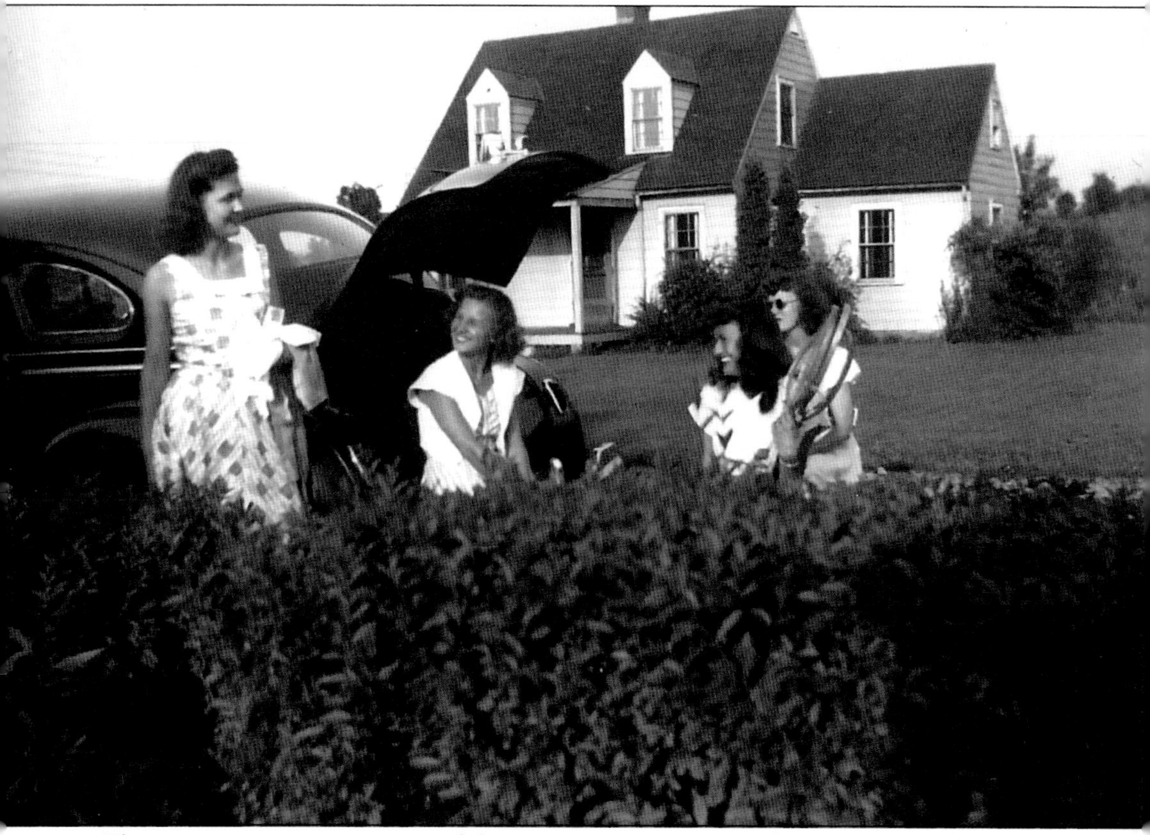

These young women just returned from a vacation at Coneaught Lake. Pictured from left to right are Doris Johnson Peterson, Irene Cibulas Balazek, Virginia Boytim Vahaly, and Mildred Johnson Kennelty. To this day, residents fondly remember Eleanor Roosevelt's contribution to their town and the well-being of their families. Roosevelt's legacy, civic pride, social responsibility, and patriotism are imbedded in this community. (Courtesy of Virginia Boytim Vahaly.)

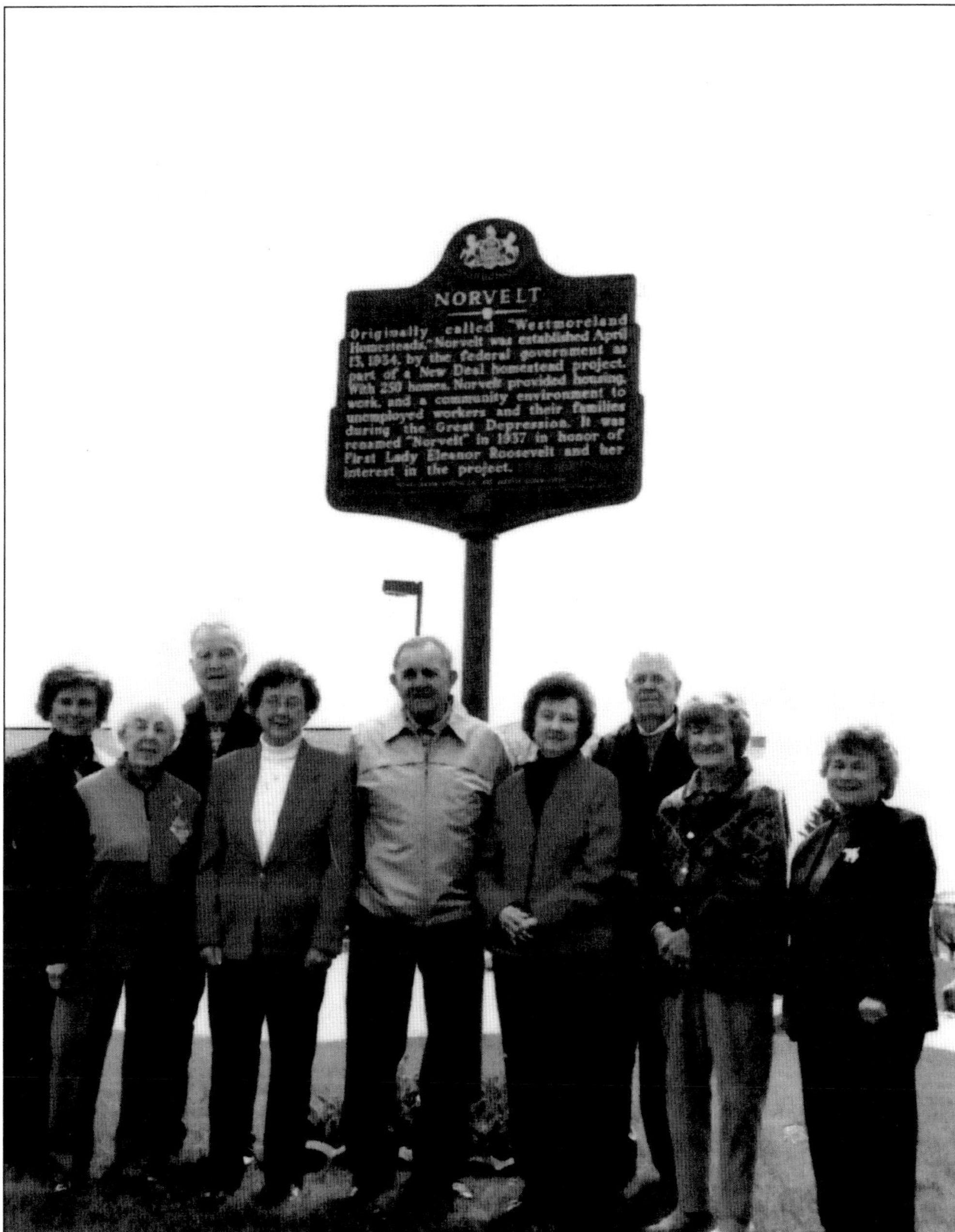

Members of the Westmoreland Homestead Historical Committee, original homesteaders, stand at the historical marker that describes the town's founding. From left to right are Valeria Sofranko Wolk, Gerry Peterson Palmer, Joseph Wolk, Lois Schlingman Weyandt, Ed Cibulas, Catherine Cibulas, Earl Saville, Virginia Boytim Vahaly, and Betty Sue Boytim Mondock. (Courtesy of Valeria Sofranko Wolk.)

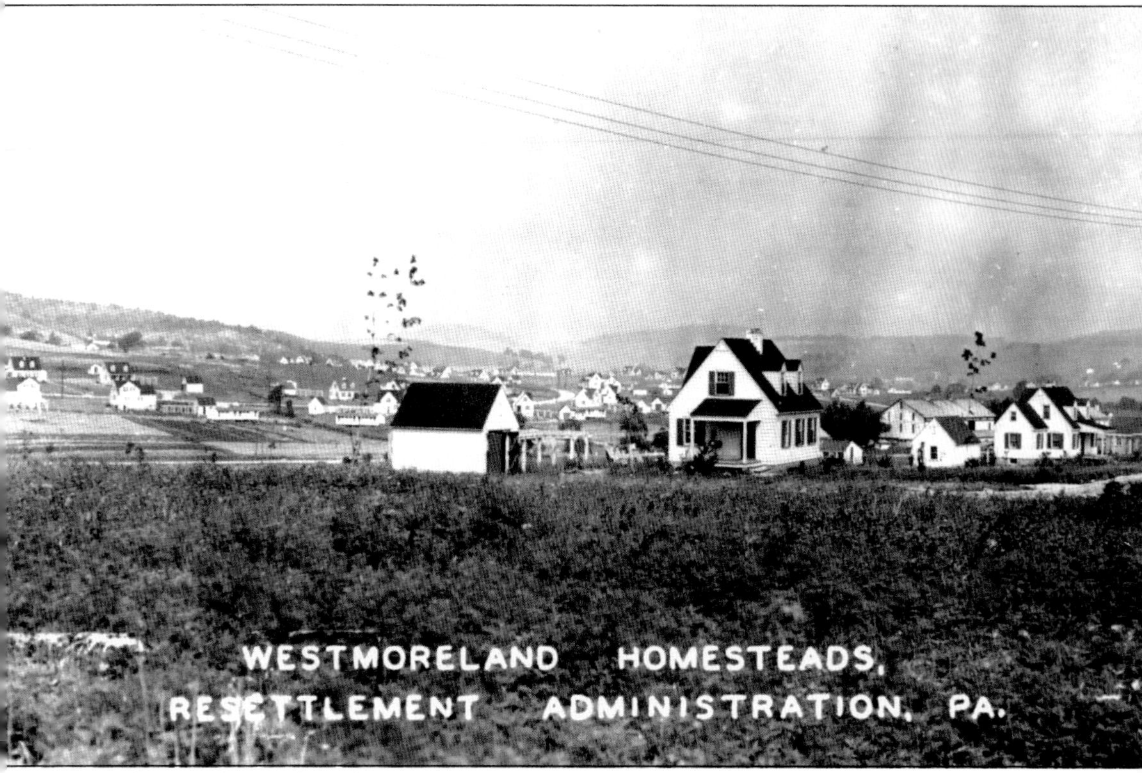

In her autobiography, Eleanor Roosevelt stated, "Only a few of the resettlement projects had any measure of success; nevertheless, I have always felt that the good they did was incalculable. Conditions were so nearly the kind that breed revolution that the men and women needed to feel their government's interest and concern." If success is measured by the quality of life the homesteaders and their families experienced for the generations to come, as well as their gratitude today, Eleanor Roosevelt would have been pleased. (Courtesy of Valeria Sofranko Wolk.)

Bibliography

Black, Allida M. ed. *Courage in a Dangerous World: The Political Writings of Eleanor Roosevelt.* New York: Columbia University Press: 1999.

Conwill, Joseph D. "Back to the Land: Pennsylvania's New Deal Era Community." *Pennsylvania Heritage* X, no. 3 (summer 1984): 12–18.

Cook, Blanche Wiesen. *Eleanor Roosevelt: Volume 2, the Defining Years, 1933–1938.* New York: Penguin Books, 1999.

Hareven, Tamara K. *Eleanor Roosevelt: An American Conscience.* Chicago: Quadrangle Books, 1968.

Hoagland, Alison K., and Margaret M. Mulrooney. *Norvelt and Penn-Craft, Pennsylvania. Subsistence-Homestead Communities of the 1930s.* National Park Service, 1991.

Kearney, James R. *Anna Eleanor Roosevelt: The Evolution of a Reformer.* Boston: Houghton Mifflin Company, 1968.

Roosevelt, Eleanor. *The Autobiography of Eleanor Roosevelt.* New York: Harper and Brothers Publishers, 1937.

"They Went in Harm's Way." *Westmoreland History* 10, no. 1 (Spring 2005).

Warren, Kenneth. *Wealth, Waste, and Alienation: Growth and Decline in the Connellsville Coke Industry.* University of Pittsburgh Press, 2001.

"Westmoreland Homesteads: A Little Touch of Heaven." *Westmoreland History* 7, No. 3 (December 2002).